American Conquest

AMERICAN CONQUEST

The Northwest Indian War
and the Making of US Foreign Policy

ANDREW A. SZAREJKO

STANFORD UNIVERSITY PRESS
Stanford, California

Stanford University Press
Stanford, California

Library of Congress Cataloging-in-Publication Data
Names: Szarejko, Andrew A. author
Title: American conquest : the Northwest Indian War and the making of US foreign policy / Andrew A. Szarejko.
Description: Stanford, California : Stanford University Press, [2025] | Includes bibliographical references and index.
Identifiers: LCCN 2024059261 (print) | LCCN 2024059262 (ebook) | ISBN 9781503643536 cloth | ISBN 9781503643819 paperback | ISBN 9781503643826 ebook
Subjects: LCSH: Indians of North America—Wars—1790-1794 | Indians of North America—Wars—Northwest, Old | Indians of North America—Government relations—1789-1869 | Northwest, Old—History—1775-1865 | United States—Foreign relations | United States—Military policy
Classification: LCC E83.79 .S98 2025 (print) | LCC E83.79 (ebook) | DDC 973.04/9700903—dc23/eng/20250305
LC record available at https://lccn.loc.gov/2024059261
LC ebook record available at https://lccn.loc.gov/2024059262

Cover design: George Kirkpatrick
Cover engraving: *View of Long-Reach*, an engraving (1805) by Georges-Henri-Victor Collot, engraved by Pierre François Tardieu, approx. 14 × 19 cm., published in *A Journey in North America: Containing a Survey of the Countries Watered by the Mississippi, Ohio, Missouri, and Other Affluing Rivers* (1826) by Georges-Henri-Victor Collot, courtesy of the University of Pittsburgh Library System.

The authorized representative in the EU for product safety and compliance is: Mare Nostrum Group B.V. | Mauritskade 21D | 1091 GC Amsterdam | The Netherlands | Email address: gpsr@mare-nostrum.co.uk | KVK chamber of commerce number: 96249943

CONTENTS

ACKNOWLEDGMENTS

I have many people to thank for helping make this book a reality. First, Andrew Bennett, David Edelstein, and Daniel Nexon offered much support throughout my time at Georgetown University. The research on which this book is based was better because of their feedback, and I appreciate their continued support.

I have received valuable responses on various parts of this book from numerous discussants, fellow panelists, and audience members at conferences over the years. I am especially grateful to these scholars: Michael A. Allen, John Arquilla, Jessica Auchter, Alexander D. Barder, Kelly Bauer, Justin Casey, Michael C. Desch, Laura E. Evans, Miles M. Evers, Brian Finch, Eugene Gholz, Stacie E. Goddard, Eric Grynaviski, Chris M. Jackson, Patrick Thaddeus Jackson, Minseon Ku, Tobias Lemke, Richard W. Maass, Paul K. MacDonald, Carla Martínez Machain, Joseph MacKay, David M. McCourt, Liam Midzain-Gobin, Paul Musgrave, Stephen Pampinella, Joseph M. Parent, Christopher Preble, Mark Raymond, Hilde Restad, Joshua R. Itzkowitz Shifrinson, Brent J. Steele, and Jelena Subotić.

I am also grateful to have received invitations to present my work at the Cultural Center of the Shawnee Tribe of Oklahoma, the University of Oklahoma's Department of International and Area Studies, the Notre Dame International Security Center's Emerging Scholars in Grand Strategy Conference, and the Cato Institute's Junior Scholars Symposium. This research also benefited from financial support from the Georgetown Department of Government and the Georgetown Graduate School of Arts and Sciences.

Before accepting my current position at Wartburg College, I held short-term positions at the University of Cincinnati and the Naval Postgraduate School. I am grateful to Brendan R. Green, whose usual classes I taught at Cincinnati while he was on sabbatical, for his support when I found myself in the odd position of teaching all those classes online due to the COVID-19 pandemic. I also appreciate Andrew R. Lewis's help in navigating that situation. The opportunity to serve as a Hans J. Morgenthau Fellow at the Notre Dame International Security Center at the same time was rewarding and surely informs this book. At the Naval Postgraduate School, I thank John Arquilla for serving as an advisor to me and the other postdoctoral fellows in the Department of Defense Analysis and for his continued support since then. I am indebted to the department for giving me the opportunity to present my research—a first draft of Chapter 4—in its seminar series. (I must also note that the views expressed throughout the book are my own and not necessarily those of any federal institution.)

Since starting a tenure-track position at Wartburg College in August 2022, many colleagues have offered a supportive, collegial environment in which to complete this book. Bret Billet has been especially helpful as my senior colleague in political science—he has kindly taken on a disproportionate share of departmental service and has otherwise been protective of my time in my first two-plus years at Wartburg. As I have started taking on more responsibilities in student advising, institutional committees, and the like, he has been an accessible mentor and a reliable sounding board. The Social Science Department more generally has been a pleasant place in which to work, and I am thankful to my colleagues for making it so. At the institutional level, I am grateful to have received the Dr. Peggy and Kendall Pruisner Early Career Scholarly and Creative Activities Award, which provided me with funding in the summer of 2023 to focus on this project. I am also grateful to my fellow now-third-year faculty colleagues with whom it has been a privilege to find our way through modern higher education. Among those colleagues, I am especially grateful to Sarah Voels, with whom conversations about this book and her dissertation certainly helped me complete this project.

Throughout all this work, my family has been a source of steady support. I thank them for their role in making this book possible.

American Conquest

One

BEYOND ISOLATIONISM

US Foreign Policy and the Northwest Indian War

The United States initiated a military campaign in 1790 to solidify its claims to land then occupied by individuals associated with the Shawnee, the Miami, and several smaller Native American groups of the Ohio River Valley. After early victories for the Native coalition stunned US political elites, the United States would raise and provide for the training of a larger, more professionalized fighting force that would ultimately mount a victorious war effort codified in the Treaty of Greenville in 1795. The Northwest Indian War, as this intermittent series of battles and abortive negotiations came to be known, was an important inflection point in early US foreign policy.[1] In this book, I will show that early US foreign policy was constituted in part by relations with Native American groups, that understanding these relations can thus help us understand US foreign policy, and that attending to these relations illuminates the ongoing processes by which America's conquest of Native lands is legitimized.[2]

Within the field of international relations (IR), the study of US foreign policy has rarely included much attention to relations with Native American groups. Some narratives of the history of US foreign policy omit it entirely and focus on the Spanish–American War of 1898 as the moment when the United States became more active in world affairs (see, e.g., Dombrowski and Reich 2019; Layne 2006). Even studies that do address this period generally give only a brief overview of roughly a century of US history, and they can arrive at a description of early US foreign policy as "isolationist" by privileging relations with European powers while downplaying relations with Native American groups (e.g., Copeland 2024; Kupchan 2020; Trubowitz 2011). When scholars of US foreign policy do give US relations with Native American groups some attention, US and Native interests are often treated as a given, with US seizure of Native land being "predetermined" and Native resistance being "doomed from the start" (Mandelbaum 2022, 88–89).[3]

What scholars miss here is that relations with Native Americans were centrally constitutive of early US foreign policy; that is, these relations helped make US foreign policy what it was.[4] The Northwest Indian War and the Indian Wars more generally should be thought of as "foreign" policy to the extent that they were treated as such, and indeed, these conflicts involved organized violence and diplomacy between the United States and other political communities. For decades, relations between the United States and Native American groups were mediated primarily by the bureaucratic entities—the Department of War and the Department of State—responsible for the conduct of foreign policy. These wars were also important: The United States devoted significant resources to the conquests entailed in its westward expansion, and these conquests involved substantial debate among political elites as to how best to prosecute them. Moreover, America's Indian Wars—as I will discuss here through a focus on the Northwest Indian War—also set important precedents and provided perceived lessons that US political elites would bring into other contexts.[5]

This book offers a corrective to narratives that see US foreign policy as constituted primarily—even wholly—through relations with European states.[6] To borrow Chief Justice John Marshall's famous 1831 formulation in *Cherokee Nation v. Georgia*, if Native American groups are thought to be "domestic dependent nations," IR scholars have most readily acted as if those groups are "domestic" rather than considering them as "nations."[7] This book rests on the premise that US relations with Native American groups are indeed international relations in important ways.[8] In short, this book is an effort to demonstrate what those of us in the field of IR—and in the subfield of US foreign policy especially—can gain from a conceptualization of US foreign policy that takes seriously relations with Native American groups.[9]

I conceptualize US relations with Native American groups not necessarily as wholly domestic or international. Rather, I view US–Native American interactions as a set of relations that different actors have tried to solidify as domestic or international—with actors pushing to make the relations domestic having had the advantage for some time—but these relations nonetheless continue to be ambiguous and contested. On the one hand, legal decisions, military force, and other instruments of state power have been used to try to crystallize these relations as purely domestic in nature. On the other hand, Native American groups have often contested these efforts and sought to preserve their sovereignty and self-determination to the extent possible. Thus, if US relations with tribes have become more seemingly domestic over time, I take that as a contingent social fact, not as the natural state of affairs or as a condition that will forever prevail. In that sense, this book is at least minimally constructivist and, more specifically, processual-relational in its theoretical approach.[10]

To accomplish my task, I ask two central questions. First, why did the United States go to war against the tribes of the Ohio River Valley? Even if the ostensible purpose was to secure US claims to the territory of the Old Northwest, how did political elites come to view the very costly option of war as necessary? Why war rather than any other response? The origins of the war, I argue, lie not just in the straightforward incompatibility of Native and US claims to territory but also in the incentives that settlers had to secure cheap land for themselves and in the process by which settlers lobbied political elites for military intervention. For scholars of US foreign policy, the origins of this conflict undermine the conventional wisdom about the role of the public in war initiation—here, the public played what would seem to be an outsized role given the typical view today that foreign policy is more insulated from public pressures than domestic policy.[11] Moreover, the nature of the conflict speaks to how we ought to conceptualize early US foreign policy; if we take Indian Affairs as seriously as US relations with the "great powers" of Europe, it is difficult to maintain that the United States ever enacted anything we could meaningfully call isolationism.

Second, I go beyond the origins of the war to ask how the Northwest Indian War can help us make sense of US foreign policy more broadly. I argue that in this first conflict between the fledgling American state and Native American groups, we can see a harbinger of things to come: The war functions in part as a model for a mode of territorial expansion secured through the construction of military fortifications and for an early counterinsurgency doctrine. Moreover, the extent to which the Northwest Indian War continues to be politicized suggests that the legitimacy of American conquests requires continual reinforcement. This is not so much an argument that acts associated with the Northwest Indian War had specific causal effects that made certain later acts or events more likely. Rather, it is an argument to the effect that these early actions at least presaged certain patterns of behavior and offered later policymakers an intellectual resource in debates about how to enact foreign policy.

In that regard, the reverberations of the Northwest Indian War extended far beyond the settlement of the Old Northwest. Indeed, the Northwest Indian War was won with a strategy that would come to define American expansion and that would become central to American defense policy beyond North America—with the use of military bases to concentrate and project power across an expanding frontier. It was in the Northwest Indian War, moreover, that the United States would learn how to wage a sort of counterinsurgency campaign that would later be implemented in other so-called Indian Wars and by veterans of such conflicts in the Philippine–American War of 1899–1902. Lacking much in terms of a formal, institutionalized "lessons learned" process, however, the US military continually forgot and relearned how to wage such counterinsurgencies; it was in the individualized experiences of military veterans, I argue, that the perceived lessons of the Indian Wars made their way abroad.

The long-term consequences of the Northwest Indian War linger not just in these military practices but also in the contested territory of American political memory. How exactly should American citizens remember the Northwest Indian War and those who fought to secure American expansion? What is at stake in the stories told about this past? In Fort Wayne, Indiana, a town named for Anthony Wayne, the victorious American general, Republican political officials and activists have recently answered these questions by establishing an annual commemoration of General Wayne that serves as an affirmation of the fundamental goodness of Wayne, the American Revolution in which he played a part, and the expansion of the United States that he helped facilitate. By contrast, some local Democrats and tribes involved in the eighteenth-century hostilities opposed this move and instead framed the Northwest Indian War as a shameful episode that ought not to be publicly celebrated—or, at the least, ought to be memorialized in a manner that allows for reflection on the war's meaning rather than trying to establish one correct view of the events. In an increasingly polarized and nationalized political context, this sort of local-level contestation over the legitimacy of American conquests seems likely to continue with tribes getting caught in the crossfire.

THEORY AND METHODS

Each of the next four chapters examines a different aspect of the Northwest Indian War and its legacies in US foreign policy. I thus discuss more specific methodological choices as necessary in each chapter, but as a general matter, I approach this subject from a theoretical perspective grounded in processual-relational and constructivist theory. Processual-relational theory helps to make sense of the extent to which early US foreign policy was defined by interactions with Native nations, and it draws our attention to the networks within which political actors seek to induce stasis or change. The latter underscores the non-inevitability of any given pattern of interaction between the United States and Native nations and prompts a concluding engagement with the narratives we construct about histories of US–Native relations.[12]

In addition to the study of US foreign policy, I contribute to an increasingly broad literature that brings relational theory into IR.[13] Such an approach has variously been described as "relational," "processual," or as some combination of those terms; here I use processual-relational and the increasingly prevalent relational label interchangeably (though processual-relational theory might be seen as a subset of relational theory). Such an approach "treats configurations of ties—recurrent sociocultural interaction—between social aggregates of various sorts and their component parts as the building blocks of analysis" (Jackson and Nexon 1999, 291–292).[14] For its advocates, relationalism is opposed to substantialism, an often tacit approach in which "entities exist before interaction and all relations should be conceived as relations between entities" (Jackson and Nexon 1999, 291). Importantly, however, "Relationalism . . . is not a 'theory' in the same sense as structural realism or Wendtian constructivism" (Nexon 2010, 100), and it is "methodologically neutral" (Jackson and Nexon 2019, 585). Rather, relationalism is a sort of ontological wager that can be cashed out in various ways—often as field theory, network analysis, or actor-network theory (McCourt 2016, 475).[15]

This relationality is present throughout the book, but it is perhaps clearest in Chapter 2 and Chapter 5. In Chapter 2, I opt for a sort of qualitative network analysis conducted through a case study, networks being "sets of relations that form structures, which in turn may constrain and enable agents" and network analysis concerning "relationships defined by links among nodes (or agents)" (Hafner-Burton et al. 2009, 560, 562). While previous research has examined the creation of social ties, the relationship between network centrality and social power, the politics of brokerage, and ability of nodes to disconnect from other nodes in their network, my argument on the origins of the Northwest Indian War differs in emphasizing the ways settlers activated or made more salient existing social ties.[16] In Chapter 5, my focus is highly processual—that is, I consider the processes by which officials and activists have sought to make one particular interpretation of the Northwest Indian War *the* interpretation that is promulgated and commemorated in Fort Wayne, Indiana.

In this regard, I diverge from perhaps the most prominent recent work to address similar questions. In seeking to explain "why states colonize and why they stop," Lachlan McNamee (2023, 32, 40) takes an explicitly "rationalist" approach to the question—he thus "assume[s] that all settler migration is voluntary and economically driven" and that "states are principally concerned with balancing wealth and security." Like McNamee (2023, 17), I see "colonization projects" as "characterized by a triangle of actors— settlers, indigenes, and the central state"—but to answer the questions I am asking, I see no need to assume that those actors have any specific motivations or degrees of voluntarism.[17] To the extent that I discuss the motivations of actors in this book, I attempt to discern those from recorded actions, but I am generally inclined not to dwell on motivations and to instead concern myself with actions, including speech acts.[18]

My goals here are more explanatory and descriptive than they are critical. If critical theoretical perspectives are intended to be in some way "emancipatory" or "liberatory," I am skeptical of my own ability to satisfy such lofty promises (Alker 2005; Booth 1991). I do, however, believe that critical work generally aims to demonstrate why things are the way that they are and how they might be made different, and this book seeks to contribute to such an understanding of US relations with Native American groups. If these relations are now largely thought of as domestic rather than international, this book helps to demonstrate how that came to be and how that might be contested. Moreover, to the extent that critical scholarship is often concerned with uncovering dynamics that other scholarship has missed, I would describe this book as critical insofar as I am interested in demonstrating continuities in US foreign policy that have been overlooked. I thus draw on critical scholarship, and while I remain agnostic here on what the future of US relations with tribes ought to look like, my concluding chapter ultimately suggests that the ways we engage with Indigenous histories may play an important part in shaping that future.

Throughout the book, I use qualitative methods, but the kind of qualitative methods I use and the way I employ them differ from much work in political science. In short, I see this as an "analyticist" project that "provides a set of more or less helpful idealizations or oversimplifications that can be used to order the complex chaos of empirical reality into more comprehensible and manageable forms" (Jackson 2011, 113). The "idealizations" in question are those surrounding the processes and relations I identify in each chapter. Importantly, this is not a neopositivist project of the sort that predominates in IR today; while the use of qualitative case studies is common in IR, I am not using cross-case variation to support an argument that aspires to "nomothetic," law-like generalization (Jackson 2011, 200). Rather, what I am doing in Chapter 2 especially takes the form of "singular causal analysis" by way of "ideal typification." There the ideal type in question is that of the activation of social ties. "An ideal-typical analytical depiction produces not a representation of any actual situation, but a *model* of it, using categories and terms that a scholar has derived from a set of value-commitments" (Jackson 2011, 146–147, emphasis in original). The process of producing such a model entails, for Max Weber, as interpreted by Patrick Thaddeus Jackson (2011, 147–148), three key claims or moves: First, "a concrete situation is never to be understood as resulting from or consisting of any one factor, but instead from a number of factors coming together in a case-specific way" (Jackson 2011, 147).[19] Second, "researchers seeking to isolate causal factors should proceed by ideal-typifying processes and causal relations, and then trying to imagine whether the observed result in question would actually occur if things had occurred in a different way, or if factors had been present which were not in fact present" (Jackson 2011, 148). Third, "This imaginative isolation of factors allows an analyst to ascertain which factors are critical to the causal configuration responsible for the outcome in question according to a simple rule: if one can imagine the outcome taking place despite the modification of some factor, then that factor is not part of the causal configuration" (Jackson 2011, 148).

Here this analyticist, ideal-typical approach manifests in part in a tight focus on the Northwest Indian War itself. I am less interested, for example, in the general question of why the United States entered wars with Native American groups or what effects such wars have than I am in looking at why the United States entered this specific war and what this first war with Native American groups can tell us about US foreign policy and its territorial conquests. Ultimately, each chapter is a sort of case study in its own right, but they are all focused on the Northwest Indian War in some way. This allows me to focus on the specifics of this war and what it tells us about the conventional wisdom across various issues in the study of US foreign policy. Some of the analytic work here relies on the identification of proposed causal mechanisms that might be generalized to other cases— perhaps to other settler states, for example—but I leave that task for future research.

To support my qualitative examination of the Northwest Indian War, I rely on primary sources where possible to supplement a wide-ranging engagement with secondary sources from across disciplines. In the first three empirical chapters—on the origins of the war, the use of military fortifications, and the nascent practice of counterinsurgency—the primary sources are often documents produced by settlers, government officials, and others involved in the processes I describe.

The fourth empirical chapter is unique in that it is essentially a digital ethnography. If the first three empirical chapters look like more conventional qualitative studies of US foreign policy—like the sort of work that could be described as "Historical IR" (Lemke et al. 2023)—this fourth empirical chapter is thus more influenced by work in the humanities.[20] Here I provide a granular description and analysis of various public-facing messages communicated by those associated with the General "Mad" Anthony Wayne Organization and made available in various online fora.[21] In relaying their public statements made on local news stations, on their organizational website, and on their organizational Facebook page, I convey how this group seeks to solidify a particular reading of Wayne's actions in the Northwest Indian War while marginalizing other potential readings thereof. In other words, this final empirical chapter is central to the relational theoretical core of this book. Relational work suggests that any given state requires a sort of tacit, daily buy-in to continue existing as such; my examination of Fort Wayne's Anthony Wayne Day is about one group's efforts to legitimize American conquest in ways that facilitate that buy-in.

These empirical and theoretical contributions do not stand alone but instead inform a broader interpretation of US foreign policy. In taking a relational approach to this study and in highlighting the settler colonial project as constitutive of US foreign policy, I ultimately come to an interpretation of US foreign policy that shifts our attention away from particular goals (e.g., power or security), political valences (e.g., liberal or conservative), or modes of statecraft (e.g., unilateral or multilateral) that might be taken to define US foreign policy. Rather, I emphasize that the making of foreign policy is constituted by the identification and crafting of distinct stances toward political others. To date, the most common labels for US foreign policy that draw our attention to self-other relations have been isolationism, a stance in which the United States would shield itself from the influence of others, and internationalism, a stance in which the United States would engage with others to make the global environment more conducive to US interests. However individual scholars parse this dichotomy, I argue, such labels are insufficient for the purpose of describing US foreign policy. In the next section, I make one of my key arguments—that attending to US relations with Native American groups in the study of US foreign policy exposes the weakness of isolationism as a way to understand historical US foreign policy.

AGAINST ISOLATIONISM

For many scholars, the early United States was isolationist insofar as it sought to isolate itself from the rest of the world. For Charles Kupchan (2020, 5), for example, George Washington's farewell address serves as the definitive statement of early American isolationism. "The great rule of conduct for us in regard to foreign nations," as Kupchan quotes Washington's 1796 declaration, "is in extending our commercial relations, to have with them as little political connection as possible. . . . It is our true policy to steer clear of permanent alliances with any portion of the foreign world." This "great rule," Kupchan argues, "prevailed for over a century" (2020, 63). Washington himself did not use the term "isolationism"—that was a later innovation—but Kupchan finds in Washington's address "a grand strategy aimed at disengagement with foreign powers and the avoidance of enduring strategic commitments beyond the North American homeland" (2020, 6). I adopt this statement as a definition of isolationism.[22] Did the United States seek "disengagement with foreign powers"? Did it avoid "enduring strategic commitments beyond the North American homeland"? Those are thus the key questions in assessing whether the United States was ever isolationist, and Kupchan answers both of those questions in the affirmative.

"In the years during and immediately after the struggle for independence," Kupchan (2020, 67) contends, "two defining elements of U.S. grand strategy clearly emerged." The first of these was "strategic dominance in their own neighborhood," while the second, which "seemed to contradict the first," was "geopolitical isolation from the rest of the world." Kupchan is thus sensitive to the tension between the purported isolation and expansion of the United States. Ultimately, however, he argues that the United States hewed to this isolationist grand strategy until a more internationalist—or even imperial—impulse started to erode support for isolationism in the 1890s. Until the Spanish–American War, in Kupchan's telling, isolationism kept the United States from acquiring more territory in Latin America, the Caribbean, and the Pacific than a more activist power would have, and acquisitions that eventually occurred—of Alaska, Hawaii, and Guam for example—were significantly slowed by isolationists in Congress (or by the perception of those in Congress that their constituents supported isolationism) (Kupchan 2020, 132–136, 150–155).

If, again, the questions here are whether the United States once sought "disengagement with foreign powers" and avoided "enduring strategic commitments beyond the North American homeland," other recent scholarship on early American grand strategy suggests that the answers are not so straightforward. For Eric Grynaviski (2018), IR scholarship's habitual overlooking of early American grand strategy—or, on the other hand, an isolationist reading thereof—does not comport with the activism of early US policymakers. That this activism was often concentrated relatively close to home does not make it any less active, he suggests. "The United States concentrated on the western hemisphere in the nineteenth century, especially the American West," Gryanviski (2018, 12) writes, "because it presented the most compelling security threats and the largest incentives for intervention and occupation." If one brings a focus on hard power and political elites to the historical record, however, one might miss the extent of this activity. "American material power was important for the country's rise, but the actual process by which the United States expanded saw the federal government rarely using its military forces to effectively subdue local or foreign populations" (2018, 12). Rather, Grynaviski argues, American expansion was made possible in large part by intermediaries who bridged "structural holes" and facilitated cooperation between US policymakers and various "non-state allies" that abetted American expansion (2018, 21–23, 46–47). For Grynaviski, these intermediaries help to explain how the United States, even as it "was not a great power," nevertheless "competed globally beyond its weight class" and ultimately "wove together an empire" (2018, 281–282).

Similar to Grynaviski, Richard Maass (2020) portrays early American grand strategy as more activist than isolationist. He focuses on the question of why the United States did not expand more than it did, however, so he is concerned not to overstate either activist or isolationist impulses in American foreign policy. "Mark Twain's country was ten times larger than the colonies that declared independence in 1776," he notes, yet "U.S. leaders were neither greedy conquerors targeting everything in sight nor calculating materialists seizing every profitable opportunity" (2020, 1, 10). The characterization of early US grand strategy as isolationist thus sits uneasily with him, but nor does Maass see US history an undifferentiated mass of expansionist projects. "The United States has never been truly isolationist . . . but by overselling continuity in the history of U.S. foreign policy, the American Empire literature has helped obscure meaningful variations within that history" (2020, 17).[23] Even if the United States was "picky," Maass leaves the reader with a depiction of a quite activist United States that sought domination in its hemisphere in various ways before 1898 (2020, 81–82, 119, 197–198).

In short, isolationism is not a satisfactory rendering of early American grand strategy. As Grynaviski and Maass help to clarify, by Kupchan's (2020) own definition, the United States was never isolationist. While early US policymakers generally sought to avoid any political commitments in Europe that could lead to their involvement in European wars, Grynaviski and Maass's works draw our attention to two problems with characterizing early US grand strategy as isolationist.

First, to say that early American grand strategy aimed at "disengagement with foreign powers" overstates the extent of any such aspiration. The United States sought to avoid binding alliances that might drag it into wars—a common fear in world politics (Edelstein and Shifrinson 2018)—while consistently seeking more transitory alliances alongside sustained economic and social engagement around the world, including on the North American frontier as US territorial claims expanded. The isolationist reading of early US grand strategy equates a relatively narrow avoidance of particular kinds of commitments for specific reasons with a broader desire for "disengagement." As one historian puts it, "American statesmen had no qualms about engaging with the powers of the Old World," to say nothing of the polities of the New World, "when U.S. interests demanded" (Sexton 2011, 29). Indeed, as Maass (2020, 10) puts it:

> U.S. leaders . . . were driven by a mix of power, institutions, and ideas: excitement about geopolitical opportunities, desires to increase their wealth and power, concerns about the domestic political balance and their own enduring influence over federal policy, visions of the grand republic they sought to build, and colored perceptions of other peoples' identities relative to their own.

The concatenation of these factors sometimes led policymakers to oppose expansion, to be sure, but they also often led to expansion, a process that involved engagement with foreign powers.

Second, one might argue that the United States did engage with foreign powers where necessary, but it did so—to come to the latter part of Kupchan's definition of isolationism—to avoid "enduring strategic commitments beyond the North American homeland."[24] As Kupchan (2020, 31) argues, "Westward expansion, determined efforts to ease European powers out of America's neighborhood, and neutralization of the threat from 'savage tribes' were generally deemed to be strategic imperatives . . . in the service of isolation."[25] This argument, however, elides the extent to which the question of what constituted the US "homeland" was constantly debated and expanded throughout this period, not to mention the commitments the US government was willing to make in North America and beyond.[26] As Maass (2020, 47) notes, for example, early "U.S. leaders relieved Britain of Transappalachia, France of Louisiana, and Spain of Florida" within the country's first four decades of existence as an independent state, and in the 1840s, the United States "continued to remove eastern Indians to the West, annexed Texas, acquired Oregon South of 49°, and conquered and obtained New Mexico and California" (Hietala 2003, ix). This process surely entailed "enduring strategic commitments" to an ever-expanding homeland.[27] Moreover, even if one maintains that early US leaders believed a broad swath of the North American continent to constitute their proper homeland from which their isolated polity could remake the world through its virtuous example, American policymakers also laid claim to numerous overseas territories even before 1898.[28] Between 1856 and 1860, for example, the US pursuit of guano (seabird and bat manure typically used as fertilizer) led it to claim dozens of island territories (mostly in the Pacific) as its own, including Baker Island, Christmas Atoll, Midway Atoll, Kingman Reef, and Palmyra Island, many of which have indeed constituted enduring strategic commitments (Evers and Grynaviski 2024, 59).[29]

To label early US foreign policy isolationist is thus, I argue, a mischaracterization. Rather, as Tzvetan Todorov (1999, 247) suggests, US foreign policy might be better characterized by a central stance toward "otherness": "Since the period of the [Spanish] conquest, Western Europe has tried to assimilate the other, to do away with exterior alterity, and has in great part succeeded." Alternatively, as Hilde Restad (2015) would have it, we might conceptualize US foreign policy as a tradition of "unilateral internationalism." At the least, we can indeed think of US foreign policy as being about relations with others, and when we consider Native Americans to be among those others, US foreign policy becomes less neatly divisible into isolationist or internationalist periods.[30] Indeed, in a telling shift, Kupchan goes from describing early US grand strategy as one of "hemispheric isolation" to "hemispheric dominance" (2020, 8, 64). Hemispheric domination would be the more apt description, and one does not dominate in isolation.[31]

THE NORTHWEST INDIAN WAR IN CONTEXT

Before outlining the remainder of the book, I will provide an overview of historical context that will be relevant to every empirical chapter. The Northwest Indian War would ultimately take place in lands that now form the states of Ohio and Indiana. The "doctrine of discovery" enshrined in Pope Alexander VI's 1493 *Inter Caetera* had granted to Spain all the lands that its subjects discovered or might discover in the New World, but Great Britain would eventually secure its own claims to the land of the Old Northwest (that is, the Northwest Territory—an area including the future states of Ohio, Michigan, Indiana, Illinois, Wisconsin, and a portion of Minnesota) (Deloria and Wilkins 1999, 3). Before any European powers claimed the territory, however, the land had been inhabited and contested for centuries by various Native groups. Indeed, the region was populated largely by the Iroquois (or Haudenosaunee) and various Algonquian tribes that fought for control of the territory in the seventeenth and eighteenth centuries. Although the Iroquoian ethno-linguistic family includes a range of tribes, among them the Cherokee and Wyandot, when referring to the Iroquois, I am referring to the Iroquois Confederacy, which was comprised of the Cayuga, Mohawk, Onondaga, Oneida, and Seneca peoples—and, beginning in the early eighteenth century, the Tuscarora, who had suffered military defeat at the hands of the North Carolinian colony (Fenton 1998, 4–5, 382). Across North America, Iroquoian peoples were often in direct conflict with peoples of the Algonquian ethno-linguistic group or on opposing sides of European conflicts. These disputes were exacerbated both by the incidental introduction of European diseases that dramatically reduced Native populations even before substantial Anglo-American settlement and by the intentional violence of settlers, including practices of slave labor (Sugden 2000, 29). By the time of the Northwest Indian War, the Iroquois had largely—but not entirely—left the Ohio region under pressure from Anglo-American settlers and policymakers, leaving incoming settlers to contend primarily with local Algonquian tribes.

The Algonquian ethno-linguistic group includes a wide array of peoples that Anglo-American settlers encountered from their initial settlement to their expansion across the continent. These groups included, for example, the Wampanoag of the Massachusetts Bay area, other Great Lakes region tribes such as the Kickapoo and Sauk (or Sac), as well as Upper Midwest tribes such as the Cree of Wisconsin and Minnesota and Great Plains tribes such as the Arapaho and Cheyenne. Where such tribes existed near each other, as did those of the Ohio River Valley, members of these different tribes often lived together in "intensely multiethnic" villages (Warren 2014, 20).[32] By the late eighteenth century, two Algonquian tribes, the Shawnee and the Miami peoples, constituted the most powerful tribes in the Ohio region.

Although the precise origins of the Shawnee (or Saawanooki) are uncertain, there were Shawnee settlements across what is now the United States by the seventeenth century: From Pennsylvania to Illinois and from there to Georgia, the Shawnee population was so dispersed that their language was often used by other Algonquian peoples to facilitate intertribal contacts (Calloway 2007, 4–5). By the mid-eighteenth century, however, the threat of expanding American settlements and the simultaneous lure of retaining access to European goods would prompt many Shawnees to move farther inland to Ohio (Warren 2014, 179).

The Shawnee, like many other Native groups, occasionally allied with European powers in their various conflicts on the North American continent. In the French and Indian War, for example, many of the Shawnee originally allied with the French before switching to the British side in 1758. In the aftermath of the war, however, the French ceded their territory in the Old Northwest to the British, and the Crown quickly enacted policies that treated the Native populations as conquered peoples. The Shawnee (among other tribes) thus went to war against the British once again in Pontiac's War of 1763–66, and although the military conflict was not decisive, the Native confederation gained policy concessions that created a less coercive relationship with the British (Middleton 2007, 167–182).[33] Perhaps most importantly, the British Crown enacted the Proclamation of 1763 early in the conflict in an effort to assuage the Native communities and to prevent settlers from provoking new conflicts (Coates 2004, 176). This edict declared a portion of the lands west of the Appalachians to be an "Indian Reserve" and barred Anglo-American settlement west of the line. Although this did not prevent every interested settler from going beyond that line, it disincentivized settlement and land speculation given that such enterprises entailed efforts to establish clear legal title to land (Calloway 2007, 44; Holton 1994, 454).

The Miami (or Myaamia) people, in contrast with the Shawnee, appear to have long had a relatively concentrated population in areas now occupied by Wisconsin and Michigan, though migration brought them to the Ohio region around the same time as the Shawnee. Although the Miami lived further west than the Shawnee and were not migrating due to the direct pressure of US expansion, they had come into conflict with the Iroquois during the Beaver Wars of the seventeenth century (Anson 1970, 38).[34] Over the course of the eighteenth century, disease significantly reduced the Miami population such that the tribe's various bands would merge into three primary bands—the Miami, the Piankashaw, and the Wea (Anson 1970, 13). All three of these bands would play a role in the Northwest Indian War, though the Miami based at Kekionga as well as the Wea at Ouiatenon would be some of the primary targets for the US military by virtue of living in some of the largest Native communities in the area.

Shortly after the British ceded all land east of the Mississippi River, north of Florida, and south of Canada to the United States in 1783's Treaty of Paris, US negotiators sought treaties with various Native nations, the Iroquois among them. The Iroquois by that time had already ceded territory in what is now Kentucky, West Virginia, and Pennsylvania to the British in the Treaty of Fort Stanwix of 1768. For those Native nations whose land the British had ceded without their consent, the US position was that their new claim to the land was valid by right of conquest (even when tribes had not supported the British or when only parts of tribes had done so).

Nonetheless, given that many tribes did not recognize the British cession of their lands, US officials generally thought it was most prudent to negotiate directly with tribes to acquire their lands, and they often portrayed this as a sign of their generosity and good faith (Prucha 1994, 24–27). Among these efforts was the conclusion of a treaty between Iroquois and US negotiators—a new Treaty of Fort Stanwix completed in 1784 in which the Iroquois ceded their claimed lands in Ohio (Sugden 2000, 84). The Iroquois council refused to ratify the treaty, however, as its representatives had not been authorized to make such concessions, and a group of Algonquian tribes, sometimes referred to as the Western Confederacy (which included the Shawnee, Miami, and other Ohio region tribes) likewise denied the validity of the treaty because most of the Iroquois by that point did not live in Ohio (Calloway 2007, 77–78). Nonetheless, the Confederation Congress of the United States ratified the Treaty of Fort Stanwix in 1785, which gave US officials reason to believe that they would be able to replicate this process with other tribes. In the years between 1785 and the onset of the Northwest Indian War in 1790, they would seek to replicate what they saw as the success of the Treaty of Fort Stanwix, but they would ultimately have to go to war to compel more tribes in the region to sign land cession treaties.

PLAN OF THE BOOK

In Chapter 2, I show how interactions between settlers and political elites led to the Northwest Indian War. I argue that settlers—amid a context in which land speculation played an important role and in which the United States could field only a small military—activated social ties to receptive political elites to push for federal military intervention in local conflicts with Native American groups. This chapter is central to my broader argument that relations with Native American groups were no less central to early US foreign policy than relations with major European powers like England and France and that "isolationism" is surely a misnomer for a period of much violent dispossession.

In Chapter 3, I show how the Northwest Indian War presaged a practice that would become central to American defense policy: the use of military bases to project power. After early US losses in the war, General Anthony Wayne received command of a force that would succeed in defeating a Native coalition largely through a reliance on the construction of forts in the Ohio River Valley. This demonstrated to political elites the value of military bases in securing control across the continent, and they would subsequently invest a great deal of resources in the maintenance of an expansive basing network well before the Spanish–American War and World War II gave the United States the opportunity to craft an even more far-flung system of bases. This ultimately bolsters my argument that the difference between pre- and post-1898 periods of US foreign policy is not as stark as some would suggest.

In Chapter 4, I turn to a different set of practices that the Northwest Indian War presaged: an early sort of counterinsurgency doctrine that informed US military forces throughout the so-called Indian Wars and beyond. Through a case study of the Philippine–American War of 1899– 1902—a war in which many of the American combatants were veterans of the Indian Wars—I argue that the perceived lessons of the Indian Wars were seen as applicable in conflicts with other purportedly "uncivilized" groups such as the Filipinos who resisted American occupation. These lessons, however, were more individualized than institutionalized because the early US military lacked formal "lessons learned" processes. This chapter helps to demonstrate the relevance of the Northwest Indian War and the Indian Wars more broadly for the practice of US foreign policy beyond the North American continent.

In Chapter 5, I show how ongoing contestation over how to memorialize the Northwest Indian War has divided partisans into groups that seek to establish one interpretation of the conflict as *the* proper interpretation or to allow for more open-ended reflection. Through a case study of recent local debates over whether to commemorate Fort Wayne, Indiana's namesake, Anthony Wayne, I show how primarily Republican political officials and activists seek to legitimize America's conquest.

In making these arguments, I offer correctives to work in IR downplaying the constitutive role of relations with Native American groups in US foreign policy. In so doing, I suggest that the common usage of 1898 and the Spanish–American War to divide the history of US foreign policy into more isolationist and internationalist periods is misguided. I instead show that US foreign policy was quite active from the beginning, that the increasingly widespread use of "overseas" military bases after 1898 had a well-established precedent in the construction of hundreds of American military bases along an expanding frontier, and that conflicts with Native American groups helped refine US military practices that were subsequently deployed in other settings.

I also offer correctives to work that sees settler–Native conflict as something of the past. While overviews of the history of US foreign policy often treat America's Indian Wars as more domestic than foreign or as events of purely historical interest, Chapters 3 and 4 show that these conflicts can help us make sense of US military practices in other contexts. Furthermore, Chapter 5 draws on relational theory to show that the United States as a putative sovereign relies on the continual reaffirmation of the legitimacy of the US dispossession of Native American groups, which has produced ongoing contestation between citizens of the United States and Native tribes. Chapter 5 also reconnects with Chapter 2 insofar as it is ultimately about how individuals push the state to provide security. In today's Fort Wayne, Indiana, individual citizens celebrate Anthony Wayne to affirm the legitimacy of the state, which is ultimately the guarantor of their own security; settlers in the eighteenth-century Northwest Territory quite similarly sought security under the aegis of a state whose legitimacy they were happy to affirm so long as it rendered them aid.

I conclude in Chapter 6 with a discussion of where further research might go from here. In bringing Indigenous politics more squarely into the study of IR and US foreign policy, I argue, we might better understand a variety of political phenomena ranging from alliance formation to the question of under what conditions and to what extent Indigenous rights claims might provoke settler state backlash. Furthermore, I consider some potential future trajectories of US relations with Native American groups and of relations between Indigenous peoples and states more generally, and I note that research in this space might at least help others understand how one trajectory or another becomes more or less likely.

Two

NETWORKED FRONTIERS

The Origins of the Northwest Indian War

On June 1, 1786, John Filson wrote to the US Congress from Vincennes, a growing settler community in what would eventually become the state of Indiana. Filson—a teacher, surveyor, and writer—had already done much to encourage westward settlement through the publication of his 1784 book, *The Discovery, Settlement and Present State of Kentucke*, which included material that would make Daniel Boone a paragon of the rugged frontiersman in the American imagination (Tichenor 2009, 4–6). But in 1786, together with the heads of seventy-one Vincennes households who also signed the letter, Filson would seek a more direct role in America's expansion by petitioning Congress for assistance in combating local Native American populations.

The settlers of Vincennes, "having lately emigrated to this district, expecting to enjoy the blessings of peace and property, and as faithful subjects to the United States," felt that their entire project was being threatened (quoted in Helderman 1938, 457–458). "[B]eing surrounded and invested with hostile savages, whose antipathy to americans, exposing daily to danger and frequent death," only Congress could offer the settlers

NETWORKED FRONTIERS   *21*

enough protection to ensure their collective venture did not fail. Not just any form of assistance would suffice—the protection of the US military was necessary:

> Being now without order, law or government by any executive, which adds greatly to our distressed situation, we humbly pray that you will appoint a regular government in this place . . . and also we pray that a strong garrison may be established here, for a support to the dignity of the Civil power, and a defence against imperious hostile savages.

If Congress could make such provisions, "the banks of Wabash would soon be inhabited by numerous valuable subjects," but a lack of such protection would produce "destruction which will totally prevent an emigration." If Congress, "the guardians of our lives, liberty and property," did not do something, the settlement would surely fail and dissuade other potential settlers from doing their part to extend the American frontier.

Congress would indeed authorize the creation of a small military fort near Vincennes, and the settlement would survive, but this was not enough to save Filson himself—he was likely killed by a Shawnee party while surveying land along the Great Miami River in 1788.[1] Indeed, settlers and Native groups would continue to engage in relatively small-scale acts of violence against each other until, after years of continued settler pressure for military intervention, President George Washington ordered the military into its first war with Native American groups.[2] After an intermittent but eventually victorious five-year campaign, the United States would formally extract land cessions from the Shawnee, the Miami, and other local Native American groups in the Treaty of Greenville. If, however, the US government was willing to go to war in 1790 and stay at war for years, it is not immediately clear why 1790 was the tipping point. Settler–Native violence had been occurring for years, and the US government first laid claim to the Old Northwest in 1783. Why wait for years to support those claims with military force? On the other hand, why not allow more time to produce a negotiated settlement with tribes?

In this chapter, I examine the origins of the Northwest Indian War to consider why US political elites ultimately decided to use military force when they did. Through this case study, I show how settlers activated latent social ties to receptive political elites to push for federal military intervention in local conflicts with Native American groups. Simply being US citizens gave settlers a legitimate claim to federal support in the views of political elites, but it was the making of that claim—through direct requests to federal policymakers or indirectly through local policymakers—that spurred US military intervention in the Northwest Indian War.[3] Combined with pressure from wealthy land speculators and a fear that settlers might seek independence from the United States, this settler lobbying ultimately helped convince political elites that they needed to intervene.[4]

This examination of the origins of the Northwest Indian War sets up the next three chapters, all of which deal with the reverberations of this war. In this chapter, I begin by outlining my argument with respect to the origins of the war, and I then detail the data and methods underlying my argument before turning to the case itself in more detail. I introduce my case study by making the case that political elites wanted to expand into the Old Northwest while avoiding war to the extent possible. As settlers like John Filson streamed into Ohio and Indiana—territories that saw the bulk of the early settlement by virtue of being closer to existing US territories and having fewer ongoing jurisdictional disputes than lands farther south— they often found Native residents to be hostile to their presence, and they therefore activated their social ties to political elites to push for federal military assistance. I then examine the network effects through which settler behaviors less directly pushed political elites toward war in this case. I also engage with potential alternative explanations, and I highlight the theoretical stakes and the potential benefits of a relational perspective on US foreign policy.

THE ARGUMENT

I argue that social networks were decisive in shaping the US response to peripheral conflict. Direct and indirect ties between political elites and peripheral actors enabled those on the periphery to effectively lobby elites for support; simply being US citizens gave settlers a claim to federal support. On their own, however, such ties do not explain anything; the link between citizen and representative does not automatically cause anything to happen.[5] I argue that the activation of these ties spurred US military intervention in the Northwest Indian War and thereby shaped the contours of the country's territorial expansion. The settlers' key *fait accompli*—the act of settling on land already claimed by Native tribes—often sparked violent conflict, but settlers in such situations did not always make use of their social ties to political elites to request military assistance.[6] Rather, to activate those social ties, settlers had to take affirmative steps to lobby for federal assistance—either directly to federal elites, as John Filson and the settlers of Vincennes did in 1786, or indirectly through local political elites. This interactive process between settlers and political elites forms the crux of this chapter.

While the activation of settlers' social ties to political elites is the focal point of my argument, a broader array of network effects also undergirded this periphery-led aspect of US territorial expansion. First, settler behaviors shaped the perceived value of land, and their actions sometimes led speculators to push political elites to protect the value of that land. That is, settlers were part of a broader political system that incentivized land speculation in the form of the purchase of land with the intent of later resale at a profit, and settler actions affected speculator actions. Given that (real and potential) patterns of settlement shaped anticipated land value, settler conflicts with Native nations gave speculators reason to lobby for federal military intervention even if settlers were not already doing so.

Second, when settlers presented policymakers with the decision of whether to intervene in an ongoing settler dispute with Native nations, they forced policymakers to reckon with the potential costs of non-intervention. That is, federal elites deciding whether to engage in military intervention in peripheral conflicts had to consider both the short-term costs of war as well as the potential long-term costs. If they did not intervene and Native American groups defeated settlers, this could potentially inhibit future settlement in that area or even elsewhere if other settlers became worried that the federal government would not assist them *in extremis*. Alternatively, settlers might question the value of a government that failed to protect them, thereby sparking secessionist movements along the frontier, a situation that could be made even more worse if newly founded settler states sought alliances with European powers. Political elites, in short, feared the stunting of settlement or the settler-initiated severing of social ties that might result from non-intervention in settler–Indigenous conflicts.[7]

Third and finally, because American settlers possessed social ties to the federal government, settler actions affected perceptions of the federal government and ultimately made federal negotiations with Native American groups more difficult. In assessing the intentions of the federal government, settler actions constituted one important source of evidence for Native American groups.[8] While settlers were generally distinguishable from federal elites as a different category of persons, settlers and elites constituted an interlinked network such that when settlers laid claim to Native American lands or attacked Native American groups, this undermined the credibility of federal promises to the effect that negotiated settlements would be upheld or that the federal government would protect its Native American groups from further settler violence.

Drawing on primary and secondary sources, I demonstrate in this chapter how settlers in the Northwest Territory activated their social ties to political elites to lobby for military assistance, thereby channeling US territorial expansion in specific directions. In the next section, I outline two key premises on which my argument rests.

EARLY US FOREIGN POLICY IN PRINCIPLE AND PRACTICE

My explanation for the origins of the Northwest Indian War rests on two premises that I argue defined early US foreign policy. First, settlers and political elites alike generally saw territorial expansion as the proper course of action for the United States. In hindsight, it may appear obvious that the desire for expansion was widespread across all US classes, but the extent to which different segments of American society favored expansion is still the subject of scholarly debate.[9] However, both before and after US independence, political elites and settlers alike articulated the natural and appropriate future of the United States as being one of expansion. Second, political elites sought to accomplish this expansion while avoiding war. The potential costs associated with military conflict were assumed to be quite high, especially in the early days of a young republic with only a small standing army, so political elites tried to promote expansion while being mindful of those potential costs.

To consider the first premise—that US settlers and political elites both sought territorial expansion—I first survey expansionist sentiments among elites. Benjamin Franklin, for example, authored a 1751 pamphlet, "Observations Concerning the Increase of Mankind," in which he predicted that US population growth would naturally lead to westward expansion—a good thing in Franklin's estimation (Dahl 2018, 26–27). Similarly, George Washington believed that a well-managed process of western settlement could be lucrative so long as the government worked to facilitate connection between western and eastern markets. On October 4, 1784, at the end of a trip that took him through Virginia, Maryland, and Pennsylvania, Washington wrote in his diary that "[In order] to fix the trade of the Western country to our markets . . . the way is plain. . . . It is to open a wide door, and make smooth a way for the produce of that country to pass to our markets." A contemporary of Washington, Thomas Jefferson, was even more explicit when writing to then-governor of Virginia James Monroe in November 1801. Still in the first year of his presidency, Jefferson wrote: "It is impossible not to look forward to distant times when our rapid multiplication will expand itself beyond those limits, and cover the whole northern, if not the southern continent" (1861, 420). After Monroe himself won the presidency in 1816, his "administration was committed to seizing Florida and securing their northern and southern boundaries against encroachment from the European empires" (Goddard 2018b, 62–63). As one recent history summarizes the elite consensus of the day, "Expansion was central to America's political identity as a unique experiment in republican liberty" (Ostler 2019, 85).[10]

Settlers similarly saw expansion in the future for the United States. Both before and after US independence, Anglo-American settlers saw lands on the North American continent as theirs for the taking, and while their sentiments were recorded less frequently than those of elites, their actions speak loudly enough. Pre-independence Anglo-American settlement became sufficiently problematic that in 1763, eager to avoid territorial disputes that might trigger a repeat of the French and Indian War, the British Crown banned settlers from squatting on or purchasing Native lands west of the Appalachian Mountains (Frymer 2017, 43). Likewise, the Crown increased taxes on the colonists and sought to enforce its tax laws more reliably to make the fur trade and smuggling—the core of the frontier economy—less profitable (Andreas 2013, 29–44; Hixson 2013, 34). Such actions gave Anglo-American settlers all the more reason to support a rebellion, and once the United States had won its independence, population growth and immigration rebounded from wartime declines, which yielded a dramatic acceleration in westward settlement that would be sustained for decades (Kluger 2007, 185).

For both political elites and settlers, moreover, their view of territorial expansion as wholly appropriate for the nascent United States was informed by Lockean ideas that became all the more influential amid the American Revolution—ideas to the effect that they had an absolute right to govern themselves and to take possession of land that they would purportedly put to better use than its current inhabitants.[11] If, for John Locke (quoted in Dahl 2018, 54–55), "political societies all began from a voluntary union" and subsequently operated on the "tacit consent" of those not present at the creation of this original social contract, many Americans took such ideas to mean that they could revoke their consent to governance that was not adequately representative of their needs. Moreover, Lockean ideas of property made a sparsely populated frontier an appealing place in which to enact self-governance. Settlers saw Native American groups as not needing or deserving all the land that they might claim as their own, and they were informed by "Lockean notions of natural right, which held that the only valid title to property is the expenditure of physical labor to cultivate and improve the land" (Dahl 2018, 132). Settlers and elites alike, however, often underestimated the extent to which Native American groups did indeed "improve the land" they saw as their own, and they likewise misunderstood Native American ideas of property. Indeed, despite what many Americans thought, "The general concepts of both property and authority were not alien to [Native American groups]. Property rights simply grant the ownership of certain resources and do not have to include private property. Also, property can be owned by groups, not just individuals" (DuVal 2006, 7). In general, Native American ideas of property focused on "need and use rather than possession and accumulation" (Richter 2001, 51). For US settlers and political elites, however, they saw the North American continent as theirs for the taking.

These ideas of who deserved what land were surely influenced by racial thought as well.[12] Amid a racialized sociopolitical order in which Anglo-American settlers positioned themselves—"whites"—as different from and superior to "black" Africans and "red" Native Americans, such racist ideas helped to legitimize the taking of Native lands (Blackhawk 2023; Witgen 2021).[13] As I have argued, US relations with Native American groups were constitutive of early US foreign policy, and the extent to which these relations were racialized helps us to understand how Native American groups were marked as others, how Native dispossession was legitimized, and how race can shape foreign policy.[14]

Despite their desire for territorial expansion, political elites in the original thirteen colonies generally wanted to avoid war with European polities and Native nations alike. This may seem contradictory, but private and public statements alike support this interpretation.[15] Policymakers differed in their justifications for this approach, but likely the most broadly held concern was a pragmatic one: "Indigenous elimination is costly to states" (McNamee 2023, 8). This concern was most significantly expressed by George Washington, who structured much of early US policy on Indian Affairs by articulating an early mandate to expand without initiating violent conflicts. In a letter that Washington wrote to Congressman James Duane in 1783, he summarized his position as follows:

> In a word there is nothing to be obtained by an Indian War but the Soil they live on and this can be had by purchase at less expence, and without that bloodshed, and those distresses which helpless Women and Children are made partakers of in all kinds of disputes with them.

Duane, a New York delegate to the Confederation Congress and the chair of the Indian Affairs Committee, presented the Congress with a report based largely on Washington's lengthy letter, and this report would be the Congress's primary statement of its position on Indian Affairs for decades.[16] Regardless of their reasons, it was the case that political elites generally supported a sort of controlled expansion. Jeffrey Ostler (2019, 86) summarizes the conundrum: "While all Americans agreed they were entitled to Indian lands, they differed about how these lands should be acquired." Washington himself would struggle and ultimately fail to achieve expansion without war, a process that I will explore in the remainder of this chapter.

If not through conquest, how was territorial expansion to occur? Washington and future presidents generally evinced a strong preference for expanding through purchase. This should perhaps not be surprising given the costs of war, but narratives of US expansion often understate the extent to which policymakers wanted to avoid war.[17] While the United States would ultimately initiate the Northwest Indian War, this did not change a general preference for purchase. This was easier and more cost-effective, to be sure, but it also had a legitimizing effect in the views of those making the purchases. To the extent that political elites sought to engage in what they saw as normatively appropriate behavior in relations with Native American tribes, they seem to have done so both for the sake of appeasing their own consciences and to maintain America's "national honor" in the eyes of their European peers (Horsman 1961, 42–43). Anders Stephanson (1995, 23) characterizes this as becoming the dominant view of policymakers at least by the time of the Louisiana Purchase in 1803: "Henceforth, purchase would indeed become the preferred and morally correct American way of expansion. Even when adding territory through war, the United States would often insist on paying something."[18] After the Spanish–American War of 1898, for example, the United States would pay Spain for the Philippines, a territory the United States would then claim as its own, and while 1898 is often portrayed as a turning point in US foreign policy, by that time such actions already had long-established precedents.[19]

As suggested above, the United States also sought to keep the costs of its territorial expansion relatively low by legitimizing its gains in the public sphere. Here elite rhetoric shifted over time to legitimize its expansion in the eyes of European powers, especially Britain. While early administrations drew on revolutionary rhetoric about the republican principles the United States would spread across the North American continent (and perhaps beyond), the Monroe administration shifted to more restrained, conciliatory rhetoric, portraying its "expansion into Spanish territory as necessary to uphold Britain's vision of an international legal regime, taking particular care to invoke the norms of self-defense, treaty law, and non-intervention at the core of Britain's nascent 'Atlantic system'" (Goddard 2018b, 62). Subsequent administrations in the nineteenth century would largely follow that precedent in an effort to lower the anticipated costs of expansion by defusing European opposition.

Political elites also sought to smooth this process of expansion through use of the regulatory tools available to them. Most significantly, the United States (under the Articles of Confederation and later under the Constitution) passed various laws to protect Native Americans from American settlers. "Regulations concerning the mode of white settlement, the encroachment on Indian land, the selling of liquor, and fair trading practices toward the

Indians were all put into effect" (Horsman 1961, 43–44). Political elites, for example, established financial inducements and restrictions through a licensing system for trade between US and Native persons, something that was intended to reduce incidents of trade-related disputes and the military conflicts that could arise from them (Prucha 1962). Political elites also established a process for "depredation claims" that acknowledged the real possibility of violence in settler-Indigenous interactions while seeking to disincentivize reprisals by reimbursing settlers and Native American individuals who could prove that one's property was damaged by the other (Skogen 1996).[20]

Alongside such tools aimed at preventing American settlers from harming Native Americans, political elites also tried to "civilize" Native nations in what was essentially an effort to create a shared identity that could deter conflict and encourage cooperation (Prucha 2000, 29, 59, 81). This civilizing effort—even as early as the 1780s—often manifested in treaty clauses that guaranteed some form of US assistance to Native nations. From the perspective of US elites, turning these populations into patriarchal, Christian, agrarian societies would civilize them in a way that would make friendlier coexistence possible or that would, perhaps even better from their perspective, eliminate the need for coexistence by fully assimilating Native American groups into the American polity—by eliminating "them" as distinct political groups and making them part of "us" (cf. Todorov 1999). Programs oriented toward agriculture were especially important to early political elites as these programs were viewed as likely having the positive side effect of allowing Native nations to live on much smaller parcels of land (Horsman 1961, 48; Lee 2019, 213–215). Both economic and social programs, however, ultimately proved costly and ineffective while settlers poured into the West (Flint 1833, 8).[21]

In principle, early US foreign policy was thus guided by elite desires for expansion while avoiding wars with European polities and Native nations. In practice, however, the US nonetheless found itself in such wars quite frequently—the country fought in fifty such wars in roughly the first hundred years of its independence.[22] The issue here is that US foreign policy was not wholly determined by political elites. Rather, studying the processes leading up to the Northwest Indian War entails focusing on multiple sets of actors, including political elites but also settlers themselves,

speculators, local elites such as county and state officials, and Native nations that often had relatively decentralized political structures.[23] Here I
come to the same conclusion as Lachlan McNamee (2023, 17): "Colonization
projects are characterized by a triangle of actors—settlers, indigenes, and
the central state." Although I am ambivalent as to whether we might locate
speculators and local elites in the category of settlers or the central state, I
am concerned with these actors insofar as they constitute ties between settlers and the central state. We might think of settlers and the central state
as nodes in a network constituted by other intermediaries, and of social
ties as being latent or active (where they exist in the first place). Ultimately,
as I will demonstrate in this chapter, the activation of settler social ties to
federal elites and related network effects created a divergence between the
principles and practice of early US foreign policy.

THE COMING OF WAR

Having detailed the historical background for the onset of the Northwest
Indian War in Chapter 1, I now shift toward an examination of the factors
that led to the US decision to use military force to solidify its claims to
the Old Northwest. I begin by focusing on a key permissive condition that
constrained and enabled action on the frontier: the presence of only a small
standing army.[24] Through the remainder of this case study, I examine the
interests of and interactions among political elites, settlers, and Native
American groups.

The United States began its political existence under the Articles of
Confederation with an exceptionally small standing army; deliberations of
the Continental Congress yielded a 700-man military drawn from state militias for the purpose of protecting "the northwestern frontiers of the United
States, and their Indian friends and allies, and for garrisoning the posts
soon to be evacuated by the troops of his britannic Majesty" (Dalton 1784,
n. 2; Millett and Maslowski 1984, 85–87). The primary consideration in these
deliberations—a point most forcefully made by New Englanders—does not
appear to have been whether the United States could afford a large standing
army but whether "the principles of republican governments . . . [and] the
liberties of a free people" could be maintained if the state relied on a larger
standing army (Dalton 1784). That is, ideas about the role of a military in

a democracy were perhaps as influential as the state's limited capacity.[25] Indeed, those in the federal government tended to assume that opposition to a large standing army was a given. During Virginia's state convention on the ratification of the new US Constitution, for example, then-Governor Edmund Randolph noted that, "With respect to a standing army, I believe there was not a member in the federal Convention, who did not feel indignation at such an institution" (Randolph 1788, 401). The military would grow incrementally for the next two decades—spurred in part by conflict with Native nations as well as domestic uprisings such as Shays's Rebellion—but a more substantial change in military personnel and organization would not come until the War of 1812 (Katznelson 2002, 95–96).

Despite this opposition to a large standing army, political elites still needed some way to enforce prohibitions on settlement in certain areas. US political elites simultaneously codified the right of Native American groups to occupy their lands (in the Northwest Ordinance of 1787) and sought to persuade such groups to sell the lands they occupied. Until the lands were sold, however, it would be necessary to prevent settler violence from undermining federal negotiations. The United States sought to discourage settler incursions on the lands of the Miami, Shawnee, and others, and at times the military even used their limited means to evict squatters (Tate 1999, 238–239).

The task of keeping the peace on the frontier fell to Josiah Harmar, lieutenant colonel commandant of the First American Regiment (the aforementioned 700-man force). When he was initially sent to the Northwest Territory in 1784, he understood a prominent part of his work to be the prevention of settlement in disputed territory (Sword 1985, 89). As he wrote about two-and-a-half years into his assignment, "I humbly conceive that the great objects I have to attend to, will be, to prevent illegal encroachments on the public lands, to secure happiness to the inhabitants, and to protect private property from arbitrary invasion, and to remove, if possible, diffidence, fear, & jealousy from the minds of the Indians; to these points I shall lend my attention" (Harmar 1787, 120).[26]

Harmar was at the same time being urged to avoid any actions that would produce a general war—that is, a war between the United States and the various tribes of the Old Northwest. Immediately prior to a 1788 treaty council, Secretary of War Henry Knox relayed to Harmar that a war "would at present be embarrassing beyond conception" (quoted in Sword 1985, 67). Harmar and his hundreds of soldiers were ill-equipped to deal with thousands of settlers and Native individuals.

Is it, however, fair to say that settlers brought political elites into wars that the elites would have preferred to avoid? I make the case below that the activation of social ties and network effects outlined here did indeed help settlers push political elites into the Northwest Indian War despite their preference to acquire territory without war.

THE DESIRE FOR EXPANSION WITHOUT WAR

In the years prior to the onset of the Northwest Indian War, political elites articulated various reasons to avoid war with Native American groups. In George Washington's aforementioned 1783 letter to James Duane, he noted that the newly independent United States would do well to avoid any wars on the frontier, but he was cognizant that settlers and others would make that difficult. "To suffer a wide extended Country to be over run with Land Jobbers, Speculators, and Monopolisers or even with scatter'd settlers," he wrote, "is pregnant of disputes both with the Savages and among ourselves." He argued in this same letter for the purchase of Native land rather than its acquisition through conflict and—until such lands could be purchased— for federal restraint of settlers:

> We will . . . establish a boundary line between them and us beyond which we will <u>endeavor</u> to restrain our People from Hunting or Settling. . . . I am clear in my opinion, that policy and economy point very strongly to the expediency of being upon good terms with the Indians, and the propriety of purchasing their Lands in preference to attempting to drive them by force of arms out of their Country.

The principle was expansion, to be sure, but elites wanted "to regulate the pace of expansion" (Ostler 2019, 93).

General Philip Schuyler, another major voice in early Indian policy, agreed. In July of 1783, Schuyler (quoted in Horsman 1961, 37) submitted a statement to the president of the Confederation Congress that laid out a view for Indian Affairs that, even though it envisioned relations proceeding without war, was ultimately more accurate (or perhaps honest) than Washington's statements on this topic in anticipating the ruinous consequences of mass settlement for Native Americans:

> It will be little or no obstacle to our in future improving the very country they may retain, whenever we shall want it. For as our settlements approach their country, they must from the scarcity of game, which that approach will induce to, retire farther back, and dispose of their lands, unless they dwindle comparatively to nothing, as all savages have done, who gain their sustenance by the chace, when compelled to live in the vicinity of civilized people, and thus leave us the country without the expence of a purchase, trifling as that will probably be.

Regardless of whether Washington privately foresaw such a future on the frontier, Washington made the case for a relatively pacific Indian policy once he was in office. In addresses to Congress, he spoke of his desire "that all need of coercion in future may cease and that an intimate intercourse may succeed . . . to advance the happiness of the Indians and to attach them firmly to the United States" and "for the improvement of harmony with all the Indians within our limits by the fixing and conducting of trading houses upon the principles then expressed."[27] By the time of those statements, however, Washington had decided that the United States would need to use military force against "certain banditti of Indians from the northwest side of the Ohio" (quoted in Sword 1985, 82). He, like many of his successors, tried and failed to promote US expansion without going to war with Native American groups; by June of 1790, just a year into Washington's first term as president, he was at war.

To elaborate on the steps early political elites took in trying to avoid war in this case, Congress—both under the Articles of Confederation and the Constitution—drew on established precedent and authorized multiple rounds of treaty negotiations. This would result in the Treaty of Fort McIntosh—a treaty signed with Ohio-region Wyandots and Delawares in January of 1785—as well as attempts to negotiate treaties in 1787, 1788, and 1790 and early congressional revisions to the Northwest Ordinance designed to make explicit the US desire to acquire Native land by purchase rather than conquest (Sword 1985, 28, 50, 62).[28] Moreover, policymakers would occasionally authorize the military to punish settlers on disputed territory. Among the new federal lands, the Ohio region saw relatively frequent attempts to push settlers off lands to which they had only dubious claims. In 1785, for example, Knox authorized Harmar "to expel from the public lands, those lawless men who have acted in defiance of the orders and interest of the United States."[29] For policymakers, however, the mass removal of squatters "was never an attractive political option," and even if they had wanted to do it on a larger scale, they did not have the military to do it (Limerick 1987, 61).

In addition to these attempts to negotiate land cession treaties and to evict settlers in violation of existing territorial laws, the federal government also sought to prevent violent disputes between settlers and Native nations and to punish settlers who might instigate such conflicts. As Knox wrote to Washington in 1789, "If so direct and manifest contempt of the authority of the United States be suffered with impunity, it will be vain to attempt to extend the arm of Government to the frontiers." It was in line with this thinking that the Confederation Congress had adopted the Northwest Ordinance in 1787.[30] The ordinance had several features designed to discourage conflict between settlers and Native nations, including administrative reorganization and restrictions on trade, travel, and residence. Policymakers sought to ensure a more unified relationship to tribes by consolidating three previous Indian Affairs departments into two (for the northern and southern regions), both with superintendents who reported directly to the secretary of war (Anson 1970, 101). Traders needed a government license to operate in the Northwest Territory, and citizens would need to secure a permit to travel to there; non-citizens were barred from residence entirely.

Once the Northwest Territory was organized as such, negotiations with tribes in the region came under the purview of the territory's first governor, Arthur St. Clair, a major general in the Continental Army and later president of the Continental Congress. St. Clair had routine communications with Henry Knox and John Jay, secretaries of war and foreign affairs, respectively, during the late Confederation period (Saler 2015). Knox and Jay stayed in their posts once Washington entered office in early 1789 (though Jay only stayed in an acting capacity through March of 1790; his successor, Thomas Jefferson, would be the secretary of state through 1793. St. Clair's orders from all these political elites were consistently oriented toward expansion without war. Indeed, the federal government took steps to ensure that settlers could not scuttle treaty negotiations, even going so far as to drive settlers off disputed land ahead of negotiations (Sword 1985, 56; Tate 1999, 238–239). The ultimate goal, however, remained expansion—at the same time that the military was being tasked with driving off illegal settlers, policymakers were authorizing land surveys and making plans to pay off US debt with land sales.

Over the course of multiple treaty negotiations, US political elites came to believe that they were successfully balancing their desire for expansion with their desire to avoid war. As late as January 1789, it seemed to these decision-makers that a nonviolent resolution was soon forthcoming. But they often (perhaps willfully) misunderstood their bargaining counterparts and what they were able to authorize: Some tribes signed away land without soliciting the agreement of other tribes that properly should have had a say in negotiations, for example, and the parties involved in negotiations sometimes did not represent all relevant decision-makers within their own tribe (Sugden 2000, 7–9).

SETTLER *FAITS ACCOMPLIS*

While political elites debated the virtues of the standing army, settlers were moving in droves to the territory that England had ceded to the United States in 1783. The United States claimed to exercise sovereignty over the ceded territory (east of the Mississippi and south of Canada, excluding Spanish Florida) by virtue of conquest, though Americans had been moving in fewer numbers onto the land of what is now Kentucky, Ohio, and Indiana for decades before the war (Hurt 1996, 76–80). As noted above, however, the British Crown banned the private purchase of Native lands in the eastern Ohio Valley in its Royal Proclamation of 1763. This important development nonetheless had some unintended consequences. "The Crown's prevention of Indian-European sales encouraged settlers and speculators to argue that American Indians had as much, if not more, sovereignty than the British government, and the British government could not prevent a sovereign people from exercising their rights as sovereigns" (Pawlikowski 2014, 337). But the Royal Proclamation did change the incentives facing settlers, and "In all, 1768 to 1773 marked a period of peace in the eastern Ohio Valley. 'Alarms' of disunion between Indians and Euroamericans 'blew over' without a disturbance to the greater interethnic community" (Pawlikowski

2014, 277).[31] To the extent that settlers instigated acts of violence during this time, outsiders—that is, non-residents or very recent settlers—perpetrated most attacks on Ohio-region Native communities (Pawlikowski 2014, 280).

The end of the Revolutionary War would see a rush of new settlers, including military veterans who sought (and sometimes received) land grants as a reward for their service (McGlinchey 2006, 129). These were mostly relatively poor individuals who left the more populous original colonies for the prospect of abundant, fertile farmland. "Many of them," wrote Judge Jacob Barnett (quoted in Hall 1905, 495),

> had exhausted their fortunes in maintaining [the war effort], and retired to the wilderness to conceal their poverty and avoid comparisons mortifying to their pride while struggling to maintain their familiarizes and improve their condition.

The most accessible paths for settlers ran through the Cumberland Gap, which is at the intersection of modern-day Kentucky, Tennessee, and Virginia, and along the Ohio River by way of modern-day Maysville, Kentucky, about 180 miles north of the Cumberland Gap. Most early settlers who reached Indiana or Ohio thus tended to establish residence in southern portions of Ohio, where there were already substantial Native populations; that later settlers would need to claim lands further north put all the more pressure on Ohio region tribes (O'Malley 1987, 19).[32]

In addition to economic factors that encouraged settlement in the Old Northwest, settlers often migrated with certain beliefs that justified the move; many were "schooled in a view of the world which described indigenous peoples as savage, uncivilized brutes" as opposed to the civilizing presence the settlers saw themselves as bringing (Coates 2004, 181; Saler 2015, 47).[33] Similarly, many migrated with a biblical justification for their behavior: The command to "Be fruitful, and multiply, and replenish the earth, and subdue it" was one of many such passages that served to legitimize their work to settle and populate new federal lands (Stephanson 1995, 25).[34] Regardless of their reasons for seeking lands in the West, federal lands to which no states made any claims were of particular interest to settlers. Given their desire to rapidly establish land ownership, fewer ongoing jurisdictional disputes were better (Ablavsky 2016, 41–42). For many, this made the Old Northwest more desirable than lands farther south, to which states like Virginia, the Carolinas, and Georgia made various claims.

Much of the small military of the United States was stationed in the Ohio region at that time in an effort to keep the peace between settlers and Native nations, but the hundreds of soldiers posted to a few frontier forts were not well-equipped to confront tens of thousands of much more diffuse settlers (Ostler 2019, 85).[35] Indeed, as a Shawnee delegation reported to officials in Spanish Louisiana in the summer of 1784, the US settlers entered the Ohio Valley "like a plague of locusts" (quoted in Calloway 1995, 166). Given that the military could deter neither settlement nor Native attacks against settlers, locals often responded to violence with violence of their own (Wooster 2009, 6–8). Brigadier General George Rogers Clark, for example, led an unauthorized force of mostly volunteer Kentucky militia members in a series of attacks on Shawnee towns (Prucha 1969, 8–11). As Secretary of War Henry Knox reported shortly thereafter, "The injuries & murders have been so reciprocal, that it would be a point of critical investigation to know on which side they have been the greatest" (1789, 3). "Lawless acts by settlers," Vine Deloria and David Wilkins (1999, 11) write, "drove the tribes toward conflict, and Congress was impelled to act."

SETTLERS, SPECULATORS, AND LOCAL ELITES: ACTIVATING SOCIAL TIES

As settlers claimed lands in the Old Northwest, they came into conflict with Native American groups that claimed the land as their own, and this would lead to direct and indirect pressures for federal assistance. I first consider the context of land speculation before turning more directly to petitions by settlers and local elites for federal intervention.

Even before the American colonies sought and gained independence, political elites and land speculation corporations occasionally sent surveyors into the Ohio region to assess the viability of the land for settlement (Johnston 1898, 106–107, n. 2). Demand for this land was real, but it was also assumed. For the federal government's part, independence came with a heavy burden of debt, which it believed it would be able to minimize with sales of newly acquired territory, including grants to members of the Continental Army who might be compensated with land. In other words, political and business interests alike had an interest in making the territory of the Ohio region ready for sale and settlement, but it was demand that preceded these interests and made land speculation a (sometimes) profitable venture. As Cathy Rodabaugh (2015, 10) puts it, "Post-revolutionary western speculation only mirrored a near-consensus that the national expansion of markets and territory offered incomparable benefits to any man willing to pursue them."

Settlers did not always respect the claims of speculators (of which they were not always aware). "The attraction of choice locations led regularly to settlement in advance of purchase—squatting, in short. . . . Thousands of such petty *faits accomplis* all over the Northwest frontier could hardly be reversed, no matter how powerful the petitioners" (Elkins and McKitrick 1954, 337). The relationship between settlers and speculators in the Northwest Territory was thus not always mutually beneficial, but there does appear to have been a degree of positive feedback. There was settler demand for land, which made land speculation a potentially profitable pursuit, and competition among speculators meant that they sometimes had to improve their lands to maintain and spark further settler demand (Hurt 1996, 171). While "improving" the land often meant mundane work like building fences or clearing fields, it was also the case that perhaps the most valuable possible improvement was to secure land from potential Native attack. For settlers and speculators alike, the ideal means of securing their lands was to off-load that cost onto another actor—the federal government. Thus, settlers and speculators alike would lobby for federal military intervention in the Northwest Territory with increasing frequency as the 1780s progressed.[36]

From Samuel H. Parsons, a one-time Indian Affairs commissioner, to Cleves Symmes, a New Jersey chief justice, wealthy elites were important players on the frontier insofar as they used their fortunes to buy and sell lands in the Northwest Territory. These speculators were often settlers themselves: They often financed and otherwise helped organize large land purchases and then assumed leadership roles in the settler communities they helped create in disputed territory. Even on the frontier, however, wealthy speculators were able to make good use of their social standing and connections; their wealth gave them the social capital necessary to mingle with and influence policymakers and other local elites, and they often used their political connections to push for federal military intervention to quell the violence being directed at settlers (Sword 1985, 45–49).

As a case in point, Parsons had served as a general in the Continental Army and was appointed a commissioner of "Indian Affairs" by the Confederation Congress after being elected to the Connecticut General Assembly in 1782. After years of involvement in land speculation, he became a director of the Associated Ohio Company in 1787 (Shannon 1991, 396, 399).[37] Together with a number of other prominent veterans of the Revolutionary War, Parsons would help to oversee one of the most expansive land purchases in the Ohio region—a purchase of hundreds of thousands of acres (in what became Marietta) made possible by the means and status of the respective investors (Clayton 1986).[38] As a notable figure in the region, Parsons had regular contact with officials and military officers like Arthur St. Clair and Josiah Harmar and was able to make appeals for aid quite directly throughout the mid- to late 1780s (Hall 1905).

Even before the Associated Ohio Company was established, Parsons had signed a 1783 petition to Congress along with 287 other officers of the Continental Army requesting that "Indian title be extinguished to what is now the eastern half of Ohio" to pave the way for American settlement (Hall 1905, 546). The petition made its way to Congress via George Washington and resulted in no action, but Parsons would continue to remind political elites of the extent to which frontier settlement would benefit from federal support. Indeed, Parsons corresponded with Washington, who had been his commanding officer in the Revolutionary War, at least as late as July 1788, and without making any specific commitment to federal aid, in a 1788 letter Washington assured Parsons "of the satisfaction I take in hearing from my old military friends and of the interest I feel in their future prosperity."

Ultimately, Parsons mirrored many political elites in his desire to acquire Native American lands through purchase, but he came to see war as the only option when efforts at purchase were unsuccessful. In 1785, Parsons wrote to William Samuel Johnson, who represented Connecticut in the Confederation Congress to express his view that purchase would be the most appropriate and efficient way forward (in Hall 1905, 475):

> Suppose the land to be our own, is it not more expedient to give content to the Indians by purchasing such tracts as they will sell, than to hold out an idea which fires their pride and alarms their fears and will probably deluge our frontiers with blood? . . . I am convinced this is the only proper route to be taken to get a knowledge sufficient to settle the Virginia accounts with justice; and Congress ought by no means to be in haste to close that account.

By contrast, when Parsons would again write to Johnson in 1788 (Hall 1905, 535), he saw war as the likely outcome given a Native refusal "to treat":

> The Indian Treaty is yet in suspense. They refuse to come here and the Governor refuses to go to them. . . . [A] war must be the issue, which, though it will probably terminate favorably, will be more expensive than a purchase of the lands as we want them. But in present circumstances, I don't see but that they must be driven away and dispersed, if they refuse to treat.

Whether by purchase or by force, extinguishing Native land claims in the Northwest Territory would allow Parsons to "sell in the counties of Pennsylvania and Virginia on this side of the mountains, so that a settlement would take place next year which will open the way to rapid sales both in and out of the State" (Hall 1905, 535). In relaying that to Johnson, by that time an incoming senator from Connecticut under the new Constitution, Parsons was activating social ties he had to political elites to build support for federal military intervention.

As for Symmes, he petitioned Congress for a purchase of land in the Ohio region, and once Congress authorized the purchase, he promptly solicited buyers for small tracts of the land by advertising its "rich easy soil for tillage" and led some settlers there himself (Hurt, 2003, 17; Rodabaugh 2015, 6). He later worked with Governor Arthur St. Clair to determine county legal codes for the territory, and after early US defeats in the Northwest Indian War, he sent a long letter on Indian Affairs to an acquaintance of his—Elias Boudinot, a congressman from New Jersey. There Symmes—a man with only limited military experience—offers Boudinot a lengthy list of suggestions for continued military attacks on the territory's Native peoples. The United States ought to focus on recruiting soldiers who were less prone to "blasphemies, drunkeness and lewdness" than those who had been defeated in earlier engagements, he argued; and cavalry "armed with a rifle-gun, two horse pistols fixed to a girdle buckled round the waist of the mean, and not fixed as usual to the saddle" would be more effective than infantry given Native tactics. "I tremble lest Congress should determine that the defence of the western country costs the nation more than it is all worth to them, and leave us to our own defence in the best manner we can make it" (Greve 1910, 97–99). Like Parsons, Symmes activated his social ties to political elites to push for a more effective federal military intervention.

While it is unclear if speculator pressure would have been sufficient in its own right to trigger federal intervention—and indeed, I can only show here that speculator lobbying in this case passes a hoop test in which the phenomenon is present but of indeterminate significance—this pressure likely shaped federal decisions about military intervention (Van Evera 1997, 31). Although there is little recorded acknowledgment by policymakers that they were swayed by speculator appeals, the evident patterns of behavior suggest some speculator influence. At least some of the descendants of those who fought in the Northwest Indian War also attribute at least some of the responsibility to speculators. In a 2019 interview with Benjamin (Ben) Barnes, at the time of this writing the elected chief of the Shawnee tribe (and, at the time of the interview, the second chief), he noted that, "People [are] selling titles for lands they know they don't hold. . . . You sell the land, then you go to the government to do [something] about it? I think those people are really the ones who . . . should hold a lot of responsibility."[39]

While many speculators were relatively well-connected, the majority of those on the frontier were not as notable as Parsons and Symmes. Nevertheless, even settlers of less social status could bring pressure to bear on local elites who could, in turn, lobby federal policymakers. In the case of the Northwest Indian War, these were often county, city, or state officials—or the relevant equivalent in territories that were not yet states. Settlers could pressure such officials both through elections and through petitions. Kentucky District settlers, for example, brought enough such complaints to their district administrators that these local elites eventually compiled a list of grievances to present settler concerns to the Virginia state legislature (to which the Kentucky District was beholden before Kentucky became a separate state). The first item of complaint was the inability of Kentucky officials "to call out the militia" without approval from Virginia officials (Clark 1993, 58–62):

> In the course of our enquiries, we find that several laws have passed the legislature of Virginia, which, although of a general nature, yet in their operation are particularly oppressive to the people of this district; and we also find, that from our local situation, we are deprived of many benefits of government, which every citizen therein has a right to expect; as a few facts will sufficiently demonstrate. We have no power to call out the militia, our sure and only defence to oppose the wicked machinations of the savages, unless in cases of actual invasion.

In short, this petition and many others like it—all of which helped accelerate Virginia's devolution of authority to Kentucky (Robertson 1998)—is evidence of settlers activating their social ties to local political elites to pressure them for greater military preparedness on the frontier.

Likewise, after an especially costly Native attack on Kentucky settlers (probably by Shawnees or Miamis), settlers pressed their concerns with local officials, who in turn expressed their complaints to the federal government. As one such official, Arthur Campbell (1789, 631), wrote to the governor of Virginia:

> It is inexplicable to some why the Indians attack our frontiers with such fury, destroying all where they come, when at the same time we are told the Governor of the Western Territory made peace with the Northern Indians last winter. . . . Will not Congress adapt some effectual measures before long respecting Indian affairs?

Campbell, who was being lobbied by Kentucky settlers to pressure political elites for military assistance, had served in the Continental Army (like Parsons) and made good use of his connections to political elites. In correspondence with figures such as James Madison and George Washington, he pushed for Kentucky's statehood and for greater federal military assistance to deter or perhaps win a war with Native American groups. "Kentuckey," he informed Madison, would keep "the Southern and Western Indians in awe," and he later wrote that the federal government ought to work to "terrify . . . the predatory Tribes" (Campbell 1785, 1787). Similarly, he wrote to Washington to suggest various ways in which settlers might be made more secure from hostile Native Americans groups, which he feared the British could use to their own ends (Campbell 1789):

> A detachment of the American Regulars, posted on the Tenasee river, near the Muscle Shoals, may if under a faithful and intelligent Officer, awe our enemies, encourage our friends, conciliate all; or if that cannot be effected, foment divisions, and play off the interests, and views of one Tribe, against that of another, so as to render the machinations of a foreign power amongst them, of little avail against us.

Settlers, in short, effectively activated their social ties to local political elites, who transmitted settler concerns to federal political elites to push for military assistance on the frontier.

Settlers also targeted their appeals more directly at local political elites. The Kentucky settlers, as I have suggested above, sought to do this with Virginia officials. For as long as the Kentucky District remained under the jurisdiction of the Virginia state legislature, its state militia could operate only within its own jurisdiction (i.e., nearly the entirety of modern Kentucky). By July 1786, however, Kentucky settlers had resolved to attack Native nations in the Ohio region with whom the settlers had long been engaged in low-level violent conflict. Kentucky District militia leaders asked the Virginia state legislature for permission to attack beyond its borders, and once it became clear that such permission would not be forthcoming, these same Kentuckians—more specifically, settlers in Jefferson Country—distributed a call for military aid from other Kentucky settlers. Although framed in terms of defending settler populations, the appeal was clearly oriented toward actively seeking out and attacking Native American groups and forcing Virginia elites to reckon with the situation. Indeed, Virginia Governor Patrick Henry felt that he had little choice but to authorize the creation of "some system for their own defense" (Sword 1985, 33).

Federal officials evinced increasing awareness of settler pressure. Knox, aware that "the Kentucky settlements were vehemently demanding protection," still saw "the small corps of federal troops located nearby on the Ohio River was far too weak to be effective for this purpose" as of July 1787 (Sword 1985, 45–47). While the young Washington administration sought to allow time to ease tensions through negotiations, St. Clair pushed the administration for clear decisions in the summer of 1789. At an in-person meeting with Washington, St. Clair told him that the pace of negotiations was allowing for retributive violence to occur. "It is not to be expected, sir, that the Kentucky people will, or can, submit patiently to the cruelties and depredations of those savages; they are in the habit of retaliation" (quoted in Sword 1985, 83). Meanwhile, in a 1789 letter, Washington assured Campbell that federal commissioners were going to "treat with the Indians" to try to avert further violence, and he asked Congress to provide "some temporary provision for calling forth the militia" while instructing St. Clair on the US interest in "a cessation of hostilities as a prelude to a treaty" (quoted in Sword 1985, 83–84).

At times, the most that military contingents based in the Northwest Territory could do was refuse assistance to settler raiding parties (Anson

1970, 107). As early as the summer of 1787, Knox had warned Congress that the number of settlers was making it increasingly difficult to remove them, and he continued to receive petitions from frontier officials through July 1790 asking for federal military assistance (Sword 1985, 45). Indeed, letters from individuals like Harmar and Harry Innes, a district judge in Kentucky and a friend of Washington, helped relay settler concerns and ultimately convinced Knox that a US military offensive was necessary, and he sought and received Washington's permission to authorize such an offensive in June 1790 (Sword 1985, 87). As settlers activated social ties to local political elites to request military assistance, those local elites faithfully relayed settler concerns to federal political elites who were eventually convinced that they needed to act.

It may have been possible for state and federal officials to resist settler pressure for longer than they did. Indeed, the federal government sought for years to avoid war with the Ohio Valley tribes before ultimately deciding to intervene. The next mechanism I discuss, however, often made elites feel compelled to provide federal military assistance to settlers.

COSTS OF NON-INTERVENTION

Once settlers conducted the *faits accomplis* of settling on land and initiating violent conflict—and especially once settlers activated their social ties to political elites by petitioning for military intervention on their behalf—they created a situation in which political elites had to decide whether to intervene. The anticipated costs of intervention—the various resources a government needed to conduct a military campaign in the 1780s and 90s, which would have been a steep price for any government, let alone a recently independent one—made for a fairly straightforward calculation. We thus see federal policymakers cite the likely costs of military intervention as a reason to give time for negotiations to play out. Less immediately obvious, however, are the potential costs of non-intervention that elites believed they would face, including the loss of territory that would come with secession and/or, perhaps even worse, settler alliances with foreign powers. If the United States did not ultimately intervene militarily to assist settlers, federal elites risked a situation in which either Native nations reclaimed their land or settlers took the land for themselves and no longer saw much need for the federal government.[40] Moreover, Knox saw it as necessary to prevent any such settler rebellions so as not to create in other settlers the belief that secession was preferable and practicable. As he wrote to the Congress shortly after the passage of the Northwest Ordinance, "If such audacious defiance of the power of the United States be suffered with impunity a precedent will be established, to wrest all the immense property of the western territory out of the hands of the public" (quoted in Lindberg 2015, 130).

As early as 1781, political elites expressed concern that settlers, once they had moved west and established communities of their own, would want independence. It was in that year that an American military commander at Fort Pitt (associated with the settlement that would become Pittsburgh) argued to his political superiors that a settler-led "invasion" of the Ohio territory would be the best way of dealing with the "Indian problem," but civilian officials rejected the idea for fear that these settlers might seek independence or come under British sway (Sword 1985, 55). Given ongoing hostilities, it was seen as an unnecessary risk. But this remained a concern well past US independence. Knox, for example, expressed his concern in July of 1787 that the "whole western territory is liable to be wrested out of the hands of the Union by lawless adventurers, or by the savages" (quoted in Sword 1985, 47). Such concerns were commensurate with the grievances put forward by local officials in newly acquired lands—for example, Walker Daniel, the attorney general of the Kentucky District, wrote to Benjamin Harrison V, then the governor of Virginia, that the federal and Virginia governments' inability "to prevent the cruelties & Depredations of the Savages," was the primary source of separatist sentiment in the west (quoted in Leadingham 2016, 343).

Contemporaries from George Washington to James Monroe echoed such concerns about the rise of "rival settler nations" (Frymer 2017, 46; Saler 2015, 14), and they had reasonable cause to do so. Indeed, Washington himself owned land in western Pennsylvania that a small Calvinist group (called the Seceders, because they rejected all civil authority) claimed by right of residence. After initiating legal proceedings to validate his claim to the land in 1784, Washington would eventually win his case and evict the squatters, who simply moved further west (Larson 2014, 43–45).

A more serious issue arose when settlers in what is now Tennessee—on land then claimed by North Carolina—established what they declared to be the state of Franklin. There the administration of Governor John Sevier actively courted Native and European allies. The administration sought the alliance of the Chickasaw and Cherokee peoples in exchange for protection against the Creek, and it eventually turned to the Spanish to seek at least a trade agreement (Flaherty 2012, 72). Sevier even authorized negotiations for a land cession treaty with the Cherokee. Franklin's diplomats only ever achieved a tentative agreement that a group of young Cherokee men said they would bring to their elders for consideration, and while the Franklinites would declare the treaty to be valid and begin settling on Cherokee lands, their fledgling state would dissolve by 1788 (Ablavsky 2016, 100–101). Settler efforts such as these were part of Madison's rationale for the design of the Constitution—among other things, he argued that it would give western settlers a greater stake in the government and all the more reason to remain a part of it (Leadingham 2016, 364). Six years later, however, the Whiskey Rebellion would reignite federal concerns of settler secession.

Just as political elites had good reason to believe that settlers might seek independence from the United States, they also had reason to fear that settlers might turn to foreign powers for assistance. US diplomats, for example, "could not cajole Britain to abide by its treaty obligation to evacuate forts in the Northwest Territory so long as Congress remained powerless to force states and individuals to return property from Tories during the American Revolution as mandated by the same treaty" (Larson 2014, 68). The British remained officially neutral in US relations with Native nations, and the Crown's representatives gave only noncommittal replies when presented with Native requests for overt aid, though British officials did hope that it could assist in subtly nudging Native nations toward the creation of a unified coalition that could provide a buffer state between the United States and Canada (Calloway 2007, 91–92). George Washington, Peter Trubowitz (2011, 48–49) notes, "worried most about British power," especially because of its continued occupation of its forts and its much more powerful navy, and these fears were exacerbated when Spain created a diplomatic crisis by seizing a British trading ship in what is now British Columbia in 1789 (Merk 1978, 145–146). Joseph Parent (2011, 62–63) agrees with this assessment in characterizing broader elite fears:

Whether or not foreign powers were actually intriguing against the former colonies, elites constantly perceived threat. . . . [M]align British influence was seen everywhere. A nonaligned or mal-aligned state could be a base for foreign intervention, an encouraging example to groups contemplating secession, and a resource drain on the Confederation's already meager aggregate power.

Despite all these concerns about the British, perhaps the most notable instance of settler collaboration with a European power came in James Wilkinson's collusion with Spanish colonial officials. Wilkinson had been a general in the Continental (and later United States) Army, but after settling in Kentucky, he became disenchanted with a government that he felt promoted eastern business interests at the expense of developing the frontier. Thus, in 1787, Wilkinson contacted Esteban Rodríguez Miró, the governor of Spanish Louisiana, and pledged loyalty to Spain if they would aid his effort to create an independent nation in Kentucky (which was still under Virginia's jurisdiction at the time) (Linklater 2009, 85–86). If Spain did not assist in this venture, however, Wilkinson noted that he and his fellow Kentuckians would likely need to turn to the British for support (Narrett 2012, 108). Within a little over a year, Miró's superiors in Spain had decided that there was little to be gained from such plans and discontinued assistance for Wilkinson's short-lived separatist movement in early 1789—the strength of which Wilkinson had inflated in his talks with Miró—but Wilkinson would continue to feed sensitive information to the Spanish to remain in their favor (Linklater 2009, 99; Narrett 2012, 112).

Although little ultimately came of Wilkinson's effort to cultivate Spanish support for this project, he was not the only one to make such an effort. William Augustus Bowles, a Maryland-born loyalist, fought for the British during the Revolutionary War and was captured by a Creek party after deserting in West Florida (McAlister 1962). He cultivated positive relationships with the Creek, however, and eventually found his way back into the British military, after which he was tasked with developing trade relations with the Creek. He would maintain this relationship as something of an intermediary for the British well after the war, although it is not clear to what extent he was acting on orders when he declared the independence of the state of Muskogee in 1799. With the support of some members of various Florida and Georgia-area tribes, including the Creek, Seminole, and Muskogee, Bowles sought to establish a state from which the British could fight against US expansion. Both the United States and Spain found this development to be a nuisance, however, and they cooperated to ensure the capture of Bowles and the end of the state of Muskogee. Hapless though these examples may seem, US political elites feared the possibility of a genuine threat to the Union emerging on the frontier, and these cases help to illustrate exactly the sort of settler secessionism mixed with foreign intrigue that political elites feared.

Ultimately, federal elites often interpreted the question of intervention on behalf of settlers as a question as to whether they should side with the "lawless adventurers" or the "savages," and although they believed any such wars would likely be costly, they suspected that a victory for Native nations could be even more costly in the long term (Ostler 2019, 119). As settlers claimed disputed territory and petitioned for federal assistance in conflicts with Native American groups, they were ultimately aided by this elite calculation in favor of "lawless adventurers" who were nonetheless American citizens. By intervening in the Old Northwest, federal elites would set something of a precedent: "[T]he use of an army became crucial to proving the value of the national government. Nothing else it did was more important in attaching people to the United States, for nothing else was a more visible symbol of the value of the government of the United States" (Cayton 1992, 47).

SETTLERS AND CREDIBLE COMMITMENTS

Alongside the activation of social ties to political elites, settlers also shaped the course of events in the Old Northwest through their assumed ties to the federal government. To the extent that the United States was able to successfully negotiate land cession treaties with some tribes, trust was often a critical component of those negotiations.[41] A lack of trust, however, made any negotiated settlement more difficult to attain. It was especially difficult for the United States to establish trust with Native nations in this period in no small part because policymakers did indeed want to expand at the expense Native peoples. But it was also the networked character of American actors that contributed to this distrust. That is, for many Native American groups, there was often little meaningful distinction between settlers, speculators, local elites, military officials, and federal policymakers to the extent that those actors all constituted a single network oriented toward Native dispossession. The actions of one American reflected on the others, and their intentions were at times taken to be basically the same: to "deceive the Indians, to defraud them of their lands," in the words of Gischenatsi, a Shawnee chief (quoted in Calloway 2007, xxiii).

It is a well-known argument in IR scholarship that an inability to credibly commit to uphold international agreements—most importantly, the commitment not to attack or otherwise take advantage of another—can be a cause of war (Fearon 1995). One thing that the Northwest Indian War helps to illustrate is that the credibility of one's commitment may not be entirely up to oneself. In this case, the federal government repeatedly sought treaty negotiations with Ohio region tribes while simultaneously being undermined by the settlers for whom it was trying to acquire land by purchase.[42] All the while, Knox was aware that settlers were subverting federal Indian policy in both the misleading commitments they made to Native nations and their continued expansion and violence aimed at securing territory for themselves. "The Indian tribes," he wrote to St. Clair in 1789, "can have no faith in such imbecile promises, and the lawless whites will ridicule a government which shall, on paper only, make Indian treaties, and regulate Indian boundaries" (quoted in Ablavsky 2016). He thus gave St. Clair standing orders to prevent any such settler expeditions and to punish any participants therein, but there was only so much the small frontier army could do.

After years of violence, divisions had emerged among and within tribes of the Ohio River Valley. There were both pro-British and pro-American sentiments within the Miami tribe by 1785, though any support for accommodation with the United States eroded through the rest of the decade as even the Miami bands most aligned with US interests suffered attacks by settlers (Rafert 1996, 47). Most tribes in the Western Confederacy appear to have believed by the late 1780s that the United States and its settlers would continue trying to expand at their expense, but different groups disagreed as to what they should do about that. Some believed their respective tribes should seek peace and content themselves with relatively small reservations that were at least on or near their traditional homes. Others, however, believed that the United States could not credibly commit to leave them alone even after making any such concessions; among the Ohio region tribes, these were the groups that ultimately decided on war, which included substantial numbers among the Shawnee and Miami nations.[43]

By April 23, 1790, the Northwest Indian War was close to breaking out. St. Clair and Harmar dispatched two final messengers with a mandate to seek peace—one of British lineage, the other French. Antoine Gamelin, the French messenger, eventually made it to a Miami town at which he met Blue Jacket, a principal warrior of the Shawnee. Blue Jacket's response indicates the distrust that had formed after repeated US promises and settler-initiated episodes of violence: "From all quarters we receive speeches from the Americans, and not one is alike. We suppose that they intend to deceive us" (Sugden 2000, 96; Sword 1985, 85). Some among the Shawnee would no longer listen to American promises, especially when they came from St. Clair, who displayed little understanding of Native cultures during negotiations and who often took a harder line in pushing for treaties than his superiors requested (Ostler 2019, 95). The actions of settlers contributed to the perception of bad faith and would ultimately result in war in the Northwest Territory.

CONFLICT INITIATION AND CONTEMPORANEOUS EXPLANATIONS

In this section, I examine the initiation of official hostilities in the Northwest Indian War and consider the stated explanations for conflict. After years of unfruitful negotiations and increasing violence between settlers and Native American groups, President Washington concluded that only a decisive but narrowly targeted military victory could stop the mutual depredations. In consultation with Henry Knox, Washington authorized Harmar to use whatever force necessary to attack those groups believed to be responsible for depredations on settlers.[44] By this point, the size of the military had increased slightly to 1,216 men (McDermott 1998, 9). US civilian leaders sought to avoid a broader war by ordering Harmar to punish only specific groups that had been involved in violence against settlers and by communicating their intentions to British officials still in the region to avoid unnecessary escalation (Sword 1985, 94). Knox, who remained skeptical of the virtues of settlers, nonetheless explained to Washington that their decision to intervene would not only "strike terror into the minds of the Indians" but also would be "highly satisfactory to the people of the frontiers" (quoted in Sword 1985, 87).

From Harmar's inaugural defeat (which I discuss further in Chapter 3) through the deciding battle at Fallen Timbers and the signing of the Treaty of Greenville in 1795, the United States frequently sought an end to hostilities and a negotiated settlement.[45] The most sustained period of negotiations came between the fall of 1792 and the spring of 1793—in no small part because the earlier defeats had significantly reduced the number of soldiers available to the already very small US military. In a proclamation made in April of 1793, for example, General Anthony Wayne noted that, as per instructions from President Washington and Secretary Knox, he would seek a treaty with the Northwest tribes and would therefore prohibit any violence against Native settlements (Knopf 1960, 218). But the Shawnees insisted that treaty boundaries be redrawn—to accord with the original 1768 Treaty of Fort Stanwix—and that the US government remove settlers north of the Ohio River. Neither was a winning proposition to US representatives given the steadily increasing settler presence, nor were US demands that the Ohio tribes simply sell the land on which settlers were encroaching (Calloway 2007, 98–101). With a negotiated settlement not forthcoming, Wayne had led US forces to victory, and the defeated Native nations signed the Treaty of Greenville in 1795, at which point settlement and land speculation in the region accelerated (Scheerer 2014, 10).

To consider elite explanations for the war, Secretary of War Henry Knox's letters and reports to Washington offer glimpses of the roles that settlers played in decision-making. In December of 1790, Knox wrote to Washington to inveigh against a proposal by Arthur St. Clair:

> It will be our true wisdom to condense our population instead of dispersing it. Besides the expense of protecting such distant settlements greatly exceeds the value of them, whether considered as purchases of the land, as consumers of articles contributing to the revenue, or as constituting a strength of any real use to the empire.

After making the case that the United States could not afford to protect even more expansive settlements, Knox (1790) asserted in the same letter that to turn the war into a land grab would sully the virtue of those involved:

To grasp an additional territory will give the expedition an avaricious aspect. . . . The motives of the expedition ought to appear as they really are—A clear and uncompromised dictate of Justice to punish a banditti of robbers, and murderers, who have refused to listed to the voice of peace and humanity.

In their correspondence, it is often this "banditti" to which Washington and Knox refer in articulating their war aims: They appear to have wanted a rather narrow, punitive strike against a circumscribed population designed to bring reluctant bands back to negotiations.

Two years after the war began, Knox (1792) provided his view of how the war started, and it is worth quoting at length (italics are my own):

It appears, that the unprovoked aggressions of the Miami and Wabash Indians upon Kentucky and other parts of the frontiers; together with their associates, a banditti, formed of Shawanese and outcast Cherokees, amounting in all to about one thousand two hundred men, are solely the causes of the war. . . . The frontier settlements were disquieted by frequent depredations and murders; and the complaints of their inhabitants, (as might be expected) of the pacific forbearance of the government, were loud, repeated, and distressing—their calls for protection incessant—till at length they appeared determined by their own efforts to endeavor to re-taliate the injuries they were continually receiving, and which had become intolerable. . . . But notwithstanding the ill success of former experiments, and the invincible spirit of animosity which had appeared in certain tribes, and which was of a nature to justify a persuasion that no impression could be made upon them by pacific expedients, it was still deemed advisable to make one more essay. [Between 1783 and 1790, Native American groups] on the Ohio, and the frontiers on the south side thereof . . . killed, wounded and took prisoners, about *one thousand five hundred men, women and children; besides carrying off upwards of two thousand horses, and other property to the amount of fifty thousand dollars. A frontier citizen possesses as strong claims to protection as any other citizen.* The frontiers are the vulnerable parts of every country; and the obligation of the government of the United States, to afford the requisite protection, cannot be less sacred in reference to the inhabitants of their Western, than to those of their Atlantic Frontier.[46]

While Knox maintained that aggression by the Ohio region's Native nations was the sole cause of the conflict, he made several important acknowledgments. The purported aggressions in question were directed at settlers, he said, and settlers sought to respond with violence of their own, apparently without any direct federal assistance or encouragement. Furthermore, he reported that 1,500 men, women, and children were killed, wounded, or taken prisoner in a seven-year period, which speaks to the volume of settlement and the related violence in what was clearly disputed territory. Knox also mentions that settlers actively sought federal intervention on their behalf, that the federal government was aware of these requests and still sought to negotiate for peace, and that in his view settlers were ultimately Americans with a legitimate claim to federal aid.

By the time he wrote a similarly lengthy letter to Washington in 1794, Knox was more explicit about the role of settlers in pulling the government into militarized disputes:

> The desires of too many frontier white people to seize by force or fraud upon the neighbouring Indian lands has been and still continues to be an unceasing cause of jealousy and hatred on the part of the Indians, and it would appear upon a calm investigation that until the Indians can be quieted upon this point and rely with confidence upon the protection of their lands by the United States no well grounded hope of tranquility can be entertained.

In other words, Knox is suggesting here that the United States would continue to find itself at war with Native nations for as long as the federal government could (or would) not reliably protect Native lands from settler depredations.

Washington himself also came to express resignation at the federal government's inability to control settlers. As he wrote in a letter in 1796 to Timothy Pickering, then his secretary of state (and earlier the successor to Knox as secretary of war), "I believe scarcely anything short of a Chinese wall, or a line of troops, will restrain Land jobbers, and the encroachment of settlers upon the Indian territory." Absent a sufficiently long line of troops, there was little else Washington felt he could do to prevent the settler *faits accomplis* that would continue to bring the United States into conflict with Native nations.

THEORETICAL IMPLICATIONS

The origins of the Northwest Indian War have implications for scholarship in IR and on US foreign policy. First, contrary to the frequently espoused view that foreign policy is naturally more insulated from public opinion than domestic policy, the extent to which settlers drove the process of war initiation in this case suggests that even if foreign policy is more insulated than domestic policy today, that has not always been the case. Indeed, early US foreign policy seems to have been rather responsive to such public opinion. I am agnostic as to the appropriate extent of public influence on US foreign policy, but if policy in this domain has become increasingly detached from public opinion over time, the Northwest Indian War helps to demonstrate that the current state of affairs is the result of contingent choices that have been made over the years; foreign policy is not naturally insulated from the public and has perhaps become more insulated over time through legislation, litigation, and executive action.[47] In part because of this early public influence, as discussed in Chapter 1, whatever we might call early US foreign policy, it is difficult to maintain that it was isolationist if we consider relations with Native American groups to be constitutive of early US foreign policy.

Second and relatedly, the origins of the Northwest Indian War suggest that political elites have historically exercised less complete control over US foreign policy than one might think. This chapter draws our attention to the ways that private citizens have directly influenced the course of US foreign policy, and this aligns with other recent work that has identified dynamics by which non-official actors can nonetheless shape policy.[48] While elites preferred to avoid war with Native American groups in the Northwest Territory, Florida, and elsewhere, an aggressive, land-hungry public was often able to force the hand of political elites and receive military intervention on its behalf. Moreover, settlers had this effect in part because of the way that they undermined the credibility of federal promises to Native populations, a phenomenon that suggests that commitment problems may be even more common than prior research suggests given that third parties can create such problems for others. There may be fewer opportunities for private citizens to provoke militarized disputes today, but findings here suggest that we ought to reevaluate two common assumptions: that it is political elites who initiate militarized disputes, whereas citizens serve primarily as an audience capable of rendering judgment on elite decisions after the fact; and that the public, especially in a democracy, generally acts as a constraint on elites who would otherwise initiate militarized disputes more frequently.

Third and finally, my reading of the origins of the Northwest Indian War complements other arguments to the effect that while territorial expansion was central to US history, the United States was not maximally expansionist. While John Mearsheimer (2001, 238), for example, might portray the United States as "the poster child of offensive realism," the contours of American expansion have long been more constrained and contested than one might assume, especially when US policymakers had to consider whether to absorb new territories inhabited primarily by substantial non-white populations (Maass 2020). That is, the United States was not an indiscriminately power-maximizing state dedicated to acquiring any territory it could. Among others, the historian Frederick Merk (1963, 261) once came to a similar conclusion: "A thesis that continentalist and imperialist goals were sought by the nation regardless of party or section, won't do. It is not substantiated by good evidence."

CODA: THE OLD NORTHWEST AND THE INDIAN WARS

In this chapter, I have focused on the origins of the Northwest Indian War, a war of conquest in which settlers exercised seemingly outsized influence in shaping the US decision to intervene militarily to secure its claims to territory in the Old Northwest. I have described the ideal typical mechanisms through which settlers activated their social ties to federal political elites, and I have elaborated on the theoretical relevance of this case. In short, the conventional wisdom of early US foreign policy as having been isolationist falls apart in the earliest days thereof. The United States sought expansion at the expense of others from the beginning. As just one of America's many Indian Wars, the Northwest Indian War is part of a broader history of conquest. As the first of these wars for the nascent United States, it helped to establish a rough template for how to go about that conquest. In wars with the Seminoles, the Utes, and myriad other tribes that US forces would confront across the continent, the perceived lessons of the Northwest Indian War would be applied along the expanding frontier.

In the next two chapters, I turn to different ways that the Northwest Indian War presaged broader trends in US foreign policy: its reliance on military bases to project power along an expanding frontier and its development of an early sort of counterinsurgency doctrine. The next two chapters are companion pieces of a sort; they offer similar readings of the Northwest Indian War as at least presaging certain foreign policy practices and perhaps locking the United States into certain patterns of behavior in places ranging from what is now the continental United States to the Philippines. After these two chapters, I continue into the twenty-first century to consider how the memory of the Northwest Indian War has become politicized in recent years.

Three

PROJECTING POWER

US Military Bases in the Ohio River Valley and Beyond

Previous to the revolution, and even since the peace, there has been a constant necessity for keeping small garrisons on our Western frontier. No person can doubt that these will continue to be indispensable, if it should only be against the ravages and depredations of the Indians.

—ALEXANDER HAMILTON (1787)

For Alexander Hamilton, it was obvious that the United States would need to establish and maintain military garrisons along a frontier that was expanding at the expense of Native American groups.[1] Such military bases would be necessary to ensure the security of settlers and would "continue to be indispensable" for the foreseeable future.[2] As the conventional wisdom would have it, however, such frontier fortifications were qualitatively different from military bases that the United States began operating on foreign territory after the Spanish–American War of 1898 or even more expansively after World War II. For many historians and international relations (IR) scholars, the proliferation of overseas US military bases marked an end of American "isolationism" and the beginning of "imperialism" or "internationalism" (Kupchan 2020).[3] The US military and its practice of establishing bases in other countries has certainly expanded since 1898, but I argue that this is a less significant departure from the past than it is often made out to be.[4]

In this chapter, I show how the Northwest Indian War presaged a practice that would become central to American foreign policy: the use of military bases to project power. As noted above, after early US losses in the war, General Anthony Wayne received command of a force that would succeed in defeating the Native coalition. As I discuss at greater length in this chapter, this American victory was in part the product of Wayne's decision to construct a series of forts that would allow the Legion of the United States under his command to project power deep into the Ohio River Valley. This demonstrated to political elites the value of military bases in securing control across the continent, and they would subsequently invest a great deal of resources in the maintenance of an expansive basing network across the North American continent. Standard narratives of US foreign policy identify the construction of overseas military bases as a significant change—a rupture dividing discrete isolationist and internationalist periods in US foreign policy—that came about after the Spanish–American War and (and after the Second World War gave the United States the opportunity to craft an even more far-flung system of bases). I argue here, however, that there is more continuity than change in the ways the United States has used military bases over time.

In making the case that US foreign policy was significantly different pre- and post-1898, scholars often reference the role of military bases. For Eric Nordlinger (1996, 52), it was the pursuit of what were framed as "defensive outposts in the Pacific" that constituted America's "first internationalist ventures." Contemporaneous debate over what to do with America's newfound possessions was often framed in terms of whether the United States was becoming an empire, however, and scholars still typically discuss this post-1898 moment as being about imperial rather than internationalist politics. "Until 1898, the United States had a very limited overseas military presence and no permanent bases. . . . The United States exhibited greater signs of formal empire following the Spanish–American War in 1898," and one key sign of "formal empire" was the creation of military bases in new territorial acquisitions such as Guantánamo Bay, the Philippines, and Guam (Yeo and Pettyjohn 2021, 24). The establishment of these permanent "overseas" bases was evidence of an "imperial turn" away from "isolationism" in US foreign policy (Kupchan 2020, 193–195). Indeed, Arthur Schlesinger (1999, 141) asks:

> [W]ho can doubt that there is an American empire?—an "informal" empire, not colonial in polity, but still richly equipped with imperial paraphernalia: troops, ships, planes, bases, proconsuls, local collaborators, all spread wide around the luckless planet.

Others emphasize the period during and after World War II as a time when—as evidenced in its expansion of "overseas military bases"—the United States became a more "extroverted" world power (Stevenson 2022, 9).

Well before the Spanish–American War and World War II, however, the United States constructed and staffed many military bases as it acquired land across the North American continent via force, purchase, treaty, or combinations thereof. The military bases the United States constructed across the continent served to facilitate its territorial expansion and might thus be thought of as harbingers of today's global US military presence. Thus, I argue, US military basing practices do not support a strong distinction between pre- and post-1898 eras of US policy. In short, America's pre-1898 military basing policy is not as qualitatively different from its post-1898 basing policy as it is often made out to be.

In the next section I elaborate on my argument, and I discuss the role of basing in early US military policy. Then I examine military basing in the Northwest Indian War of 1790–1795, a conflict in which victory relied significantly on the development of basing infrastructure to enable relatively quick transit between fortifications, and I follow that with a discussion of how the bases used in this war compare to later bases.[5] I conclude with a look at how this case and the subsequent expansion of military bases across North America cuts against any sharp distinction between a pre-1898 isolationist and a post-1898 imperial foreign policy.

US MILITARY BASES IN THEORY AND PRACTICE

I argue that US military bases have served the same basic purpose throughout American history: to allow for the projection of US military power. This power is generally concentrated in military bases with the goal of influencing others through deterrence and/or compellence, and different bases have different functions in supporting those ends. Some might serve primarily to ease logistical challenges through the storing of otherwise difficult-to-transport materiel or through the maintenance of lines of communication, whereas others might host military personnel meant to serve as a "trip-wire."[6] But most fundamentally, bases serve to concentrate military power in specific locations to enable its use.[7] This premise may seem uncontroversial or even banal, but it is important in establishing the continuity that I argue exists in US foreign policy; the United States has utilized military bases throughout its history, and it has used them to the same basic effect.

Arguments for some important discontinuity in US military basing tend to focus on the fact that early US military bases were established on what policymakers saw as US territory. The years leading up to 1898, as this narrative goes, were defined by expansion across the continent but also by attempted isolation from the rest of the world (Kupchan 2020; Morgenthau 1969). With its territorial acquisitions after the Spanish–American War, as then president of Princeton University Woodrow Wilson opined, "The nation has stepped forth into the open arena of the world" (quoted in Herring 2008, 335). The practice of maintaining military bases in unincorporated territories and in countries recognized as sovereign surely represented a shift in the territorial scope of the US military's footprint. If we take Native American claims to sovereignty seriously, however, we might not so readily accept that all early military bases were on US territory (Deloria and Wilkins 2000; Prior 2020). That is, US claims to land are not the only ones we ought to consider. Even if we maintain a domestic/overseas distinction in pre- and post-1898 basing, I argue, the differences between early and later US military bases are less significant than the more fundamental similarity in the purposes US policymakers have pursued through basing policy.

There are surely some salient differences in pre- and post-1898 US military bases. First, overseas bases present challenges that domestic bases present to a lesser extent. Getting a foreign sovereign to acquiesce to the maintenance of a US military base on its soil can be a challenge in its own right, and if the base is to be a lasting presence, both the host government and the US government need to have reasonable confidence that the local population will tolerate the base's presence. It takes political work to make military bases unobtrusive enough that they do not provoke costly back-lash.[8] "Most bases have managed to slip into the daily lives of the nearby community," but that does not happen automatically (Enloe 1990, 66).[9] Indeed, it is precisely when major changes in a base's operations disrupt the status quo that activists are most likely to mobilize in opposition to the expansion or continued operation of a base (Kim 2023).

Second, early US basing policy primarily used fortifications to help ease the process of American expansion, whereas today's bases are oriented more toward maintaining a post-1945 status quo that has been relatively favorable to the United States. That is, early basing was about supporting a more clearly revisionist American foreign policy.[10] Regardless of whether we identify 1898 or 1945 as demarcating periods of increasingly expansive goals in US foreign policy, however, I argue that the United States has used military bases throughout its history for the same basic purpose of pro-jecting power. The projection of power can, however, be oriented toward varying ends.

Studies of US military basing have occasionally acknowledged the early use of bases across the North American continent while asserting that those bases were different in kind from later overseas bases. Michael Allen and co-authors (2022, 207) acknowledge, for example, that, "The US established its first overseas base in Cuba in 1898; however, the concept of placing the US military among people who it does not directly represent is much older, as the US established bases in indigenous territory during westward expan-sion." But this changed after 1898 (Allen et al. 2022, 10):

> The US began actively sending troops overseas on long-term deployments after the Spanish-American War. . . . Where earlier US bases in North America were designed to help maintain control over territory the US gov-ernment sought to absorb, the bases the US began to develop throughout the 1900s were designed to help assert US influence and project military power to more distant locations).[11]

Those earlier bases, I argue, were designed just as much to "help assert US influence" and to "project military power" even if their geographic reach was not as far (due in no small part to technological constraints). While dif-ferent bases serve different purposes, they have generally served to project power and to thereby expand the scope of US influence.

For Allen and co-authors (2022, 9), the key difference between pre- and post-1898 bases lies in the fact that pre-1898 bases were on territory that policymakers sought to make or assumed to be "a part of the country itself":

> The US has a long history of using military bases to expand its influence. The process of westward expansion across the North American continent was accompanied by the construction of numerous military bases to aid in the projection of military power against Great Britain, Spain, France, Mexico, and Native Americans, as it sought to assert control over the increasingly vast territories settlers occupied. It also used these bases to try to protect commerce as the flow of settlers pushing West often outpaced state control. However, the US ultimately sought to extend direct control over these territories, making them a part of the country itself.[12]

But throughout its history, for Allen and co-authors (2022), the United States has used military bases "to expand its influence," and I argue that there is more to make of that continuity.[13] The core purpose of US military basing has not meaningfully changed over time: Whether in the 1790s or in the 1990s, US military bases have been used to the extent possible to project power.

EARLY AMERICAN MILITARY BASING

The US military surely staffs more bases today than it did on the early American frontier. The Department of Defense's occasional Base Structure Report is a frequently cited source on recent US military installations, and as of 2006, Alexander Cooley (2008, 5–6) details, the United States maintained 2,888 military installations within the country, 77 in its unincorporated territories, and 766 in other countries.[14] Drawing on the 2016 report, Andrew Yeo (2017, 130) identifies 587 US bases in 42 foreign countries—at least as publicly identified by the Department of Defense. Claudia Kim (2023, 13) cites the 2018 report as listing 518 overseas bases, which suggests a significant decline between 2006 and 2018 that is likely related to the diminishing intensity of the Global War on Terror in that time. Little has changed since then; the most recent version at the time of this writing—the 2023 report—lists 511 overseas bases. A rise in the number of military sites in unincorporated territories—from 77 to 159 between 2006 and 2023—only partially compensates for the decline in total overseas bases.[15] This compares to an American military that spent many of its early years staffing only dozens or scores of bases on the North American continent, but this was a rather substantial commitment for the small military of the time (Prucha 1964).

Early US military bases primarily took the form of coastal fortifications or frontier encampments. In the mid-1790s, coastal fortifications became a priority for policymakers as the British and French rivalry started to threaten US shipping. In response, Congress made a sizable investment in key ports (Weigley 1977, 42–43):

> Congress voted in 1794 to rehabilitate coastal fortifications of the Revolutionary era and to erect new ones to protect sixteen principal ports and harbors. . . . These fortresses, it was hoped, would protect the most important points on the coast from any sudden hostile *coup de main*, would compel any invading force which might arrive to land at less vital places while American forces assembled to deal with them, and would provide bases and places of refuge for an American Navy.

Moreover, these fortifications were not purely about hardening American targets but were also meant to enable the projection of power (Weigley 1977, 43):

> With the vital parts of the American coast secured by forts, the American Navy would be free to range out to sea, to threaten an invading expedition before it reached American shores and perhaps deter it from attempting to land, while also protecting the waterborne commerce so important to the growth of the economy and harassing enemy commerce.[16]

While the United States considered fortifying the eastern seaboard, it also had a western frontier to secure. With Britain having ceded land encompassing territory east of the Mississippi River and South of Canada, early US political elites widely agreed on the need for further expansion. This was "axiomatic, because external threats exacerbated the fragility of the political union," and as discussed in Chapter 2, this was a broadly shared sensibility (Priest 2021, 34).[17] "Most fundamentally, the American *Weltanschauung* contained an intense, seemingly moral imperative to expand the country's 'experiment' in liberal democratic government beyond its original borders, which required an aggressive strategy along the western frontier" (Maslowski 1994, 207). Native American groups that might resist such expansion were ultimately seen as a threat to US interests, and as discussed in Chapter 2, settlers were anxious for the security that a federal military presence would provide. Early elites thus looked to the erection of fortifications on the frontier as having the potential to influence those groups in various ways. Most fundamentally, fortifications would allow for the projection of power, ideally in such a way that Native groups might be awed into submission.[18] Moreover, given that settlers often wanted to be close to the protection offered by the US military and that settler activities would disrupt local ecosystems on which Native Americans relied for sustenance, some political elites hoped that the spread of military fortifications along the frontier would incentivize Native groups to relocate without bloodshed (Frymer 2014, 121–122). Ultimately, if necessary, frontier military sites would enable the use of force against tribes. Military bases—along the coast and across an advancing frontier—were thus central to early American defense policy.

The United States, as I detailed in Chapter 2, began its history with a very small military in part due to economic distress after the Revolutionary War and in part due to a widespread belief that large standing armies were not conducive to the maintenance of a representative democracy. "Thus the Confederation sold the Continental Navy's last ship in 1785 and maintained as its 'army' only the 1st American Regiment, at an authorized strength of 700 men" (Maslowski 1994, 208). George Washington was among those who called for a more substantial military—he proposed a force of 1,908 infantrymen and 723 artillerymen—but it took years for Congress to authorize increases in the size of the military up to that point (Prucha 1969, 5). Fort Pitt (in Pennsylvania) and West Point (in New York) would be the two most substantial US military bases in its early days (Prucha 1969, 6). As soon became clear, however, the nation's expansionist goals demanded a more substantial military apparatus. The inability of the United States under the Articles of Confederation to quickly put down Shays's Rebellion, as well as its inability to effectively police a frontier along which settlers frequently sparked conflicts with Native American groups, gave impetus to efforts to replace the Articles with the Constitution, under which the ability to fund and field a military was more effectively centralized in the national government. The US Army's "foremost domestic role" would be "to police the so-called Indian frontier" (Maslowski 1994, 212).[19] That frontier would soon be demarcated by US military bases.

Across the frontier, military bases helped to secure US territorial acquisitions. By 1898, hundreds of bases had been constructed across the North American continent: "While many scholars date the creation of the first US bases abroad to the seizure of Guantánamo Bay during the 1898 Spanish–American War, more than 250 frontier forts helped enable the seizure of foreign, Native American territory across North America" (Vine 2019, S161–S162).[20] To some extent, however, the US Army was simply following patterns of settlement rather than actively shaping them, and the construction of military bases intended to protect settlers had the unintended consequence of encouraging settlers to move even farther west as they assumed that the now-nearby military would be better placed to protect them (Utley 1977, 5). Before the dramatic expansion of this basing network in the nineteenth century, however, the Northwest Indian War helped to establish that the United States could indeed concentrate military assets in bases to effectively project power and influence Native American groups.

PROJECTING POWER IN THE OHIO RIVER VALLEY

In this section, I examine the use of military bases in the Old Northwest in the years prior to and during the Northwest Indian War. Victory in the Revolutionary War left the United States with a new problem: The Treaty of Paris entailed British land cessions, but Native American groups in that territory did not believe they had made any such cessions. Some of these tribes, as discussed in Chapter 2, were rather large and militarily capable. The United States nonetheless claimed those lands by virtue of conquest; tribes accused of aiding Britain in the war were portrayed as being on the losing side. George Washington was aware of the issue this presented; settlers would think the lands to be rightfully theirs, and they would likely clash with Native populations. It is worth returning here to Washington's 1783 letter to Congressman James Duane: "To suffer a wide extended Country to be over run with Land Jobbers, Speculators, and Monopolisers or even with scatter'd settlers . . . is pregnant of disputes both with the Savages and among ourselves." In my reading of this letter in Chapter 2, I noted especially Washington's view that the purchase of Native lands would be more cost-effective than military conquest. Here, however, I would place more emphasis on Washington's advice for how to avoid those disputes: "We will . . . establish a boundary line between them and us beyond which we will <u>endeavor</u> to restrain our People from Hunting or Settling."[21] The "boundary line between them and us" would be comprised of military fortifications.

The process of asserting control of the Ohio River Valley, the first major flash point in conflicts over the Northwest Territory, would ultimately depend on the construction of forts from which military personnel could try to restrict illegal settlement while also deterring Native attacks and enabling US military action against the tribes. Figure 1 shows the location of many of the relevant forts in this case; of particular relevance to the Northwest Indian War are those on the western side of the map.

While some forts in what would become the Northwest Territory were built during or before the Revolutionary War, the post-revolutionary 1780s and 90s saw a significant expansion in US military basing in the Northwest Territory. As violence between settlers and Native American groups continued and Congress sought treaty negotiations with tribes, Fort Harmar would be constructed in 1785 to serve as a frequent site of negotiations. Likewise, Fort Washington's construction farther to the west (modern Cincinnati) in 1789 would allow for additional negotiations meant to forestall war. Not long after, however, some of the first expeditions of the Northwest Indian War would depart from there (Wooster 2009, 8–10).

It was Josiah Harmar—the lieutenant colonel commandant of the First American Regiment—who was tasked with enforcing national policy in the Northwest Territory starting in 1784 and who ordered the construction of Fort Harmar to facilitate this mission (Sword 1985, 89). As noted in Chapter 2, Harmar understood his task to be "to prevent illegal encroachments on the public lands, to secure happiness to the inhabitants, and to protect private property from arbitrary invasion, and to remove, if possible, diffidence, fear, & jealousy from the minds of the Indians" (Harmar et al. 1957, 38). These ambitious goals required a permanent base on the frontier, and Fort Harmar would be the primary location from which the early American military would project power in an effort to prevent illegal settlement and to deter Native American attacks on settlers.

Throughout the Northwest Indian War and in the years leading up to it,

FIGURE 1: U.S. forts in the Northwest Territory.

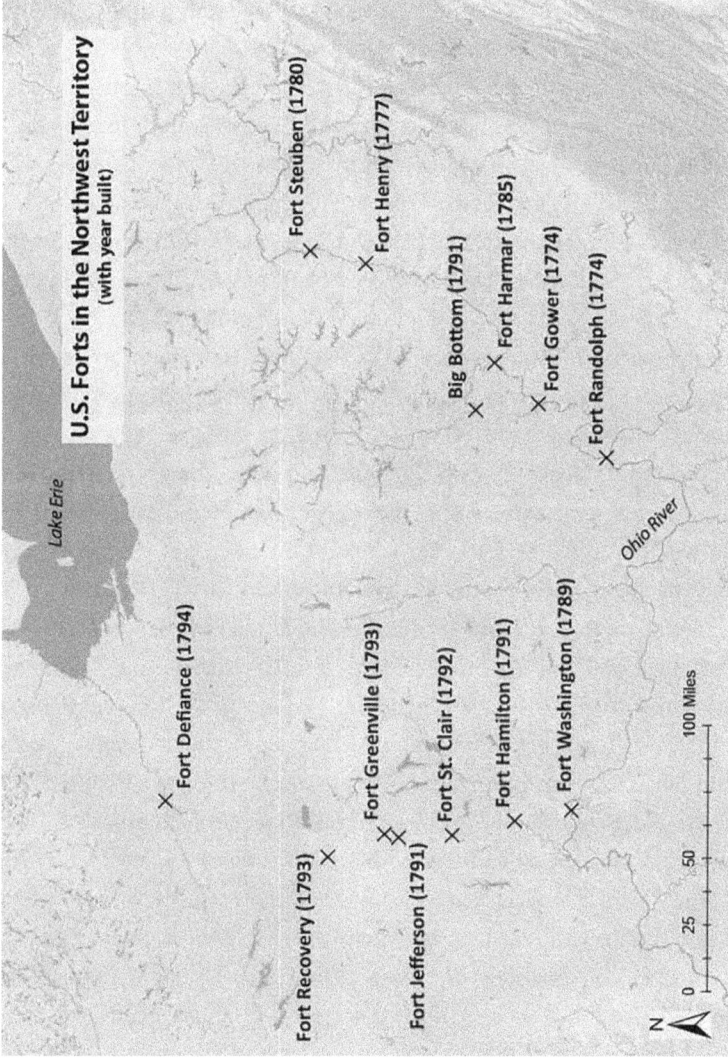

U.S. Forts in the Northwest Territory
(with year built)

Lake Erie

Fort Defiance (1794)

Fort Recovery (1793)

Fort Greenville (1793)

Fort Jefferson (1791)

Fort St. Clair (1792)

Fort Hamilton (1791)

Fort Washington (1789)

Fort Steuben (1780)

Fort Henry (1777)

Big Bottom (1791)

Fort Harmar (1785)

Fort Gower (1774)

Fort Randolph (1774)

Ohio River

0   25   50   100 Miles

N

Source: Keller et al. (2011, 29). Original map based on Shetrone and Sherman, The Historical Marker Database.

these forts (and the preexisting network of which they were a part) were central to US efforts to project power in the region. The process began at older forts such as Fort McIntosh, which had been built in 1778 in what is now Beaver, Pennsylvania. Having been abandoned since the end of the Revolutionary War, a portion of the small military would accompany US negotiators to the fort in January 1785 and would help refurbish it.[22] The negotiations produced the Treaty of Fort McIntosh, and Harmar would afterwards stay there to try to keep settlers and Native populations apart. The limited manpower of the early US military, however, meant that its efforts were only minimally successful: "From Fort McIntosh the colonel sent out detachments to disperse settlers who had settled illegally on the northern side of the Ohio, but he could hardly keep pace with the influx" (Prucha 1969, 8).

As the settler military presence in the Northwest Territory increased, so too did the construction of new US forts.[23] In October 1785, Congress would authorize the construction of another fort—the aforementioned Fort Harmar— to be placed between the Muskingum River and the Great Miami River to enhance the small military's power projection capabilities. The location was "in a good position to exclude intruders on the public lands, protect surveyors of the Seven Ranges, and convince the Indians that Congress meant to protect legal settlers on the lands that had been ceded by treaty" (Prucha 1969, 8). Shortly thereafter, Captain John F. Hamtramck was tasked with protecting surveyors in the area, and his detachment constructed Fort Steuben in the winter of 1785–86 (Prucha 1969, 9). A small detachment led by Captain Walter Finney would establish a temporary Fort Finney near the mouth of the Great Miami River in September 1785 before moving to a more suitable location farther south in August 1786 (Prucha 1969, 10).

Given continued clashes between settlers and Native populations through 1786, in April 1787 Congress authorized the deployment of additional troops to Vincennes—the location from which, as discussed in Chapter 2, John Filson wrote to petition Congress for military aid. Fort McIntosh and Fort Harmar would remain lightly staffed, and Harmar would concentrate much of this expanded military force in the newly constructed Fort Knox at Vincennes. Harmar himself would then return to Fort Harmar and leave the since-promoted Major Hamtramck in command at Fort Knox (Prucha 1969, 11).

By the time President Washington authorized federal military action in 1790, Harmar was in place at another new fort—Fort Washington, located at the mouth of the Little Miami River (Prucha 1969, 20). Having been constructed in 1789, it was ideally located to enable a military campaign against the tribes of the Ohio River Valley. Harmar's initial attacks on the Western Confederacy—on Miami towns in particular—proceeded from Fort Washington with a force of 320 federal regulars and 1,153 state militiamen who had been called into federal service (Prucha 1969, 20). Despite assumptions that the US force would easily rout Native American forces, Harmar's contingent fruitlessly searched for members of the Native coalition before suffering a surprise attack and incurring substantial losses, largely due to an undisciplined performance by militiamen who scattered upon first contact. Seventy-five regulars and 108 militiamen were killed while inflicting few casualties on the Miami in their first two engagements (Prucha 1969, 21). Harmar was relieved of command as the War Department sought answers as to how the US forces could have been defeated by Native American groups that white Americans generally saw as lesser peoples.

Determined to make up for their early losses, Congress authorized the raising of an additional 912 infantrymen and 2,000 militia cavalry in March 1791, but it was assumed that additional forts were also necessary to more capably project power in the Ohio River Valley. The frontier contingent would be placed under St. Clair's command with the orders to first send negotiators to sue for peace and, if they were not successful, to then attack the tribes on the Wabash and Maumee Rivers (Prucha 1969, 22). To ensure any such military efforts were successful, St. Clair was also meant to establish another fort as his headquarters and to construct a series of supporting forts that would link this new headquarters back to Fort Washington (Prucha 1969, 23–24). St. Clair's force would construct Fort Hamilton and then Fort Jefferson as supply depots and communication hubs on their march north from Fort Washington (Prucha 1969, 24–25). St. Clair and his men would continue north toward some of the larger Native settlements in the area, but they would not have the opportunity to construct a third fort before being attacked on November 4, 1791. Native forces once again overpowered the surprised Americans in an even more resounding defeat than Harmar's. Winthrop Sargent, St. Clair's adjutant general, estimated that 35 officers and 588 noncommissioned officers and privates were killed (Prucha 1969, 26). St. Clair himself escaped, but like Harmar he was summoned by the House of Representatives to explain himself. Congress ultimately found no fault in either man's command, but both men would resign from the military in disgrace.[24]

With military efforts in the Northwest Territory having been frustrated twice already, Congress would soon pass an act bolstering the military once again. It authorized the raising of another 2,880 federal regulars on the condition that their terms would last no more than three years or until "the United States shall be at peace with the Indian tribes" (quoted in Prucha 1969, 28). Major General Anthony Wayne was given command of this new fighting force in April 1792, and he focused on training this new Legion of the United States at Fort Pitt (Prucha 1969, 29–30). To deprive his troops of "the blandishments the city offered his men," Wayne set up a new camp called Legionville (about twenty-two miles south of Pittsburgh) in November 1792. In the meantime, as discussed in Chapter 2, the United States continued to send negotiators to meet with the Ohio River Valley tribes, but no mutually satisfactory agreement was forthcoming.[25]

While Wayne was training his troops in Legionville, Brigadier General James Wilkinson commanded a smaller portion of the US Army at Fort Washington starting in March 1792. He had been tasked by Knox with gaining any relevant information he could on the local tribes, assuring the Native population of America's peaceful intentions, and strengthening the line of forts that St. Clair had started, which ran north of Fort Washington (Prucha 1969, 34). A key aspect of this work was the construction of Fort St. Clair, roughly halfway between Fort Hamilton and Fort Jefferson, which made the trip from one fort to another less perilous simply by shortening the time that forces would spend exposed to potential attack.

After training through the winter of 1792–1793, Wayne was authorized to join Wilkinson in the Ohio territory in April 1793, and he encamped with the Legion just south of Fort Washington as he continued drilling his men. Wayne was told in September of that year that negotiations had failed and that, while it was too close to winter to mount a campaign, he ought to prepare for hostilities, which entailed constructing more forts closer to Native population centers. Wayne would march the Legion north past Fort Jefferson and order the construction of a new fort called Fort Greenville. From that base his troops would construct yet another fort farther north, Fort Recovery, in December (Prucha 1969, 35). These forts were central to military action in the next year.

The Legion continued fortifying its positions into the summer of 1794 until members of the Western Confederacy, confident of victory given their previous engagements with the Americans, attacked Fort Recovery at the end of June (Prucha 1969, 36). Unlike previous surprise attacks that caught US soldiers outside their fortifications, this one was unsuccessful.[26] The well-trained soldiers and well-developed fortifications allowed Wayne's Legion to successfully repel the attackers, and the Native forces retreated. Shifting to the offensive, Wayne marched a total of 3,500 men toward Native population centers near the confluence of the Maumee and Auglaize Rivers on July 28, and on August 8, he would stop his march to have his men construct Fort Defiance—a location at which a small rearguard would remain to ensure that the main fighting force could not be surprised from behind (Prucha 1969, 36). From there, Wayne's Legion would continue north until it met about 500 men representing the Western Confederacy on the battlefield. Given its numerical, tactical, and technological advantages, the Legion easily won what is now called the Battle of Fallen Timbers in about forty-five minutes, but Wayne continued to fortify old positions such as Fort Defiance and construct new ones such as Fort Wayne to solidify American control in the region as long as Native land cessions were pending (Prucha 1969, 37; Wooster 2009, 20). Having been defeated in battle, the Ohio River Valley tribes agreed to undertake negotiations with Wayne at Fort Greenville, and they ultimately ceded much of what is now Ohio and a portion of Indiana to the United States on August 3, 1795 (Prucha 1969, 38). The US military had succeeded in using military bases to project power in the Ohio River Valley.

FRONTIER FORTS AND OVERSEAS BASES

US success in the Northwest Indian War bolstered arguments for the continued use of military fortifications along the frontier and presaged the global network of military bases that the United States now maintains. Despite early elite concerns about the creation of a standing army, Wayne's success in the Old Northwest secured Congress's support for the maintenance of a military of about 3,000 men, and some of those men would continue to staff forts constructed during the Northwest Indian War. Knox's successor as secretary of war, Timothy Pickering, was sufficiently convinced of the utility of military forts that he would authorize the construction of new ones elsewhere on the American frontier to further project US power oriented toward influencing Native American groups (Wooster 2009, 23, 25). Once it was established that the federal government would keep "operational control over the process of Indian war-making" on the frontier, military basing became the primary tool by which the government could control that process (Maulden 2016, 21). The Northwest Indian War became a model of how to effectively use military forts to project power; in the early days of the War of 1812, William Henry Harrison, then the governor of the Indiana Territory (and an earlier secretary of the Northwest Territory and, briefly, a later president) would write that Wayne's "penetrating the Country of the Enemy and securing the possession by a chain of Posts" offered a "tardy" but "effectual" model that could be applied amid renewed hostilities with British and Native forces (Maulden 2019, 112).

In the frontier forts built for the Northwest Indian War, I have argued, we can see a harbinger of things to come: That is, the claiming of overseas territory and the creation of overseas bases associated with the Spanish–American War and World War II are less a departure from the American past and more the continuation of it. Frontier forts and overseas bases, I have argued, serve the same fundamental purpose—to project power and thereby influence others. Having noted the extent to which the Northwest Indian War offered a model of how to use military fortifications effectively, I consider in the remainder of this section how we might create a typology of military bases that captures the different ways that bases allow for power projection.[27]

In a Global Posture Review ordered by the George W. Bush administration, the Department of Defense distinguishes between three types of overseas facilities: "main operating bases," "forward operating sites," and "cooperative security locations." Main operating bases are "where American combat troops (and usually their families) are permanently stationed in facilities controlled and secured by the US military"; forward operating sites house a smaller "support presence" and are used "for temporary deployments or training"; cooperative security locations involve "a minimal footprint and level of control, use of which is contemplated mainly for contingencies" (Stevenson 2022, 15). Such facilities surely differ from those used in the Northwest Indian War, but what all these types of facilities do is "act as 'force multipliers' and enable U.S. planners to rapidly project power both within and across regions" (Cooley 2008, 5). By providing "access to neighboring assets, territories, or resources" or by providing "service and repair facilities, storage, training facilities, and logistical staging posts," today's military bases enable the US military to project power and influence others (Cooley 2008, 5). That is, while the US government might divide its overseas military facilities into three types based in part on its degree of control over the site, it may be worth thinking of these facilities as falling into one of two categories when describing the purposes military bases serve: Bases can enable power projection either by facilitating the mobilization of military forces or by ensuring the readiness of military forces.

This dichotomy is apparent in the ways the US military used forts in the Northwest Indian War. The forts that Anthony Wayne's Legion constructed during their campaign were largely intended to facilitate the mobilization of military forces. These forts were meant primarily to give the Legion a safe place from which to depart on their mission to compel the Western Confederacy to cede Native lands. Other forts of the Old Northwest served more to ensure the readiness of the early American military.[28] St. Clair's Fort Hamilton and Fort Jefferson, as noted above, were intended less as bases from which his fighting forces would initiate attacks and more as sites of logistical support. Fort Pitt, where Wayne trained his Legion, was a site well-equipped for such training by that point. As these examples suggest, whether a site is meant to facilitate mobilization or ensure readiness may have a relationship to distance: Fort Pitt was a good place to train given its significant distance from the places of active hostilities with Native American groups.

This is only a brief sketch of a typology of military bases, but in considering how bases are used to enable power projection, the distinction between facilitating mobilization and ensuring readiness (i.e., readiness to be mobilized) offers an ideal typical way of thinking about military bases ranging from eighteenth-century frontier fortifications to twenty-first- century overseas facilities. In line with my argument, this typology suggests a fundamental continuity in the purposes that military bases have served throughout the history of US foreign policy. This further reinforces my position that the United States has never been isolationist: It has used military bases to project power and to thereby influence others in similar ways throughout its history.

CODA: TO THE PACIFIC

If US military bases after 1898 "were designed to help assert US influence and project military power" (Allen et al. 2022, 10), it would seem difficult to maintain that bases like Fort Washington or Fort Recovery served fundamentally different purposes in the Northwest Indian War. Bases were an effective way of projecting power, and they served to decisively influence actors on the frontier. Hundreds more bases would be constructed across the ever-expanding frontier for similar purposes, and the network would reach the Pacific Coast by the mid-nineteenth century (Prucha 1964).

US basing policy of the twentieth and twenty-first centuries, in short, has more in common with basing policy of the eighteenth and nineteenth centuries than is typically assumed. While the military and its global footprint have grown over time, US policymakers have been using the strategic placement of military bases to influence others for centuries. The sharp divisions scholars sometimes make between American foreign policy before and after 1898 or before and after 1945 are ultimately at odds with the ways that US leaders have wielded military force from the beginning.

This continuity also means that the study of modern basing policies might gain from more sustained engagement with earlier US basing policy. In the same way that modern US bases are not contested by local populations with equal intensity, not all Indigenous tribes attempted to violently resist US encroachments that were tangibly realized in the construction of frontier bases. Research on the causes of more or less intense anti-base activism (such as that by Allen et al. 2022 and Kim 2023) might thus interrogate similar dynamics on the early American frontier.[29] Also, those who seek to understand how elites rhetorically legitimize the creation and maintenance of military bases (e.g., O'Shea 2019; Salter and Mutlu 2013) might examine discursive support for earlier bases that were maintained despite the general public's hesitance to support a large standing army. Further study of early US military basing practices may help us to better understand the practices of the more recent past and the present.

This continuity between early and modern basing practices also reinforces a broader argument that I make throughout this book. That is, the continuity in US military basing over time suggests that early US foreign policy was less clearly isolationist than some suggest. As I noted earlier in this chapter, whether early US bases were indeed on their own territory was a contested issue rather than a neutral statement of fact, and the early use and proliferation of military bases across the American frontier came at the expense of Native American groups and European powers whose claims to North American territory were rapidly extinguished. At the same time, the United States sought to avoid permanent alliances for fear of becoming committed to costly conflicts, but that hardly amounts to isolation. In short, if the modern US basing network constitutes a "hybrid empire-liberal hegemonic organization," this organization did not emerge spontaneously in 1898 or 1945; early frontier bases were a harbinger of things to come (Cooley and Nexon 2013, 1,044). Indeed, this is not the only way in which the war presaged later developments. As I discuss in the next chapter, the Northwest Indian War helped the US military develop a sort of early counterinsurgency doctrine that would be refined in America's subsequent Indian Wars and, as the United States extended its reach across the Pacific Ocean, in the Philippines.

Four

LEARNING COUNTERINSURGENCY

Bringing the Indian Wars to the Philippines

The Northwest Indian War was constitutive of early US foreign policy, as were the many subsequent Indian Wars extending through the nineteenth century; they made US foreign policy what it was. In this chapter, I consider how engaging in conflict with Native American groups in the Ohio River Valley and across the North American continent helped cultivate a military with significant experience fighting what we might now call counterinsurgency campaigns. Here I go beyond America's continental conquest to show how the military practices enacted in the Indian Wars shaped military practices enacted overseas. In the Philippine–American War of 1899–1902, I argue, individual military men with experience in the Indian Wars applied what they perceived to be the lessons thereof and arrived at a sort of counterinsurgency doctrine that had been continually learned and relearned on the expanding American frontier.

The Spanish–American War of 1898 is often cited as an inflection point in US foreign policy. This is where many claim that the United States emerged from isolation to become an imperial or at least a more active global power. While I have already argued against seeing 1898 as that significant a rupture in the history of US foreign policy, the Philippine–American War that followed deserves consideration here for the ways that US military men analogized this war to the Indian Wars. After a victorious United States acquired the Philippines from Spain in 1898 and refused to grant the Philippines independence, a Philippine independence movement engaged in violent resistance to US rule. The US military response to this, I argue, was to eventually come to think of the war as similar to the eighteenth- and nineteenth-century Indian Wars and as therefore requiring similar responses.

It is often assumed or argued that America's Indian Wars influenced later US military doctrine. Perhaps those experiences established a template for later counterinsurgency campaigns or created precedent for the use of especially harsh tactics against enemy combatants believed to be "uncivilized." It often remains unclear, however, how exactly US military engagements with Native American groups affected later military actions; I seek to clarify how they did so in the Philippines. It is useful to examine the Philippine–American War to shed light on this question because, given its timing, it was a conflict in which many US participants had served in the Indian Wars. Moreover, as I show in this chapter, those North American experiences were frequently invoked by US soldiers in the Philippines. In a mode similar to my engagement with military basing practices in Chapter 3, I demonstrate here how the Northwest Indian Wars presaged later US military practices.

THE ARGUMENT

I argue that the Northwest Indian War saw the United States develop an early sort of counterinsurgency doctrine—one that borrowed from earlier precedents and that was enacted throughout the Indian Wars. There was little institutionalized learning of lessons from the Northwest Indian War or other Indian Wars, however, and the US military thus frequently found itself relearning the same lessons throughout the eighteenth and nineteenth centuries. To the extent that a counterinsurgency doctrine was learned in the Northwest Indian War or other Indian Wars, I argue, it was therefore applied on a more individualized basis. More formalized doctrine would only start to crystallize after the United States relearned the art of counterinsurgency in the Philippines.

I argue that individual soldiers brought perceived lessons of the Indian Wars with them to the Philippine–American War and that the Indian Wars were seen as an applicable analogy because Native Americans and Filipinos were assumed to be similarly "uncivilized." In other words, I argue that the effects of the Indian Wars were most significant at the tactical level of warfare, where individual soldiers could directly implement what they took to be the lessons of the Indian Wars, and the lessons ultimately related to the supposed character of the enemy. At the strategic level of warfare, the Indian Wars had prompted little organizational learning over the course of a century. Rather, the US military maintained its doctrinal focus in this period on more traditional campaigns associated with interstate war among Europeans (i.e., large-scale conventional warfare with engagements resolved through decisive battle), and the application of counterinsurgency techniques in the Philippines would ultimately start as a bottom-up process.[1]

That US participants in the Indian Wars learned something from the experience is not a novel claim.[2] My argument, however, offers a clarifying distinction between individualized learning that could be implemented tactically and organizational learning that could structure higher-level strategic choices. Moreover, my argument prompts a second question. That is, if US soldiers learned something from the Indian Wars, what sort of knowledge did they acquire? I argue that we should think of the knowledge acquired in the Indian Wars and applied in the Philippines as *habitus* (implicit background knowledge) and *phronesis* or *phronetic* knowledge (practical, context-dependent knowledge distinct from epistemic or technical knowledge).[3] As I discuss at the end of this chapter, moreover, *phronesis* offers a useful warning to those seeking lessons learned from military experiences. We ought to be careful not to turn those lessons into nomothetic generalizations (*episteme* or epistemic knowledge) to be applied unproblematically to future campaigns.

In the next section, I provide an overview of claims that have been made about how or to what extent the US military learned from the Indian Wars and applied that knowledge in the Philippines. I then provide a case study of the Philippine–American War that demonstrates how lessons learned from the Indian Wars were applied in that context. I then discuss the nature of the knowledge acquired from experience in the Indian Wars, and I conclude by considering the more general issue of how to think about what lessons can be learned from specific military experiences. In short, this chapter offers an argument to the effect that the US conquest of Native lands had consequences far beyond the North American continent. That is, I have argued that US relations with Native American groups were constitutive of early US foreign policy, but these relations also had lingering effects, even as Indian Affairs increasingly came to be treated as domestic issues in the United States (Szarejko 2022).

LEARNING FROM THE INDIAN WARS

In this section, I outline the debate over the extent to which the US military drew on its experiences in the Indian Wars to fight the Philippine–American War. I focus on specifying the reasons to believe the Indian Wars had some influence on later US military policy, and I conclude the section with a discussion of reasons why we might alternatively believe the influence of the Indian Wars to be overstated.

In the aftermath of the Spanish–American War of 1898, the United States claimed control of the Philippines. Many Filipinos welcomed the voiding of Spanish claims to the islands, and having already contested Spanish dominion, some offered violent resistance when the United States assumed Spain's claims. The resulting conflict is often referred to in English-language historiography as the Philippine–American War and is dated from 1899 to 1902. The United States, having spent much of the previous century at war with Native American groups, was in some tellings rather well-prepared for this sort of counterinsurgency campaign. There is no consensus, however, on how to conceptualize the relationship between the experiences of the Indian Wars and the occupation of the Philippines. Was organizational learning on display here? Was this a case of individualized learning in which many soldiers happened to converge on the same "lessons learned" from similar experiences? Was the analogy of Filipinos to Native Americans simply a manifestation of racism that bifurcated the world into civilized whites and barbaric non-whites? Or are there other ways to understand the link between the Indian Wars and the Philippines?

The extent to which the Indian Wars influenced US operations in the Philippines remains unclear, but most who have written on this topic seem to think that the experiences of the Indian Wars had some effect here. Many of those who fought in the Philippines, including all four US military governors and those who oversaw the occupation from afar, compared US operations in the Philippines to those that had been conducted against Native American groups to consolidate American control of what is now the contiguous United States. "Because of their experience fighting Indians, United States Army leaders in 1900 were probably better equipped to fight a guerrilla war than at any subsequnt [*sic*] time in the twentieth century" (Williams 1980, 828). Likewise, the experiences of war on the expanding American frontier, in Stuart Miller's (1982, 195) telling, produced habits or inclinations that were replicated in the Philippines:

> Virtually every member of the high command had spent most of his career terrorizing Apaches, Comanches, Kiowas, and the Sioux. Some had taken part in the massacre at Wounded Knee. It was easy for such commanders to order similar tactics in the Philippines, particularly when faced with the frustrations of guerrilla warfare. And the men in their command, many of whom were themselves descendants of old Indian fighters, carried out these orders with amazing, if not surprising, alacrity.

In short, some read the Philippine–American War as having been influenced at the tactical and strategic levels by the military's cumulative experiences in the Indian Wars.

One might also emphasize the extent to which civilian policymakers used the Indian Wars as an analogy for operations in the Philippine–American War.[4] In considering how to govern Filipinos, for example, policymakers were quick to see Native American groups as analogues. Henry L. Dawes, a former senator who remains most notable for his successful push to disrupt communal ownership of Native lands in the late 1880s, wrote in 1899 that with respect to the "other alien races whose future had been put in our keeping [due to the Spanish–American War] . . . our policy with the Indians becomes an object lesson worthy of careful and candid study" (quoted in Williams 1980, 814).[5] Similarly, Senator Henry Cabot Lodge argued that the legal authority for US governance of the Philippines was grounded in the same authority that legitimized US governance of Native nations (quoted in Williams 1980, 818):

When our great Chief Justice John Marshall . . . declared in the Cherokee case that the United States could have under its control, exercised by
treaty or the laws of Congress, a "domestic and dependent nation," I think
he solved the question of our constitutional relations to the Philippines.[6]

Some, such as Senator Horace Chilton, rejected the analogy, but they
ultimately did little to draw a distinction between Filipinos and Native peoples beyond, for example, making ill-specified assertions to the effect that,
"Indians occupy a peculiar situation" (quoted in Williams 1980, 821). This
analogy thus became embedded in official US policy—President William
McKinley (quoted in Williams 1980, 823) instructed the Philippine Commission in 1900 as follows:

In dealing with the uncivilized tribes of the islands the commission should
adopt the same course followed by Congress in permitting the tribes of our
North American Indians to maintain their tribal organization. . . . Such
tribal governance should, however, be subjected to wise and firm regula-
tion; and . . . active effort should be exercised to prevent barbarous practices and introduce civilized customs.

Academics and members of relevant civic associations likewise saw US
governance of the Philippines as an opportunity to apply the lessons of past
experiences with Native nations. Walter Williams (1980, 819), for example,
cites a contemporary University of Chicago political scientist as affirming
Lodge's legal analogy: "uncivilized nations under tribal relations [in the
Philippines] would occupy the same status precisely as our own Indians."[7]
"The most influential advisory group on Indian policy," the Lake Mohonk
Conference of Friends of the Indians, quickly turned its activities toward
the Philippines starting in 1898, and throughout subsequent meetings, the
organization would officially recommend broadening its orientation "to
include other dependent races" for which their assimilationist position on
Indian Affairs (to bring them into "Christian civilization") should likewise
be applied (Williams 1980, 814–815). The most prominent civic association
against the acquisition of the Philippines, the Anti-Imperialist League, did
not reject the analogy but opposed expansion nonetheless: "Our treatment
of the Indians cannot be dignified and made a precedent or a defense for
like policy in foreign lands" (quoted in Williams 1980, 822).

Returning to the military, it is not just that the experiences of the Indian

Wars might have informed practices in the Philippines; rather, US soldiers in the Philippines directly invoked the Indian Wars as a salient analogy. American troops stationed there were informed "that the Filipinos were savages no better than our Indians" (Williams 1971, 162). To the extent that US soldiers in the Philippines analogized their situation to the Indian Wars, they were at least partly following the cues of public political discourse. "The impact of imperialist rhetoric on actual events in the Philippines, especially during the 1899–1902 insurrection," Williams (1980, 827) argues, "influenced the feeling among United States troops that this was merely another Indian war." It may have been the case, moreover, that the soldiers stationed in the Philippines were already predisposed to think and speak of the conflict in similar terms; most regiments were from western states with relatively recent experience in the Indian Wars.

Analogies to the Indian Wars were not limited to the lower ranks. Most officers, as one contemporary author wrote, "have seen much service in fighting Indians on the western frontier. Many of them do not regard the military problem as one of any great difficulty" (Robinson 1901, quoted in Williams 1980, 828). For some, fighting Filipinos was "worse than fighting Indians," while others saw it the other way around: "If these Filipines [*sic*] could ambush like our Indians, we would have a bad time; but they have not the grit" (quoted in Aune 2021, 420).[8] Indeed, twenty-six of the thirty American generals who served in the Philippines between 1898 and 1902 also served in conflicts with Native American groups; the remainder all had at least some military experience in the American West (Williams 1980, 828). All four of the US military governors of the Philippines—Wesley Merritt, Elwell Stephen Otis, Arthur MacArthur, Jr., and Adna Chaffee—had significant experience with the Indian Wars.[9]

The key question here, however, is whether the use of the Indian Wars analogy indicates any actual influence on the actions of the US military in the Philippines. Stefan Aune (2021, 429), for example, argues for the presence of this influence by way of General Henry Ware Lawton, who led some of the earliest campaigns in the Philippine–American War: "As much as Lawton was the embodiment of the discursive aura of an Indian fighter, he also put into practice tactics which directly drew on his experience in frontier violence." Aune (2021, 429–430) frames those tactics—especially "surprise attacks on villages," "the use of smaller mobile units alongside Indian scouts," and "the incarceration of Native non-combatants"—as practices that were taken to constitute to the "lessons" of the Indian Wars (Aune 2021, 429–430). If, for Aune (2021, 421–422), "such a connection [between the Indian Wars and the Philippine–American War] exists," the nature of that connection is a straightforward one in which officers learned from fighting in the Indian Wars and applied what they took to be the lessons thereof in the Philippines.

Despite all this evidence that the Indian Wars influenced US military operations in the Philippines, there are reasons to doubt that the Indian Wars served as a sort of master analogy guiding US policy in this case. Early stages of the war were fought as rather conventional engagements, and while many officers had experience in the Indian Wars, it is not clear that they all learned much from the experience. At the least, they did not seem to draw the same lessons. The Philippine–American War occurred at a time when the US military possessed no formal counterinsurgency doctrine, and the Indian Wars were not the only conflicts that officers saw as having relevance for the conflict; they relied on analogies from European contexts as well. As Julian Go (2003, 9) remarks, while there are "continuities and precedents" here, "the discontinuities and novelties cannot be overlooked, either"—some of the key discontinuities being the novel legal category of "unincorporation" that would be applied to the Philippines and the need for the Philippines to be "internally financed" through tax collection and the construction of an administrative apparatus to facilitate that. As Aune (2021, 447) puts it, "'Indian fighting' was not the only lens through which U.S. soldiers understood their time in the Philippines, but it was prominent and powerful, able to enmesh the soldiers in one of the United States' most enduring narratives about violence." There is thus much reason to believe that the Indian Wars had some effect on US military operations in the Philippines, but it was certainly not the only influence on those operations, and it is difficult to say with precision how strong its effect was.

In an effort to clarify exactly what the US military took from the Indian Wars and brought to the Philippines, I argue that the experience of the Indian Wars differed in its salience for US military operations in the Philippine–American War across different levels of warfare. More specifically, the lessons of the Indian Wars had little influence at the strategic level and more influence at the tactical level of warfare. At the strategic level, the

Indian Wars were largely ignored in US military doctrine throughout the nineteenth century. Rather, when engaging in those wars and when later engaging in the Philippine–American War, military doctrine at the strategic level remained largely concerned with prototypical conventional wars between European states—wars fought by large Napoleonic forces in which conflict termination was presumed to come about through a single decisive battle.[10] At the tactical level, however, the individual experiences of service in America's Indian Wars helped to guide practical decision-making.[11] Individual soldiers learned from their frontier military engagements, and when they came to see the Philippine–American War as similar in nature, they sought to apply their perceived lessons of the Indian Wars. Before turning to a case study of the Philippine–American War, however, I must further specify what I mean by "learning" in this context.

Following Andrew Bennett (1999, 3), I define learning here as "changes in belief systems or 'cognitive structures' as the result of experience or study." This is a rather inclusive definition; "cognitive structures" can include especially important elements of decision-making such as "specific historical analogies, schemata or operational codes, and ideological beliefs," and we can treat such structures as present at both individual and organizational levels of analysis (Bennett 1999, 79–81).[12] While I focus on both individuals and organizations here, Bennett focuses more on the processes by which organizations learn—that is, "by encoding inferences from history into routines that guide behavior," including "the forms, rules, procedures, conventions, strategies, and technologies around which organizations are constructed and through which they operate" (Bennett 1999, 98). Learning, however, does not necessarily imply improvement in performance or the accuracy of any purported "lessons learned."

As a subset of organizational learning, military learning is most visible in formal processes, especially those that involve the publication and dissemination of new guidelines (Nagl 2002, 7):

> An army codifies its institutional memory in doctrine. . . . Doctrinal
> changes are not the only way in which military organizations demonstrate
> learning, although the published nature of formalized doctrine makes it
> convincing evidence of change. Learning is also demonstrated in the cur-
> ricula of military schools and training institutions, in the structure, of
> military organizations, in the creation of new organizations to deal with

new or changes situations, and in myriad other institutional responses to change.... Responsive, flexible military institutions often publish "Lessons Learned" notes incorporating information gained locally during the course of a conflict, and pull forces out of a conflict for periodic retraining in new techniques or new weaponry.[13]

Like many other contemporary militaries, however, the US military did not have institutionalized learning processes for much of the eighteenth and nineteenth centuries. Indeed, John Nagl (2002, 10) maintains that "The [US] Army began its journey to becoming a learning organization in the 1970's." The occupiers of the Philippines had nothing approximating *FM 3–24*, the counterinsurgency manual published by and for the US military amid the war in Iraq in 2006; the word "counterinsurgency" itself did not enter the US military's lexicon until the 1960s (MacKay 2023, 29). Rather, in the Philippine–American War, it was individual soldiers who fought in the Indian Wars who "were the main repository for that sort of institutional knowledge" (Aune 2021, 429).

In practice, the counterinsurgency campaign of the Philippine–American War was guided not by official doctrine but by the experiences of "Indian fighters": "The army had no official doctrine for Indian fighting, though it had a foundation of practices and principles from which it could draw and, with some modification, apply" (Echavarria 2014, 95). Those "practices and principles" can be summarized in two parts. They entailed, in turn, "finding and destroying the Indians' material capacity to resist" and "giving relentless pursuit so they had no opportunity to reconstitute it" (Echavarria 2014, 95).

"[F]inding and destroying the Indians' material capacity to resist" entailed a willingness to use military force to target not just enemy combatants directly but also anything that was a part of the support system on which they relied. Underlying this first principle was thus a willingness to attack civilians and related infrastructure: "Early Americans created a military tradition that accepted, legitimized, and encouraged attacks upon and the destruction of noncombatants, villages, and agricultural resources" (Grenier 2005, 10). This notion of destroying an enemy's material capacity to resist was sometimes paired with the idea that one could, rather than attacking the population of which enemy belligerents were a part, separate combatants from noncombatants and attempt to provide the noncombatant population with inducements to accept a settlement or otherwise distance themselves from combatants, a principle we might now call population-centric counterinsurgency.[14]

"[G]iving relentless pursuit so they had no opportunity to reconstitute it" required highly mobile forces—ideally cavalry (or, later, mechanized transportation) where possible. Moreover, this put a premium on information; simply knowing where enemy combatants might flee and being able to distinguish combatants from noncombatants was important. This principle also encouraged a willingness to use local scouts to find and effectively pursue the enemy.[15] The US military thus entered the Philippines with little in the way of formalized counterinsurgency doctrine on which it could rely, but the experiences of the Indian Wars had inculcated some general principles for such conflicts in individual soldiers. In other words, there is reason to expect that learning from the Indian Wars will be more evident at the tactical level of warfare than at the strategic level.

Among America's Indians Wars, these two principles had first been enacted in the Northwest Indian War. The first principle—"finding and destroying the Indians' material capacity to resist," which included "attacks upon and the destruction of noncombatants, villages, and agricultural resources"—was consistently applied in the Old Northwest. Knox's orders to Harmar and St. Clair established the parameters of the mission: They were to "'extirpate utterly, if possible, the . . . banditti' committing 'depredations' in the Ohio country" (quoted in Ostler 2015, 607). To do so, they sought to find and defeat Native combatants in battle (a task at which, as discussed in Chapter 3, their initial attempts failed), and they did indeed take "noncombatants, villages, and agricultural resources" to be valid targets (Maulden 2019, 45; Ostler 2019, 101–102). Anthony Wayne took the underlying goal to be that "by the sword we must procure peace," and he spent the days leading up to the Battle of Fallen Timbers "destroying Indian villages and fields" (quoted in Grenier 2005, 201).[16] Moreover, all of these commanders made vigorous use of scouts to assist in their finding Native groups in the first place; Wayne's Legion would use hundreds of men at a time for scouting purposes (Nelson 1985, 260–261, 263).

The second principle—"giving relentless pursuit so they had no opportunity to reconstitute it"—was likewise central to US conduct of the Northwest Indian War. Although Harmar and St. Clair ultimately failed, they both set out with the goal of destroying the Native capacity for resistance and denying them the ability to reconstitute it. They both engaged in days- and weeks-long pursuits of Native forces, and they burned lodgings and agricultural products that Native peoples abandoned due to their advances (Prucha 1969, 20–21). The relatively small early US military did invest in some cavalry that assisted with the "relentless pursuit" of others, and indeed, cavalry was quickly decisive at Fallen Timbers (Nelson 1985, 266). Even after his decisive victory at Fallen Timbers, General Wayne spent days "destroying for miles about the helpless natives' crops and villages" to ensure that they lacked any "opportunity to reconstitute" their capacity for resistance (Nelson 1985, 267).

Returning to current military doctrine, official doctrine in the United States (among other places) divides warfare into three different levels—strategic, operational, and tactical. However, I follow Brett Friedman (2017) (who, in turn, is following Clausewitz 1976), in maintaining that the most useful conception of different levels of warfare omits the operational level. Indeed, the operational level of warfare—a level generally associated with "corps headquarters and higher, the command echelons at which campaign planning and execution and the design of operations traditionally occurred"—is a comparatively recent addition to US military doctrine having been introduced to the army doctrine in the 1980s and to the rest of the services by the 1990s (Echavarria 2014, 57). A model of warfare with only tactical and strategic levels, however, better conceptualizes war itself. Tactics ("actual combat between opposed military forces") further strategy, and strategy ("the overarching plan for using tactical engagements to achieve the ends as set forth by policy") succeeds only through tactics, while operations are sets of tactics or "noncombat activities" that support tactics (Friedman 2017, 3, 155). I argue that in the Philippine–American War, the lessons of the Indian Wars operated primarily at the tactical level. At the strategic level, decisions were structured more by the relatively thin degree of military doctrine the US military had developed by that time, doctrine that was oriented toward a European tradition of military-to-military engagements rather than guerrilla warfare, small wars, or counterinsurgency.

In the next section, I provide a description of the actions taken by the US military in the Philippine–American War. I focus primarily on US actions in the First District, which was the district in which the military most rapidly defeated the Filipino insurgents—the area in which any learning from the Indian Wars should be most evident. Along the way, I note where learning is evinced at the tactical and strategic levels of warfare. This case study ultimately helps to establish that US relations with Native American groups had consequences beyond the North American continent.

(RE)LEARNING COUNTERINSURGENCY IN THE PHILIPPINES

Shortly after the US victory over Spain in the Battle of Manila Bay on May 1, 1898, partisans of Filipino independence under General Emilio Aguinaldo would declare their independence. This was at odds with American plans for the Philippines, which US policymakers saw as their rightful possession by virtue of their victory over Spain. Indeed, neither the United States nor Spain recognized Filipino independence, and Spain officially ceded the Philippines to the United States when the Treaty of Paris was signed on December 10, 1898.[17] News reached the Philippines in January 1899 and made clear to Aguinaldo and his followers that independence was not forthcoming (Silbey 2007, 62).

There were plausible alternative routes available to policymakers, but none was taken. The United States might have sought control of one or more but not all islands in the archipelago or perhaps a relationship in which the independent Philippines would grant the United States special economic and/or military privileges. But ultimately, US officials from across domains arrived at one reason or another to maintain control of the Philippines (Miller 1982, 13–20). For civilian officials, they generally saw control of the Philippines as a helpful step toward facilitating trade relations with China, as a winning stance with President McKinley's key constituencies, and/or as a moral obligation given the purported inability of Filipinos to govern themselves appropriately. Military officials argued that controlling the entirety of the Philippines rather than a segment thereof was necessary to keep the US military position there defensible. The preexisting rebel movement in favor of Filipino independence, however, did not accede to American claims, and amid rising tensions, fighting between the United States and Aguinaldo's independence movement began on February 4, 1899 (Silbey 2007, 64).

Early military engagements between the United States and Aguinaldo's insurgency played to American strengths. Aiming both to improve battle-field performance and to demonstrate their "high level of civilization" to the Americans, Aguinaldo and his followers initially organized their military force along conventional lines—a departure from the relatively successful guerrilla tactics they had previously deployed against Spain (Linn 1989, 12). This was, however, exactly the sort of combat for which the US military was best prepared, and the Filipino resistance movement's relative dearth of training made for many early US victories. Ultimately, "The American battlefield victories in early 1899 owed a great deal to Aguinaldo's decision to adopt conventional tactics and to rely on regulars instead of guerrillas" (Linn 1989, 12).

Mid-1899 saw relatively little combat as the resistance movement restructured its forces and its leadership struggled, although Aguinaldo would prevail and continue in his position after having a rival assassinated (Linn 1989, 14).[18] At the same time, American forces were similarly restructuring due to the belated realization that the occupation of the Philippines was going to necessitate a sustained war effort. For the United States, its strategy continued to be guided by standard doctrine at the time—the military effort was still oriented toward a conventional war in late 1899. The Republican Army, as Aguinaldo's force was known, having failed in conventional warfare, began to shift more toward unconventional tactics. A three-pronged US military effort to defeat the Republican Army in decisive battle converged in northern Luzon (the island home to the capital of Manila and most of the Filipino population) in mid-November, and while the revolutionaries suffered significant losses in personnel and property, they had already made the shift to guerrilla tactics (Linn 1989, 14, 16). Aguinaldo decentralized the Republican Army's command structure—Luzon would now be divided into three regions (and subdivided further into districts), and he would directly oversee military operations in only one region. At the tactical level, the focus turned to hit-and-run operations by small groups who could then blend back into the civilian population, part of which was already working in noncombat—and often clandestine—support roles for the Republican Army. The goal was not so much to defeat the American military as it was to make the war sufficiently costly and protracted to prompt the United States to leave the Philippines (Linn 1989, 16–17). What had begun as a rather conventional war had become an insurgency.

The Republican Army's shift to guerrilla tactics proved frustrating to the US military. General Elwell Stephen Otis, then the military governor of the Philippines, had set two primary goals upon the initiation of hostilities: capture Aguinaldo and destroy his army's capacity to continue fighting (Aune 2021, 426). If the US military could do this, Otis believed—and he did think it could do so with the 25,000 to 30,000 troops already stationed in the Philippines—the rest of the population would likely accept American rule and the "benevolent assimilation" policymakers had declared to be their aim (Aune 2021, 427). As the Republican Army shifted to guerrilla warfare, however, it became apparent that the US military would have more difficulty as it entered rougher terrain that lent itself to "harassing tactics" (Aune 2021, 427).

It took time for the US military to adapt to the Republican Army's shift to guerrilla tactics, and initially officers looked to European warfare for guidance rather than to wars with Native Americans. Brigadier General Samuel B. M. Young, for example, was tasked on December 20, 1899, with maintaining order in the (newly created) District of North-Western Luzon, and for him, the methods of "European nations," including "summary executions, concentration of the civilian population, and complete military rule," were the ones to emulate (Linn 1989, 34).[19] His recommendations were often ignored by his superiors, but the American military nonetheless remained enthralled with European strategic doctrine for some time, especially insofar as it legitimized harsh treatment of enemy combatants and noncombatants alike, despite its apparent inability to quash the Filipino rebellion.

The US military slowly adapted to the Republican Army's guerrilla warfare with what we might now call a counterinsurgency campaign. From the beginning of the occupation, US policymakers, chief among them President McKinley, had insisted that the occupation must be shown to be beneficial to Filipinos. The creation of schools, for example, and the provision of basic government services were central to the US occupation and its strategy of disincentivizing violent resistance (Gates 1973). The plan was to occupy the territory and "tutor" the Filipinos until the US government deemed them fit for self-government—a point in time that remained unspecified throughout the war (Miller 1982, 2). Broadening these efforts at civil administration into a cohesive civil-military strategy took time. Otis, the military governor of the Philippines from August 28, 1898, to May 5, 1900, held that position at the time when the Republican Army's transition to guerrilla warfare was happening, and he never seemed to recognize that transition. After the November 1899 battles in Luzon, Otis maintained that "war in its proper meaning had ceased to exist" (quoted in Linn 1989, 21). For the rest of Otis's tenure, fighting— by virtue of Aguinaldo's shift to guerrilla warfare—was relatively sporadic and minimal in casualties, and Otis took this behavior to be more criminal than military in nature (Linn 1989, 21).

As guerrilla warfare continued, Major General Arthur MacArthur, Jr. (the father of Douglas MacArthur) succeeded Otis in May 1900, and he more readily recognized the nature of the ongoing conflict (Linn 1989, 22–23). MacArthur also believed, however, that the US military was overextended across Luzon and that the Filipino population favored the insurgents over the occupiers. Given this position, MacArthur's first major step was the announcement of an amnesty for all former insurgents who surrendered and swore allegiance to the United States, but there was otherwise little strategic change from the military at first (Linn 1989, 22).[20] Rather, it was a more tactically driven innovation that would result in broader changes to US military policy in the Philippines.

At about the same time that MacArthur assumed his new position, Lieutenant William T. Johnston published the findings of an investigation he had been ordered to undertake to assess rebel tactics (Linn 1989, 42).[21] Johnston served under the command of Colonel William P. Duvall, the commander of US Army forces in La Union, a province of the First District in Northern Luzon. Having received his orders to undertake this investigation in March 1900, Johnston's "Investigation into the Methods Adopted by the Insurgents for Organizing and Maintaining a Guerrilla Force" was published on May 21. This report helped to clarify the relationships among different actors within the Filipino resistance movement and made wholly clear for all involved that the US military was indeed dealing with an insurgency that had adopted guerrilla tactics. The necessary changes to the American approach, however, were more readily made at the tactical level than the strategic level. Duvall reoriented his approach to target guerrilla bands in the countryside but also their support networks in towns, an approach that entailed the continued use of military force but also an increased emphasis on surveillance and localized policing. Duvall also cultivated a network of Filipino collaborators, many of whom were prisoners, to whom Duvall could promise their freedom in exchange for support in the American campaign. Importantly, however, these changes were initially only taking place in Duvall's area of command and not being recommended more broadly by MacArthur.

In Ilocos Norte, another province in the First District, Lieutenant Colonel Robert L. Howze, a veteran of the Indian Wars on the Great Plains, likewise tailored his approach to the growing insurgency (Linn 1989, 48). With a sparser troop presence there than in La Union, Howze quickly came to rely on regular troop patrols to keep himself apprised of the situation in the province. Modern understandings of counterinsurgency place a high priority on information—in particular, information about who supports whom—and contact with the population is generally necessary to acquire that information (see, e.g., Galula 2006). Indeed, its intensified patrols throughout the first few months of 1900 ultimately produced intelligence indicating that a revolt in Ilocos Norte was imminent, and Howze successfully anticipated the attacks on US military sites and ensured that the insurgents suffered heavy losses compared to relatively few American casualties.

More expansive counterinsurgency policies were slowly implemented across the First District—under the command of Brigadier General J. Franklin Bell—starting in late May 1900. Brian Linn (1989, 49) describes the first such move as follows:

> On 22 May 1900, First District Headquarters issued Circular Letter no. 1, requiring all males in the Ilocos and La Union were required to have a registration certificate. Moreover, no male inhabitant over age eighteen was allowed outside the jurisdiction of his *pueblo* without a pass from his *presidente*. People arriving or departing from a *barrio* had to report to the *barrio* head, or *cabeza*, within twenty-four hours, who in turn had to report to the *presidente*. The *presidents* were obliged to keep a register of their *pueblos'* inhabitants and to arrest all people without passes.

Further directives were issued on June 15 prohibiting the supply of food, shelter, and information to insurgents and on June 25 prohibiting the possession or hiding of firearms (Linn 1989, 49). Between January and August, the First District organized a 250-man unit of local scouts to assist in regular patrols and in the information acquisition that was becoming central to the war effort. Combined with an increase in the US military presence in the district (from 3,985 soldiers in August to 5,866 in November) and increased collaboration with local elites, these policies helped the occupiers defeat an insurgent offensive in the latter months of 1900 (Linn 1989, 53–54).

Building on military successes in the First District, counterinsurgency came to the country more broadly by December of 1900, when MacArthur imposed martial law in the Philippines and established harsher penalties for civilians who assisted the guerrillas and those who engaged in hostilities while switching between military and civilian garb (or without adopting any military identifier) (Linn 1989, 23–24). The existing Bureau of Insurgent Records, which maintained records of known insurgents, was also upgraded to a more expansive Division of Military Information in December 1900 as there was increasing demand for detailed mapping and information on insurgent leaders (Go 2024, 113). Several months after more localized commanders had shifted their tactics toward a model approximating that of frontier warfare—"finding and destroying the Indians' material capacity to resist" and "giving relentless pursuit so they had no opportunity to reconstitute it" (Echavarria 2014, 95)—MacArthur shifted the military away from traditional doctrine toward something approximating a counterinsurgency doctrine. This new approach, he wrote, was "based upon the central idea of detaching the towns from the immediate support of the guerrillas in the field, and thus also precluding the indirect support which arose from indiscriminate acceptance by the towns of the insurrection in all its devious ramifications" (quoted in Linn 1989, 24).

A new peak in the number of US personnel in the Philippines—70,000 members of the US Army—would help enact this strategy (Linn 1989, 24–25). Throughout 1901, the Army would more actively seek to destroy small groups of insurgents while also taking a more punitive approach to civilians who could be linked to the revolutionaries (by, e.g., confiscating their property and arresting or otherwise harassing their family members) (Linn 1989, 25). US forces increasingly utilized "open order mobile units"—small, mobile detachments often used for "search-and-destroy" missions that were directly informed by experiences in the Indian Wars.[22] At the same time, local elites who more readily cooperated with the United States often received significant rewards in the form of money, resources, or political power in the American civil government (Linn 1989, 25–26). This was also the phase of the Philippine–American War that saw the introduction or more frequent use of "population concentration" (i.e., forcing diffuse populations into concentration camps that could be more easily surveilled and regulated) and "the water cure" (i.e., a torture technique in which victims are made to feel that they are drowning) (Linn 1989, 25, 145).[23]

By May 1, 1901, the insurgents in the First District had surrendered. In March of that year, Aguinaldo was captured, but the insurgency remained, and conflict would continue until June 1902 (Linn 1989, 59–60). Along with the measures noted above that were designed to separate the general public from the insurgents and to deprive the latter of necessary resources, sheer manpower helped ensure the success of the American campaign. The size of the military presence in the district allowed for a portion thereof to be dedicated to the persistent harassment of insurgents in the countryside—in line with the warfighting model of the Indian Wars. While this did not yield a decisive battle with insurgents, the piecemeal destruction of insurgent supplies and infrastructure gradually degraded the insurgency's ability to sustain its operations. This campaign came to an end as the US military targeted the province of Abra and the remaining holdouts among the insurgents. By prohibiting all travel or trade in or out of the province and by destroying suspected insurgent property (including food and storehouses), the US military compelled the surrender of the remaining insurgent leaders in the First District, some of whom would shortly thereafter accept positions in the American civil government (Linn 1989, 59–60).

While Otis had ignored or failed to recognize the growing insurgency and MacArthur had belatedly introduced counterinsurgency policies after receiving a report from his subordinates indicating that he should do so, provincial and district-level military commanders more readily adapted to the Republican Army's use of guerrilla warfare and ultimately helped win the war. "Army officers in the field," Linn (1989, 22) notes, took the initiative in structuring counterinsurgency programs to deal with conditions in their areas." William H. Taft, the first civilian administrator of the Philippines, wrote accordingly to Secretary of War Elihu Root in July 1900 that "the pacification of the Islands seems to depend largely on the character of the military officer in charge of the particular district" (quoted in Linn 1989, 22). Many of the military officers in this case could draw on their experiences of the Indian Wars; such knowledge helped make Filipino insurgent tactics legible to American officers on the ground. In this sense, the lessons learned in the Indian Wars helped the United States succeed in the Philippines, but the experiences of the Indian Wars appear to have been most influential at the tactical level of warfare.[24]

LESSONS LEARNED? *PHRONESIS* AND *HABITUS* IN MILITARY PRACTICE

While scholars have debated the extent to which the US military learned any purported lessons from the Indian Wars, the nature of any knowledge acquired from those experiences has received less attention. In trying to make sense of what exactly was happening in the Philippines when soldiers cast their actions in terms of the Indian Wars, however, we should indeed ask not just whether those experiences somehow influenced later military practices but also how or through what mechanism those experiences did so. If, as I have argued, US relations with Native American groups were constitutive of US foreign policy, here I consider exactly how those relations shaped the implementation of US policy in the Philippines. I focus on two concepts that one might argue could capture much of the knowledge acquired from experiences in the Indian Wars—*phronesis* and *habitus*.

Phronesis, often translated as "practical wisdom," "practical judgment," or "prudence"—is taken from Aristotle's distinction between three "virtues of thought": *episteme, techne,* and *phronesis.*[25] *Episteme* refers to "knowledge where non-reflexivity is the rule," or "knowledge which is invariable in time and space" (Brown 2012, 445; Flyvbjerg 2001, 55).[26] This would include, for example, laws of physics. *Techne* refers to knowledge about how to manipulate material (but not social) things; it is the artisan's technical know-how, something that is more context-dependent than *episteme* (Flyvbjerg 2001, 56). For Aristotle, however, *phronesis* is more social, more contextual, and ultimately more important than both *episteme* and *techne* in that it involves discerning "the truth . . . concerned with action about things that are good and bad for a human being" (quoted in Brown 2012, 445). It is "the active condition by which someone discerns the right means to the right end in a particular circumstance," and while this is similar to *techne*'s context-dependence, *phronesis* concerns social interaction rather than material production (Emery 2021, 17).[27]

Habitus, as developed by Pierre Bourdieu (1990), refers to an understanding of what constitutes competent practice in a given field; it does not reduce to the plain meaning of "habit." This sort of knowledge "is a function of how discourses and past experiences imprint upon [an actor's] subjectivity and become an embodied disposition" (Pampinella 2021, 4). The key distinction between *habitus* and *phronesis* for my purposes is that *habitus* is generally conceptualized as implicit or unconscious, passive background knowledge while *phronesis* involves more active, conscious judgment.[28] *Phronesis* and *habitus* can thus both be seen as products of learning or experience, but they have different qualities.[29]

With respect to US military practices in the Philippines, I argue, the Indian Wars shaped the *habitus* of some individuals and perhaps allowed for *phronetic* decision-making. The experiences and perceived lessons of the Indian Wars seem to have (at least partly) constituted the *habitus* of soldiers deployed to the Philippines. Between their own experiences of the Indian Wars and the ways that those conflicts came to be represented in public discourse, soldiers arriving in the Philippines would have had much salient background knowledge with which to make sense of the conflict.[30]

From this perspective, we might thus see the frequent invocation of the Indian Wars by military personnel in the Philippines as indicative of a *habitus* constituted by a learned hierarchy—an explicitly racialized hierarchy in which civilized white peoples fought in one way, uncivilized non-white peoples fought another way, and the use of uncivilized tactics demanded certain military responses. Indeed, US soldiers often pejoratively compared Filipinos and Native Americans to African Americans.[31] This was consonant with broader trends in political thought at the time. For both English and American imperialists and pacifists at the turn of the twentieth century—for thinkers such as Alfred Thayer Mahan and Norman Angell— their proposed policies were typically justified with reference to some such hierarchy with "us" at the top and others below. The allegedly less civilized, racialized others "could not be trusted to govern themselves or recognize their own best interests" (Ashworth 2022; MacKay 2023, 16).

Insofar as Americans racialized Filipinos, this allowed for or prescribed the use of certain forms of violence. "Much like the dehumanization of Native Americans during Westward expansion, America's racial adversaries abroad were racialized to the extent that the frameworks governing warfare were rendered largely moot" (Barder 2021, 91). That is, limits on the enactment of certain forms of violence that might have been seen to apply in conflicts with white, "civilized" opponents did not apply in the Philippine–American War. I would reframe this somewhat in arguing that there were different frameworks governing warfare for conflict with civilized and uncivilized peoples, the latter being significantly more permissive in terms of what violence was considered acceptable.[32] Thus, in framing the Philippine–American War as an engagement with uncivilized peoples, members of the US military were shifting from a field defined by one form of competent performance to another. In short, to the extent that members of the US military learned anything from the Indian Wars, the clearest lesson was that of a civilizational hierarchy in which competent combat performance against racialized others allowed for or necessitated the use of certain tactics.[33]

Once the background knowledge of *habitus* came to the fore, individual soldiers adapted in ways that we might describe as the enactment of individualized *phronesis*. While guided by doctrine that focuses on conventional warfare, some at the tactical level of warfare were indeed able to see the changing circumstances of the war and adapt in such a way that they could more effectively attain their objectives.

DISCUSSION

US soldiers who fought in the Philippine–American war brought their experiences in the Indian Wars with them. Learning from war, however, is not straightforward. Different individuals will take different lessons from the same experience, and not all organizations are well-equipped to assess the varying lessons they might take from a given experience. Indeed, it is not clear if the US military as an organization took any lessons from the Philippine–American War: "The military largely failed to create any doctrine or educational record that would preserve institutional knowledge acquired during the occupation" (Aune 2021, 441).[34] We might thus be skeptical about whether the US military learned anything from the Indian Wars; available evidence does not provide much indication that there were any clear "lessons learned" or "best practices" widely understood to have been derived from the Indian Wars. *Habitus* and *phronesis*, however, offer ways of conceptualizing the individualized ways of thinking about similar conflicts.

Today's US military, however, attempts to be a more self-consciously learning organization. The US Army, for example, established the Center for Army Lessons Learned in 1985, though it is difficult to assess the extent to which it has helped improve performance (Funkhouser 2007). There are limits to what the military can do in this regard: Even if the military learns lessons from the conflicts in which it engages, its ability to act on those lessons is always subject to the demands of civilian leaders.[35] But its attempts to learn from previous conflicts have been especially visible in recent wars in Iraq and Afghanistan, both of which involved insurgencies and attempts to learn the lessons of previous counterinsurgency campaigns, albeit typically with reference to the Vietnam War, France's Algerian War, or other such campaigns of the mid- to late twentieth century. David Galula offers a case in point, which is obvious simply through the date of its original publication (1964) and its reissuance (2006). The Indian Wars and the Philippine–American War, by contrast, are rarely referenced today as examples from which to learn.[36]

Multiple US agencies are already engaged in their own "lessons learned" processes to determine what to take from the war in Afghanistan. The Office of the Special Inspector General for Afghanistan Reconstruction (SIGAR), for example, published its eleventh "lessons learned report" in August 2021. The report, "What We Need to Learn: Lessons from Twenty Years of Afghanistan Reconstruction," serves as a retrospective on the war effort and promises "critical lessons [that] will save lives and prevent waste, fraud, and abuse in Afghanistan, and in future reconstruction missions elsewhere around the world" (SIGAR 2021, ii). The seven lessons derived from the entirety of the US experience and framed as applicable to "other conflict zones around the globe" are as follows (SIGAR 2021, vii–xi):

1. Strategy: The U.S. government continuously struggled to develop and implement a coherent strategy for what it hoped to achieve.

2. Timelines: The U.S. government consistently underestimated the amount of time required to rebuild Afghanistan, and created unrealistic timelines and expectations that prioritized spending quickly. These choices increased corruption and reduced the effectiveness of programs.

3. Sustainability: Many of the institutions and infrastructure projects the United States built were not sustainable.

4. Personnel: Counterproductive civilian and military personnel poli-cies and practices thwarted the effort.

5. Insecurity: Persistent insecurity severely undermined reconstruc-tion efforts.

6. Context: The U.S. government did not understand the Afghan con-text and therefore failed to tailor its efforts accordingly.

7. Monitoring and Evaluation: U.S. government agencies rarely con-ducted sufficient monitoring and evaluation to understand the impact of their efforts.

The way today's "lessons learned" processes are unfolding brings me back to the concept of *phronesis*. That is, there will be a temptation to for-mulate any lessons learned as *episteme* or epistemic knowledge—as lessons that transcend time and space and that can be straightforwardly applied in any similar conflicts in the future. However, I argue that the less univer-salizing, more context-specific judgment of *phronesis* is a more helpful way of thinking about any lessons that might be taken from US experiences in Afghanistan. Some experiences in Afghanistan may help future soldiers make sense of and respond competently to a new situation, but the knowl-edge acquired from those experiences ought not to be taken as constituting *episteme*. For better or worse, America's experience in Afghanistan will not yield epistemic knowledge about how exactly to conduct future military operations.

CODA: "HOW TO FIGHT SAVAGE TRIBES"

The sort of indiscriminate violence practiced at times by the US military in the Philippines would later receive vigorous defense from Colonel Elbridge Colby. The notion that one can separate combatant from noncombatant, for Colby, was false—and increasingly so in an age of industrialized war-fare. He describes "the theory that war should affect only armed men" as a "theory" that "began in the mind of an idealistic philosopher" and that had become "useful propaganda" (Colby 1924, 367).[37] In this context, he derides "President McKinley's instructions to American commanders in the field" to the effect that "'We come not to make war upon the people of the Philip-pines'" (Colby 1924, 369.) Rather, quoting then-Assistant Secretary of War

Dwight L. Davis, Colby maintained that "'We must realize that there may be no noncombatants'" (1924, 373).

Colby would later argue in an article entitled, "How to Fight Savage Tribes" (1927, 287) that while international law might regulate war-fighting between "civilized" states, these states were not obligated to apply laws of war in conflicts with "uncivilized people who do not know international law and do not observe it, and would take advantage of one who did." "[A]mong savages," he argued, "war includes everyone. There is no distinction between combatants and non-combatants" (Colby 1927, 281).[38] For Colby, this did not quite imply that indiscriminate violence was necessary in such conflicts—"Ferocity and ruthlessness are not essential"—but it did mean that commanders must have license to do anything necessary to prevail (1927, 287–288):

> The really controlling element in the handling of a field force is economy. Economy of effort, economy of force, maintained by a well-knit and well-disciplined army directed toward the most direct and proper attainment of the end in view—these are the precepts by which the commander will govern his actions. Bearing these things in mind, he will use against uncivilized peoples, as the British Manual says, "the discretion of the commander and such rules of justice and humanity as recommend themselves in the particular circumstances of the case."

In his own way, Colby makes an argument for a sort of *phronesis* here; commanders must be able to use their own practical wisdom to make judgments, and such judgments might occasionally (and, for Colby, rightly) dispense with "rules of justice and humanity."

Today, Elbridge A. Colby, Colonel Colby's great-grandson, is a former deputy assistant secretary of defense for strategy and force planning under President Trump in his first term; at the time of this writing, he has been nominated to serve as undersecretary of defense for policy in Trump's second term. In between those terms, when Colby's Republican Party was out of power, he frequently wrote about his vision for a Republican foreign policy, and he occasionally turned to the Indian Wars to do so. In comparing the rise of the United States with the rise of China, he noted that China's best strategy to maximize its power and influence in the long term would be to emulate the nineteenth-century United States, which effectively pursued a "hide and bide" strategy of avoiding costly conflict while growing more powerful—"[w]ith the exception of small conflicts like the War of 1812, the war against Mexico in the 1840s, and the Indian Wars" (Colby 2021, 111). The more important lesson of the Indian Wars for the younger Colby (2021, 81), however, is that they demonstrate the importance of power and the limits of strategy:

> Military strategy, though elemental in all conflicts is less important when one combatant is much more powerful than the other. In such conflicts, so long as both sides are reasonably resolute, the stronger side typically prevails. Sitting Bull may have outsmarted George Custer at Little Bighorn, but the Americans were ultimately far too powerful for the Sioux to withstand, no matter how effective their military strategy was.[39]

I remain agnostic as to whether this or any other lessons that US officials have drawn from the Indian Wars are indeed the right lessons to learn from the wars. It is notable, however, that even some of today's foreign policy elites seem to believe that the Indian Wars hold lessons that are applicable to current US foreign policy. Indeed, as I demonstrate in the next chapter, the Indian Wars continue to provoke political contestation even today.

Five

LEGITIMIZING CONQUEST

The Politics of Memory in Fort Wayne, Indiana

Having discussed the origins of the Northwest Indian War and the ways it presaged early trends in US foreign policy, I now consider how Americans continue to legitimize the conquest that this war entailed. Until recently, the Northwest Indian War had received little public commemoration in the United States. Indeed, this is true of many of America's Indian Wars. To the extent that they are memorialized, they are often treated as somewhat embarrassing aspects of the national past that are best consigned to unobtrusive plaques or to the sober work of museums.[1] I examine a recent effort by local policymakers and activists in Fort Wayne, Indiana, to celebrate their town's namesake, General Anthony Wayne, and to commemorate his military accomplishments, which included actions in the Revolutionary War as well as the more controversial victory in the Northwest Indian War. This effort is demonstrative of the ways that selective historical memory is used to assert the legitimacy of America's conquest of lands once claimed by Native American groups. Moreover, I argue, given that the United States (like any state) depends on the continual reproduction of its claims to legitimate statehood, we should expect the justice of its conquest of Native lands to remain central to ongoing nationalist projects and for Native claims to rights to generate backlash under some conditions.

MEMORIALIZING WAR

Wars and other forms of political violence are memorialized in myriad ways, and any sort of public commemoration is an inevitably political process insofar as it is subject to public contestation and involves the potential dedication of public resources to commemorative practices. "What does 'memory' do, who 'does' memory—and what is being done by politically utilizing memory—are the central concerns for the study of memory politics" (Mälksoo 2023, 1). Here I am concerned primarily with "who 'does' memory" and "what is being done by politically utilizing memory." My answers focus on local political entrepreneurs—especially those associated with the General "Mad" Anthony Wayne Organization—and the extent to which their actions affirm the legitimacy of America's dispossession of Native nations.

There are various political purposes to which commemorations of historical events might be put. In general, however, those political purposes tend to fall into one of two categories (Mälksoo 2023, 3):

> By and large, political collectives' dealing with the past can be reflective (or geared towards remembering by thinking through) or more oriented towards establishing mnemonical security (or remembering by making sure that a particular, politically preferable version of the past sticks publicly).

That is, public commemorations of historical events invite community members to remember those events, but such commemorations will tend to depict the historical event in such a way that either invites or disallows questions about the proffered historical narrative.

Borrowing this ideal typical distinction from Maria Mälksoo (2023), I describe these two different kinds of mnemonical practices in the following terms. First, *reflective* mnemonical practices allow for open-ended questioning and interpretation of past events. They allow for a multiplicity of interpretations and for "thinking through"—that is, for consideration of how certain events transpired and why they did so. Second, *hegemonic* mnemonical practices aim at the attainment of mnemonical security. That is, hegemonic mnemonical practices seek to establish one interpretation of the past as *the* interpretation of the past. Rather than asking you to think through past events for oneself, hegemonic mnemonical practices tell you what to think. While one might ascribe a moral valence to these different positions—here "reflective" might be taken to mean "good"—I treat these solely as analytic, ideal typical categories here.[2]

I argue that in memorializing the Northwest Indian War, recent efforts to commemorate General Anthony Wayne have taken the form of hegemonic mnemonical practices. I describe how hegemonic mnemonical practices manifest in this case, but I also seek to explain why one would pursue hegemonic mnemonical practices in the first place. In other words, if reflective mnemonical practices entail "remembering by thinking through," why would one object to that? Or, rather, why would one see mnemonical security as being important enough to warrant hegemonic mnemonical practices? Given that there was no Anthony Wayne Day in Fort Wayne until recently, moreover, I ask a second question: Why do certain mnemonical practices arise when they do? Or, what explains the timing here?

To answer the question of why one would prefer hegemonic to reflective mnemonical practices, I argue, some appear to see reflective mnemonical practices as undermining the United States itself—that is, undermining the ability of American citizens to say that their country is a legitimate claimant to sovereignty over its contested territory. In favoring mnemonical security rather than reflective remembrance, those who emphasize the former position themselves as guardians of a satisfactory status quo that is allegedly threatened by their critics. As for the question about timing, shifting political conditions appear important in this case. To the extent that questions about what the United States owes to Native American groups have become a salient part of American culture wars—a racialized and increasingly polarized national political environment—that may help to explain why local political entrepreneurs may find themselves fighting more and more mnemonical battles.

There often seems to be a partisan bent to mnemonical battles, with liberals and conservatives typically proposing reflective and hegemonic mnemonical practices, respectively.[3] This is indeed the case in Fort Wayne: The political entrepreneurs proposing hegemonic mnemonical practices, as I will demonstrate, align themselves with conservative, Republican causes even as they strive to publicly portray their initiatives as non-partisan.[4] The vote to establish General "Mad" Anthony Wayne Day did not wholly break down along partisan lines, but it was an initiative undertaken by a conservative Republican that has since been backed most strongly by other conservative Republicans. Moreover, similar dynamics are observable in other national contexts as well.[5] I do not, however, have the data necessary to sustain an argument about any relationship between partisanship and mnemonical practices, nor (as I have noted elsewhere in the book) do I seek to establish nomothetic generalizations here.

In short, mnemonical practices can serve different purposes, but they tend toward either the affirmation of a singular history or the opening up of history to multiple interpretations. There is nothing inherently "reflective" about establishing mnemonical practices; their intended and realized effects are myriad. Indeed, the realized effects might diverge from the intended effects. "The placement of . . . memory objects in public spaces, and synchronizing occasions for their reflection, resonate and redound in ways that reinforce, but also unsettle, the self and collective identities of individuals and groups" (Steele and Campbell 2023, 48). For many, the goal of mnemonical practices is to "reinforce" a specific narrative or identity, while for others the goal is to "unsettle," even if the results are ultimately unpredictable.

In the United States, mnemonical practices are used for varying political causes, but I am most interested here in the memory of US settlers and their conflicts with Native American groups. Beyond the Northwest Indian War, mnemonical practices of varying kinds have often been used to affirm US claims to land. Settler grave sites strewn across the Overland Trail, for example, served from the nineteenth century onward to claim that space as their own: "On Independence Rock, emigrant signatures appeared alongside—and, likely, on top of—Native carvings. The same was true at Wyoming's Names Hill, a thousand-year-old rock art site emigrants rechristened and began remarking in the 1840s" (Keyes 2023, 145).[6] Similarly, Christine DeLucia (2018, 5–6) catalogues the various ways in which Anglo-Americans have memorialized King Philip's War (1675–1678) through various modes of commemoration at sites related to the fighting. Activists in Fort Wayne similarly commemorate General Anthony Wayne's victory over a Native coalition to affirm the legitimacy of American claims to the land.

THEORY AND METHODS

I take mnemonical practices to be one of the many tools available to participants in political processes of contestation. I draw here on relation theory,
and having already discussed relationalism at length, I would only add here
that it involves a commitment to the notion that "a substantial part of social
reality consists of transactions among social units, that those transactions
crystallize into ties, that they shape the social units involved, that they con-
catenate into variable structures" (Tilly 2002, 75). I draw on relationalism
here while also engaging in ideal typification. In this case, the ideal types
involved are two different forms of mnemonical practices—hegemonic and
reflective. That is, "hegemonic" and "reflective" mnemonical practices are
"instrumental idealizations of phenomena," which "means that the concept
or theory or ideal-typical description both simplifies and misrepresents,
and does so for pragmatic reasons" (Jackson 2011, 143). The pragmatic
reason in my case is to highlight what I posit to be the central goals of those
involved in contesting the memory of the Northwest Indian War.

What relationalism means for the politics of memory in this case is that
the United States—or any other claimant of sovereignty—is dependent
upon a sort of daily buy-in, even if only tacit, from some critical mass of its
population. Hegemonic mnemonical practices can thus be a way to make
this buy-in concrete—to publicly affirm the legitimacy of American conquest and the continued virtue of the American project and to invite others
to join in this affirmation.[7] Reflective mnemonical practices, by contrast,
might trouble the existing power structure by denaturalizing it, by questioning its virtue, and by suggesting the possibility of alternative arrange-
ments.

In terms of methods, this case study is a sort of interpretive digital
ethnography. My task here is "an interpretive one in search of meaning,"
and the "data" here are "constructions of other people's constructions of
what they and their compatriots are up to" (Geertz 1973, 5, 9). My focus
here is on "context-specific meanings" rather than "generalized meaning
abstracted from particular contexts" (Schwartz-Shea and Yanow 2012,
23).[8] As Lisa Wedeen (1998, 522) notes, "falsifiability" is a common concern
among political scientists—an unfalsifiable theory generally being seen as
"unscientific"—but the "ambiguity and indeterminacy" that is frequent in

interpretive accounts of political phenomena does not amount to unfalsi-fiability. In my case, a falsification of my argument would entail demonstrating that the statements and images I discuss below do not amount to hegemonic mnemonical practices or that I misconstrued the meanings of various statements.

Rather than a traditional ethnography that entails fieldwork and perhaps participant observation in a physical location, my research for this chapter took place entirely online and purely as an after-the-fact observer.[9] I am ambivalent about using the term "ethnography" to describe such work, but it is at least consonant with Clifford Geertz's (1973, 20) "thick," "ethnographic description":

> [I]t is interpretive; what it is interpretive of is the flow of social discourse; and the interpreting involved consists in trying to rescue the "said" of such discourse from its perishing occasions and fix it in perusable terms.

Indeed, I am trying to make clear what was "said" in various settings below; the "low data" I am using captures "the everyday, mundane representations" through which memory is often contested (Weldes 2014, 234).[10]

MEMORY POLITICS IN FORT WAYNE, INDIANA

In Chapter 3, I discussed the fortifications that Anthony Wayne's Legion and his predecessors constructed to win the Northwest Indian War. One of those was named for the general himself—Fort Wayne. As occurred with many such frontier forts, Fort Wayne would become an important trading outpost and a place of relative security for settlers. In 1818, the Treaty of St. Mary's saw the Miami cede more territory—much of what is now Indiana—and by 1819, the perceived threat from Native peoples had diminished to the point that the fort could be decommissioned, and settlers could more readily claim territory in the area. Fort Wayne, the seat of Allen County, has since become Indiana's second-largest city with 423,038 people as of the 2020 census.

Until recently, the city of Fort Wayne did not have any routine commemoration of its namesake. There is a statue of Anthony Wayne on horseback in a downtown square and a historical recreation of Fort Wayne that serves as a tourist attraction, but the memory of Anthony Wayne and his campaign in the Northwest Indian War otherwise received little sustained local attention until lately. This was put on the agenda, moreover, by conservative Republicans. Fort Wayne, like many American cities, exhibits a disjuncture between citywide and more localized elections—Democrat Tom Henry was reelected to a fifth term as mayor in 2023, and he often won with substantial majorities.[11] The city council, however, remains more conservative—six of the council's nine members are currently Republicans, and Republicans have held a majority of those seats for at least a decade.[12] In 2015, Republicans had an even-more lopsided 7–2 advantage on the council. This was thus a relatively permissive political environment for local conservative politicians.

Among the Fort Wayne City Council's members elected in 2015, Councilman Jason Arp was a Republican newcomer representing District 4. Coming into politics with only private-sector experience and having won his election with 4,783 votes to his opponent's 4,354 (52.3 percent compared to 47.6 percent), Arp proceeded to make a name for himself by being perhaps the most conservative member on the council.[13] Arp would eventually be the primary driver of efforts to establish General "Mad" Anthony Wayne Day in Fort Wayne, a commemoration that I argue was intended to establish hegemonic mnemonical practices.

On February 12, 2019, shortly after the February 8 deadline to file paperwork to run in the May 7 city council primary elections, Arp introduced resolution R-19-02-12: "A Resolution Proclaiming July 16th as General 'Mad' Anthony Wayne Day in the City of Fort Wayne."[14] The text of the resolution reads as follows:

> WHEREAS, Fort Wayne, Indiana is named after Major General Anthony Wayne, Senior Officer of the United States Army (1792–1796); and
>
> WHEREAS, General Wayne earned the nickname "Mad Anthony" for successfully leading the bayonets-only night attack on a British camp at Stoney Point, NY on July 16th 1779. It is likely that this victory saved the American fort at West Point, where General George Washington was encamped, from capture; and
>
> WHEREAS, General Wayne defeated British led Native forces at the Battle of Fallen Timbers, allowing the establishment of Fort Recovery and our beloved Fort Wayne.

**NOW, THEREFORE, BE IT RESOLVED BY THE COMMON COUN-
CIL OF THE CITY OF FORT WAYNE, INDIANA, AS FOLLOWS:**

SECTION 1. Fort Wayne, Indiana proclaims July 16th of every year
hereafter to be "Mad Anthony Wayne Day."

SECTION 2. That this Ordinance shall be in full force and effect from
and after its passage and any and all necessary approval by the Mayor

This resolution, in short, sought to establish Anthony Wayne Day on the
basis of Wayne's military accomplishments during the Revolutionary War
and the Northwest Indian War.[15] As I discuss further below, it misleadingly
frames the latter conflict by claiming that the "Native forces" were "British
led," but it places more emphasis on Wayne's actions in the Revolutionary
War.[16] Indeed, Arp and other supporters consistently refer to Wayne as a
Revolutionary War hero while making brief (or no) reference to the Northwest Indian War.

Two weeks after introducing the resolution for review, Arp brought the
resolution to the city council for a vote. He began with a prepared speech
and slide presentation that I reproduce here at length:[17]

I had a constituent contact me a couple years ago on July the 16th and
said, "Hey, we should have an Anthony Wayne Day in the city of Fort Wayne.
July 16th is the anniversary of the victory at Stony Point, New York." And
so that kind of got me on to this, and I talked about it a couple years ago,
but I met an author of a book on the subject that actually lives here in Fort
Wayne, and I've done a couple years' worth of research on Anthony Wayne,
so I have a little presentation.

[The slideshow presentation's title slide shows a photograph of a statue
of Wayne on horseback; the title reads "Anthony Wayne Day," and a subtitle
adds "Celebrating Our American Heritage." The slide to which Arp turns at
this point includes solely black text on a white background: "'Our Officers
and Men Behaved Like Men Determined To Be Free': The Battle of Stony
Point, 15–16 July 1779".]

This was a quote Anthony Wayne sent to General Washington after the
victory at Stony Point. [Arp recites the quotation.] And to me, that just
gives me chills; it inspires me. It's what—as Americans, we should all want
to be free. It's kind of the embodiment of what it means to be an American.

[Arp transitions to the next slide.]

So here's a list of the accomplishments that Anthony Wayne had during the War for Independence.

[The slide, which includes a photo of Wayne in uniform and standing next to a horse on the right-hand side of the picture, includes the following items listed beside bullet points: "Formation of a Pennsylvania militia unit 1775; Appointed Colonel of 4th Pennsylvania Regiment; Lead the Continental Army at the Battle of Stoney Point, 1779; Tactical Victories enabled Triumph at Yorktown 1781; Siege of Savannah 1782 to force British military to withdrawal." Before reading the list, he asks someone to move a camera so he can more clearly see the screen on which the slides are presumably presented. He reads through the first bullet point before an alarm seemingly rings in the audience; Arp jokes, "I guess I'm out of time." Another member of the council quips, "Can we use this more often? I like this." Arp then continues through the list of bullet points, but he pauses on Stony Point.]

So let me give you a little bit of context—how many of you have heard of Benedict Arnold? Benedict Arnold basically told the British command where General Wayne was encamped, and he was encamped at West Point, New York. They had the British Army surround West Point with their biggest encampment being at Stony Point, and they were preparing for a raid at West Point the next day. Washington was made aware of the plan from his own spies and instructed Anthony Wayne to intervene. So Anthony Wayne took about 500 of the men in a midnight raid, told his men to leave the ball and powder back at the camps—that way it wouldn't wake anyone up—and it was a bayonets-only attack at Stony Point. And the defeat of the British at Stony Point allowed Washington and General Knox and Greene and the rest of the commanders to escape New York and [inaudible] continue to fight the American Revolution.[18] If not, it would have been over that day. So we can thank Anthony Wayne for the fact that we have a United States of America.

[Arp then continues to talk through the remaining bullet points and further discusses the Battle of Stony Point before turning to another slide with a book that he claims to have read for his research, Alan D. Gaff's *Bayonets in the Wilderness: Anthony Wayne's Legion in the Old Northwest.*[19]]

This book was published by the Oklahoma University—I guess they publish books there. . . . A little bit of background about the Northwest campaign.

As Arp recounts a brief history of the Northwest Indian War, his presentation ultimately reduces the conflict to four bullet points that read as follows:

- October 22nd 1790 Little Turtle's Miami defeated General Harmar at Kekionga;

- November 4th, 1791—Miami and Shawnee alliance led by Little Turtle and Blue Jacket defeated General St. Claire;

- July 1792- President Washington appoints General Wayne Commander in Chief of the Legion of the United States;

- August 20th 1794- Victory at the Battle of Fallen Timbers.[20]

Arp notably uses the surprising defeat of Arthur St. Clair to point to a more recent moment of American insecurity—it was "kind of like a 9/11 of their day."[21] Wayne, however, is portrayed as someone who ultimately restored a sense of security and who was more merciful to his foes than they might have been to him:

> When Wayne was assigned this assignment . . . he studied his [Julius Caesar's] methods—of going along, building forts along the way, making sure that you had lines to both refortify with and to retreat to, you want to make sure you can maintain your forces. . . . The casualties of the British and Natives, most accounts show them [Native Americans] at less than fifty people from that side. So he basically forced them to sign a surrender treaty and did not do any kind of mass execution or anything like what had happened to St. Clair's people a couple years previously.[22]

"So why an Anthony Wayne Day?" Arp sets up his concluding question and answers it with another slide. The first bullet point is "Important to know our history." The second is one line followed by another series of bullet points: "We have a history we can be proud of—bravery, determination, persistence, patience, mercy." Arp concludes by noting that he only learned everything in his presentation after his aforementioned constituent suggested an Anthony Wayne Day.

There is then some discussion among the council members, and the Republicans on the council (including Thomas Didier, who more recently prevailed over Arp in a mayoral primary election) mostly speak favorably about the proposal.[23] A Democrat and the council's only black member at the time, Glynn Hines, was the only one to raise concern about commemorating a man whose most notable feat was the violent facilitation of Native dispossession:

I, too, was a history major at Manchester [University], and Dr. David Waas was my best professor, and he used to tell us that the conqueror tells the story, and that's why they call it "history."[24] And I'm a little taken aback—I won't be supporting this because the Native Americans were *Native* Americans. And instead of peaceful negotiations, opportunities to purchase land, it ended up being war. And the genocide of the Native Americans—you talked about the Miami, the Shawnee, and things of that nature—but as we know, historically, correctly, the genocide of the Native Americans impacted those Americans who were here first. And we talk about everyone seeking freedom—the one thing I read the other day about the Underground Railroad . . . is that they were for freedom of all Americans. . . . But I think we have to be considerate of those Native Americans' ancestors who still live here and their feelings as it relates to—what you refer to as "wilderness"—what they refer to as their homes. And there was many Indian nations, Native American nations that existed, and I thought rather than negotiating for land or purchasing land, the option that was chosen was to take the land, so I will not be supporting this.

At that point, Republican (and Council President) John Crawford asks Arp if he anticipates "any negative reaction to this from other groups like Glynn was just alluding to." Arp responds:

Yeah, I mean, obviously there's always going to be people that are detractors of things, and there's lots of people that don't care for America or American history. There are people that are just not patriotic. And that's their right, obviously. But that doesn't mean that we don't still continue to celebrate this day.

Arp then gets cut off by Crawford, who seems interested in postponing a vote. He asks if they should vote on the resolution in that evening's meeting, and he notes that the resolution did not receive a lot of publicity beforehand. He asks if they should instead "let it have a couple weeks to percolate and see what we hear." Arp supports going forward with a vote in that same meeting; he notes that it has been on the agenda for "a few weeks now," so any potential backlash likely would have already materialized. Hines intervenes at that point to offer a rejoinder to Arp:

Real quick, I was just going to say, the characterization of people not being patriotic because they don't accept your proposal is actually a misnomer. I think you have patriotic individuals who have served . . . which, still, if they were [of] Native American ancestry, would be somewhat offended by the idea of recognizing a specific date. We have the statue, we have, obviously, the Fourth of July, we have celebrations of all types. But just because they don't support this idea would not make them not patriotic.

Other Republicans on the council, however, indicated their support for the resolution, and when Arp ultimately moved to approve the resolution, and it received six aye and three nay votes.[25] Among the council's seven Republicans and two Democrats, the aye votes included five Republicans and one Democrat, Geoff Paddock, who did not say anything in the meeting and who later relayed to a reporter that he thought "it would look bad for the city if its council spurned its namesake" (Savage 2020). Only later would Paddock work to correct the record and make amends with the Miami Tribe of Oklahoma.[26] On the other hand, two Republicans, Crawford and Russ Jehl, voted against it. Crawford, as noted earlier, was apparently interested in delaying the vote; as a seemingly more centrist Republican than Arp, he raised a concern regarding potential backlash. Jehl made no comment at the meeting and had no comment when reached by Charlie Savage for his reporting on the issue, so it is not clear why he objected.

Arp's introduction of a resolution creating an Anthony Wayne Day, the discussion for and against it, and the passage thereof reflect different views as to how to memorialize a city's namesake and the military actions for which Wayne is known. Arp especially seems to see the need for hegemonic mnemonical practices, and Hines opposed it precisely because he saw it as such. Ultimately, passage of the resolution works to reaffirm the legitimacy of American "conquest" (a term Councilman Paul Ensley used in warning against "viewing historical events through a lens of modern morality"). "In a settler society," Kevin Bruyneel (2021, 14) argues, "the work of collective memory serves to reaffirm the settler claim of belonging to, appropriation of, and authority over lands, on the one hand, and the disavowal of the genocide, dispossession, and alienation of Indigenous peoples, on the other hand." The creation of General "Mad" Anthony Wayne Day, whatever the intent of individual members of the Fort Wayne City Council, surely lent itself to that sort of crafting of a collective memory that valorizes the victorious US forces while eliding the costs borne by Native nations.

PUTTING A RESOLUTION INTO PRACTICE

The Fort Wayne City Council's passage of a resolution recognizing July 16 as an annual General "Mad" Anthony Wayne Day did not commit the city to any particular form of commemoration; those efforts have been led by individuals associated with the General "Mad" Anthony Wayne Organization.[27] This is not coincidence. The individuals who officially formed the nonprofit organization after the passage of the resolution were the same individuals who first pushed Councilman Arp to create an annual Anthony Wayne Day. As Savage (2020) reports, Michael Loomis, a lawyer with a history in Republican politics and a constituent of Arp's, first contacted Arp to suggest the idea: "After reading about the Battle of Stony Point in 2017, he wrote a Facebook message to Arp pitching the notion. 'It could be a day of service, or a day of celebration, or both,' Loomis wrote."[28] Loomis and others associated with the organization have publicly maintained that their purpose in celebrating Anthony Wayne is purely educational.[29]

In this section, I engage in a close reading of the organization's website, MadAnthonyWayne.org,[30] to demonstrate that regardless of any protestations to the contrary, the organization's celebrations of Anthony Wayne are indeed political. I argue that the organization uses its website to project an image of objectivity—that is, of an organization concerned purely with the transmission of knowable, wholly neutral, educational facts.[31] I argue further that this image is belied by the selective manner in which it organizes historical facts—by its privileging of items that paint Wayne in a positive light while ignoring items that might do the opposite.[32] Moreover, many of its claims are not straightforward factual claims about historical events; they are interpretive or normative claims about how the reader ought to evaluate historical events. In short, the organization's website is just one place where its efforts to legitimize American conquest through hegemonic mnemonical practices becomes clear.

The General "Mad" Anthony Wayne Organization maintains a publicly available website. The home page of the website includes contact information and links to other pages on the site as well as the website's first substantive statement about the organization: "Our mission: to enhance area education about relevant history." This mission statement immediately stakes a claim to objectivity. They are simply seeking "to enhance area education," a domain typically associated with the transmission and acquisition of fact-based knowledge. This statement also speaks to the organization's very local focus—this is about "area" education, and "relevant" history is presumably only history that has some very clear ties to Fort Wayne.

The home page also underscores the version of Anthony Wayne they are celebrating. Underneath a welcome message is a photo of Fort Wayne's statue of Wayne. Mounted on horseback and looking up toward the horizon, Wayne's left hand holds the reins; his right hand holds an unsheathed sword. Dressed in a general's uniform, this is the Wayne that is central to the organization's depiction of him as a military hero. As discussed below, there is little else that the organization would be able to valorize even if it wanted to, but this focus on Wayne's military service is an important aspect of the selective memory the organization practices. The viewer is meant to see Wayne first and foremost as an important military officer.

The group also emphasizes Wayne's military role in other ways. As the user continues scrolling down the page, one encounters another section—"General 'Mad' Anthony Wayne"—which simply provides another photo of the town's statue of Wayne. Below the photo, text offers the services of a living historian: "If your organization would like General 'Mad' Anthony Wayne to make an appearance, then please email us at 'madanthonywayneorg.com'." The use of a living historian—someone representing a historical figure (generally in period-appropriate attire) but not necessarily an academic historian—is an important feature of the organization's efforts. Their living historians (which have included two different men to date) are staples of the organization's events, and these individuals often serve to perpetuate the same selective memory that appears on the organization's website. These individuals consistently make public appearances in military dress and serve to underscore Wayne's status as a military hero.

A new section header—"What we do"—informs the user that they are about to learn how exactly the organization's mission statement is put into practice. In this section, the organization lists four main items: "Local History," "Honoring Our City's Namesake," "The Military Victory at Stony Point, New York," and the "QUEST Tournament."[33] Each item is accompanied by a short statement and an image, and text under "Local History" reads, "Our primary mission is to enhance area education about local history." This restatement of their mission statement at the top of the page makes clear that this is only their primary mission; there are other aspects to the mission as well. The item is accompanied by an image of a Revolutionary War battle in which American soldiers are breaking through British lines.

The remaining aspects of the group's mission follow similarly. Under the second item, "Honoring Our City's Namesake," text reads, "Fort Wayne is named for General Anthony Wayne. We're involved in activities that keep alive the memory of our city's namesake." Here again, the organization makes a claim to objectivity. Fort Wayne is indeed named for General Anthony Wayne, and the text suggests that they are merely passing down knowledge that can help others understand why Fort Wayne bears that name. Under the third item, "The Military Victory at Stony Point, New York," text reads, "Honoring all U.S. military veterans by remembering and commemorating an important American Revolutionary War victory on July 16, 1779 under the leadership of General 'Mad' Anthony Wayne." Here the group's claims to objectivity are strained—that Wayne's victory at Stony Point was "important" and that one can and should honor "all U.S. military veterans by remembering and commemorating" the victory are interpretive and normative claims more than straightforwardly factual ones.

While seemingly less central to their mission, the website once featured a fourth item, the "QUEST Tournament," which had the longest description:

> We also present QUEST Tournament on WPTA 21, Saturdays at 7:00 p.m. from June 11-July 30, 2022. This high school quiz show is a single-elimination academic competition of of [sic] 4 team members, each in 9th-12th grades as of the Fall 2022. Sweetwater Music is providing prize money of $3,500, with $500 to 3rd Place; $1,000 to 2nd Place; and $2,500 to 1st Place. A beautiful trophy has also been contributed by Imperial Trophy & Awards. See https://www.questtournament.com[34]

Why would an organization focused on Anthony Wayne bother with a high school quiz show? The organization offers no explicit rationale for this, and the fact that this item has since been removed suggests its tangential connection to the organization's mission, but it surely helps to bolster the image of the group as one purportedly dedicated to objectivity and to a sort of civic-mindedness.

The "About Us" page lists those involved in the organization, and it includes a photograph of David Rousculp, the "living historian" who has made in-costume appearances as Anthony Wayne at the group's events in recent years.[35] The roles within the organization surely communicate its interest in education. Having a liaison to educators, an official historian, and a researcher would surely convey to most readers that this is an organization that simply seeks to promulgate uncontroversial historical facts about Fort Wayne's namesake.

As one navigates across the website, the content begins to belie the group's claims to neutral objectivity. The "Mary Penrose Wayne" page, for example, is a call for an "actress to portray Mary 'Polly' (Penrose) Wayne at our functions and events." (This was the case as of June 2024. As of February 2025, the page has been updated with details of a newly hired actress.[36]) The page includes an application form in which applicants acknowledge that "I understand and willingly accept the responsibility to attend functions in honor of General 'Mad' Anthony Wayne presented by the General Mad Anthony Wayne Organization, Inc., and I will dress in the attire of the period, closely resembling what Mary Penrose Wayne would have worn." Describing the events this actress is meant to attend as being "in honor" of Wayne suggests that there is more than a purely educational purpose to the functions—they are meant to valorize Wayne and, given that they are always in reference to "General" Wayne, to affirm the virtue of his military service.[37] Indeed, the application form for Mary Penrose Wayne's performer concludes with a note that adds further detail to their mission statement:

> General "Mad" Anthony Wayne Organization, Inc. is a 501(c)(3) entity dedicated to enhancing area education about relevant history. It was created on March 19, 2019 to support efforts to recognize the General, after the Fort Wayne City Council voted on February 26, 2019, to honor General Wayne in Fort Wayne on July 16 of each year, in celebration of General Wayne's leadership during the Revolutionary War at the Battle of Stony Point (N.Y.) on July 16, 1779, where he successfully led a "bayonets only" charge at midnight against a British garrison on the Hudson River.[38]

Here the link to the Battle of Stony Point is further reinforced, and the celebratory nature of the organization's work is made explicit.

The "National Award" page is perhaps even more clarifying of the organization's politics in its description of the "Legion of the United States Award" that the organization has given annually since 2021.[39] Anyone can be nominated for the award, and to date, the award has been used to celebrate three winners. The first winner was a local educator who served as the first living historian for the organization, and the second was an Indiana public health official who served as a political appointee in the first Trump administration.[40] The third winner was a broader group—the 122nd Fighter Wing of the Indiana Air National Guard, which is based in Fort Wayne.[41] In short, the award has been used to honor people and groups that fit a certain self-presentation—of the organization as interested in education and public service—but the particular recipients also suggest the group's conservative politics.

The "National Award" page is the only place on their website where the organization details Wayne's post-Revolutionary career and his connection to what is now Indiana. The description that follows is a very positive account of Wayne:[42]

> General Wayne was later called out of retirement by President George Washington in early 1792 to command the "Legion of the United States", the nation's first professional military forced created to defend the shores of the now-independent country, and to facilitate the national policy favoring westward expansion. General Wayne became the Senior Commander of the entire Legion, and he is the only person in U.S. history not serving as President of the United States to have received the title of "Commander-in-Chief". The Legion of the United States was renamed the "U.S. Army" in 1796, the year that General Wayne died.
>
> At the time of President Washington's appointment of General Wayne as Commander-in-Chief" of the Legion of the United States, our nation begun to grow from the original 13 American Colonies. The "Northwest" territory was considered to be Ohio, Indiana, Illinois and Michigan, not Oregon and Washington, Idaho and Montana. General Wayne commanded the Legion of the United States until his death on December 15, 1796. General Wayne was known for his talent in strategy and logistics.[43] He was also a peacemaker, and after winning the Battle of Fallen Timbers in 1794, he wrote the northern Native American tribes, in French, calling for peace. (See "The First American West", Special Collections Research Center, University of Chicago Library; available through "American Memory", Library of Congress.)

The oldest unit of the now-U.S. Army is the 3rd Infantry Regiment, "The Old Guard", which traces its lineage to the Legion of the United States. It is the sentinels of The Old Guard who protect the Tomb of the Unknown Soldier. The Tomb has been protected 24 hours a day since Midnight on July 2, 1937. Since June 6, 1948 (then called "Army Day"), it is The Old Guard that has been tasked with that assignment. General Wayne is therefore the First Commander of the regiment charged with protecting the Tomb of the Unknown Soldier. Thus, the City of Fort Wayne has a strong connection to the Tomb of the Unknown Soldier in this regard.

The Legion of the United States Award is intended to honor those who served in the Legion under General Wayne's command. The Award recognizes "excellence in education" and "dedication to community service", which attributes are consistent with our Mission Statement.

This statement shows how the organization tries to valorize Wayne while deflecting potential criticism and intermingling interpretive statements alongside more neutral, descriptive statements. Here, Wayne is someone who helped the United States secure its claim to legitimately acquired territory, and he was an exceptionally good military commander. Lest the reader think of Wayne as enacting conquest, "He was also a peacemaker, and after winning the Battle of Fallen Timbers in 1794, he wrote the northern Native American tribes, in French, calling for peace." That might sound like a stretch, but the organization wants you to know that you can check their facts with a parenthetical reference directing you to their source at the Library of Congress. It appears that the collection is no longer hosted on the Library of Congress's website, but secondary sources do agree on the point that Wayne wrote to the defeated tribes after the Battle of Fallen Timbers to request treaty negotiations that he later oversaw. Whether this supports the interpretation that Wayne was "a peacemaker" or, rather, that he was simply someone in a position to request an opponent's surrender is another question entirely.

In short, a review of the website helps to show that the organization seeks to enact hegemonic mnemonical practices insofar as it suggests that there is one appropriate view of Anthony Wayne and his actions in the Northwest Indian War—that is, a very positive one. Moreover, the website presents this hegemonic mnemonical project as a purely objective, educational mission even as some of its content suggests a more self-consciously conservative political perspective.

"MAD" TV: PROMOTING ANTHONY WAYNE DAY ON THE LOCAL NEWS

The General "Mad" Anthony Wayne Organization's public website is one of the primary venues in which they have promoted their message, but I now turn to other two outlets: televised interviews and the group's Facebook page. I examine their televised interviews with local news outlets first and then consider their Facebook presence. These data sources help establish the hegemonic nature of the group's mnemonical project and the conservative politics thereof.

The first celebration of General "Mad" Anthony Wayne Day was held in 2019, and when given attention by local news outlets, the organizers used such opportunities to promote their positive view of Anthony Wayne while also trying to maintain an air of objectivity. Michael Loomis (the chairman), David Rousculp (the living historian), or Alan and Maureen Gaff (the official historian and researcher, respectively, and jointly the national award co-chairs) are among the organization's most frequent interviewees.[44] A mid 2019 interview with the Gaffs on local television news station WANE 15 began with one of the anchors offering a prompt: "Tell me why this is a special day for the city."[45] Alan responded,

> It's a special day because people who live here don't know very much about Anthony Wayne. We've gone around the city, and if you ask about Anthony Wayne, there's like, "Well, maybe there's a statue of him somewhere," or, "Wasn't he a general in the Revolution?" They really don't know the history of Anthony Wayne and why he was here.

As with much of the text on the group's website, Alan's response suggests a degree of objectivity and purely educational interest while eliding more difficult topics such as why Wayne "was here" in the first place.

A co-anchor then asked, "So how are you going to be recognizing the day?" Maureen responded in detail:

> Well, we're going to start out the day with a memorial at the statue at 10 o'clock in the morning. The DAR—the Daughters of the American Revolution—and the Sons of the American Revolution are gonna participate in that. And we're just going to honor him as our namesake, and there will be a wreath placed at the monument. And then at 1 o'clock, there will be events at the Fort—the Old Fort. The state secretary of the Sons of the

American Revolution is going to present a copy of the payroll—missing soldiers who served under Anthony Wayne—and then there's going to be a flag ceremony there. And General Anthony Wayne and his wife will be there for the public to meet.[46] And then there's events later in the day.

Alan then interjects:

Yeah, 4 o'clock there's going to be [a] presentation at the public library downtown, and through the courtesy of Curt Witcher and the genealogy department, there will be a display, which includes the Wayne family Bible, a letter written by Wayne during the Revolution, as well as a portrait and other materials.

Maureen's statement to the effect that "we're just going to honor him as our namesake" suggests a relatively circumscribed commemoration of Wayne. As I have outlined in the prior section, however, the organization frequently goes further in its valorization of Wayne. Indeed, Alan's reference to "the Wayne family Bible" adds another layer of praise for Anthony Wayne: Beyond being a good general, Wayne is presented as a good Christian.

Continuing in the same interview, the lead anchor then prompts the couple: "So General Mad Anthony Wayne—you mentioned a lot of people don't know much about him; I don't know much about him. Really briefly, a little bit of a, maybe a tease into the history for people who would want to come out." Maureen responds:

Well, the main reason that July 16th was chosen as Anthony Wayne Day— because that is the date when he won the Battle of Stony Point in the Revolutionary War—July 16, 1779. It was a turning point for the Revolutionary War, and the Battle at Stony Point was a surprise midnight attack on the British, and he basically changed the course of the Revolutionary War— helping our side, of course—and it's just really important that, you know, young people should know that we have a Revolutionary War soldier as our namesake.

Here the emphasis is entirely on the Revolutionary War and what Wayne did for "our side." That "young people should know that we have a Revolutionary War soldier as our namesake" again frames the organization's objectives as educational and ultimately unobjectionable.

Despite Wayne's connection to Indiana coming only from the Northwest Indian War, the Gaffs do not mention the conflict until the co-anchor raises a related issue: "And so, I do want to bring up the Miami Tribe of Oklahoma has taken an issue with this day. What would you say in response to that?" Alan took the question:

> I think in response, I would say that our committee embraces any part of Fort Wayne history. As far as myself personally, and I'm not speaking for the committee, I think Little Turtle has been greatly overlooked in Fort Wayne. I would love to see his statue in a more prominent place like in a park or in another location in downtown Fort Wayne so more people can see the statue, ask about it, and become interested in that aspect of Fort Wayne's history.

This response cedes little ground. There is no acknowledgment that Wayne's actions might have been harmful to others or that the Miami Tribe of Oklahoma might have any legitimate grievance. Even if Wayne's actions did harm, they are "part of Fort Wayne history" and deserve to be commemorated on that basis alone. That the organization has a positive, celebratory view of Wayne is clear; when pressed on the purported virtues of his actions, however, they can retreat to the claim that they are merely interested in preserving history. Alan offers only that the city's statue of Little Turtle could perhaps be more prominently displayed. The interview then concludes with the co-anchor thanking Alan and Maureen for "stopping by."

WANE 15 gave more sustained attention to the controversy generated by the proposal in an earlier video posted on March 25, 2019.[47] Footage of the town's Anthony Wayne statue appears on screen, and a reporter's voice introduces the topic:

> Should the city of Fort Wayne observe General Anthony Wayne Day? A Native American tribe with roots to the Summit City says no.[48] They're demanding the city council rescinds a resolution which will honor Fort Wayne's namesake with his own day.

Meanwhile, a physical copy of the letter is displayed on screen. The footage then cuts to Councilman Arp—WANE 15 microphone being held in front of him—who frames the tribe's actions negatively. Arp, dressed in a beige corduroy blazer, a dark sweater, and a light, checked button-down shirt, notes that, "I was disappointed that, you know, the letter went out to the press—actually, you probably read it before I did—and so that was a little bit disappointing." Arp, who worked with the General "Mad" Anthony Wayne Organization in its early days, helps to further the organization's claims that it is good to celebrate Anthony Wayne and bad to oppose such celebrations.

The footage then returns to a depiction of the letter—this time, relevant text has been highlighted and marked in pen. The reporter details the letter's accusations as the camera pans over the text:

> The Miami Tribe of Oklahoma cites historical inaccuracies in the resolution. It states that in one battle, tribes were led by British officers instead of by their own captains. The letter goes on to say, "The resolution does not recognize the negative impact on tribal nations caused by the U.S. Army under Wayne's leadership." The group argues holding Anthony Wayne Day would only commemorate those actions. Councilman Jason Arp says history shows otherwise.

The footage returns to the town statue of Wayne and then again to Arp, who says, "I mean, obviously there's a different point of view there. If you look at the writings that Anthony Wayne and his lieutenants and generals had during that time period with their command staff, they had pretty good documentation that there were British forces involved."[49] The tribe's "point of view" is presented only to be dismissed by Arp, who presents himself as having objective, historical facts on his side.

The footage returns once more the statue of Wayne, and Arp is given one final chance to underscore why Fort Wayne residents ought to commemorate their city's namesake. "The decision by the city council last month was not unanimous," the reporter notes. "Three councilmen voted against it. Councilman Arp, who led the charge, said he expected some negative feedback, but rescinding the resolution now is something he won't entertain." The camera returns to Arp to conclude the segment: "There's nothing wrong with having strong, courageous men leading our country, and we should take our hat off to Anthony Wayne, and I look forward to doing that on July the 16th."

Here we have a more substantive engagement with the claims of the tribe; rather than merely noting that "the Miami Tribe of Oklahoma has taken an issue with this day," the reporter outlines specific grievances. Ultimately, however, the views expressed by the tribe and Arp are presented as differences in "point of view." At least in the footage we see, however, Arp only attempts to rebut the charge that the resolution was wrong about the extent of British involvement in the Northwest Indian War; he does not address the question of whether the resolution failed to "recognize the negative impact on tribal nations caused by the U.S. Army under Wayne's leadership." He also—in terms resonant with Donald Trump's brand of Republicanism—uses gendered language to group Wayne in with other "strong, courageous men leading our country." As noted above, moreover, Arp himself hedges his words, but he seems to be overstating British involvement. The emphasis on the British presence would seem to make the Northwest Indian War something akin to the Revolutionary War—a just war—with the United States simply using force to secure what had been guaranteed to it in the 1783 Treaty of Paris. Framing the Northwest Indian War as a British–American conflict avoids the more fraught framing of it as a one-sided war of conquest intended to dispossess Native peoples with legitimate claims to the land.

WANE 15 also gave at least brief attention to Anthony Wayne Day in the years after it began to be officially celebrated.[50] In a video posted to their website on July 17, 2022, an anchor introduces the topic:

> People gathered yesterday for the observance of General "Mad" Anthony Wayne Day. On February 26th of 2019, the Fort Wayne City Council approved a resolution to established July 16th as General "Mad" Anthony Wayne Day. It was on that day in 1779 that General Wayne led an attack on a British camp in Stony Point, New York, that is believed to have saved the American fort from being captured. Several members of the Fort Wayne Honor Guard want people to come out to this event in the future.

After the anchor concludes the main portion of her comments—by noting that "Several members of the Fort Wayne Honor Guard want people to come out to this event in the future"—the camera cuts to footage in which the living historian David Rousculp, microphone in hand, is presumably addressing a prompt from the reporter. A member of the Fort Wayne Honor Guard stands beside him, and three additional members stand behind them in the background (clearly standing there for the camera). Rousculp is the only one of them who speaks:

Well, of course, always we're looking for support financially. We also just like having people wave the flag. Bring the young people out—that's what we always want. [The man standing next to Rousculp nods his head and mouths "Yup."] Bring your young people out so we can tell the story, 'cause a lot of people here in Fort Wayne don't even know who General Anthony Wayne is. They just—"uh, it's Fort Wayne"—it's giving them something to understand. It's all about education.

The camera then returns to the anchor, who informs the viewer that "The event took place at Freimann Square."

The anchor's recitation of the story of the Battle of Stony Point gives that narrative an air of credibility. The sparse details of the battle she provides are spoken as if they are uncontroversial facts. The battle "is believed to have saved the American fort from being captured," but it is unclear by whom it is "believed." Surely, the viewer who knows little about minor Revolutionary War battles can comfortably defer to those who know enough about such battles to believe things about their tactical rewards, and those associated with the General "Mad" Anthony Wayne Organization are presented here as exactly the sort of people who would know about such things. That the celebration is marked by various patriotic symbols and that Rousculp concludes his comments by noting that "It's all about education" surely conveys to the viewer that this an appropriate way to honor the city's namesake and to convey uncontroversial historical facts.

In short, through televised coverage of their celebrations, those associated with the General "Mad" Anthony Wayne Organization present the day as a proper way to celebrate an important historical figure—Fort Wayne's namesake—while eliding or deflecting criticism of Wayne. They at times do this by disavowing any notion that they are, in fact, celebrating Wayne; rather, they sometimes retreat to a claim that they are merely offering education about historical events. Televised coverage also allows the group's use of visual symbols such as red, white, and blue decorations to communicate a sort of patriotism that they would presumably see as entirely uncontroversial and that they might want viewers to associate with Wayne and with their own organization. Those representing the organization engage in hegemonic mnemonical practices on television by presenting their reading of history as *the* proper reading of history, by dismissing alternative readings thereof, and by representing themselves as wholly objective. That this aligns with a conservative politics is at times apparent in televised interviews, but that is perhaps clearest on its Facebook page.

GETTING "MAD" ONLINE: PARTISAN POLITICS ON FACEBOOK

While the General "Mad" Anthony Wayne Organization's website has been relatively static, the group offers more routine updates on its Facebook page, which has offered much valorization of Wayne, deflection of criticism, and explicitly partisan politics.[51] In this section, I continue to make the case that the organization is engaged in hegemonic mnemonical practices in its commemoration of Anthony Wayne, and I provide further evidence to the effect that this comes from a conservative political position.

The organization's first public activity on Facebook was political insofar as it made clear its valorization of Wayne and its links to Councilman Arp. The addition of its first profile picture (a portrait of Wayne), occurred on July 19, 2019, just a few days after the observation of the inaugural Anthony Wayne Day celebrations on July 16. The update was "liked" by two people, one of whom was Arp.[52] Later on July 19 and in subsequent days, the organization posted various photos and comments on the inaugural celebrations; one post on July 20, for example, describes the July 16 event as an "Honor and Appreciation Event." A post on July 21 specifies that Arp "gave the keynote address" at the event. This collaboration with an especially conservative councilman with a clearly hegemonic mnemonical project belies any notion that the organization is apolitical or objective.

Beyond simply cataloguing the organization's activities, the Facebook page is a place where the organization has tried to deflect criticism, especially relating to Wayne's treatment of Native American groups. A November 18, 2023, post includes a photo with a background of stylized feathers and text reading "November National Native American Heritage Month."[53] Accompanying the photo is the following text:

> On August 3, 1990, President George H. W. Bush declared the month of November as National Native American Heritage Month. Our Organization respects the culture, traditions, music, crafts, dance and ways of life of our Native Americans. We also enjoy teaching the history of such things, and we try to use the celebration of historical events to teach history. If your Native American organization would like to participate with us, please send us a message.

About a year earlier, on November 25, 2022, the organization had posted a shorter message to the same effect: "Happy Native American Heritage Day!"[54] A picture of several Native American individuals in ceremonial garb (tribal affiliation is not specified) accompanied the post.[55] The organization has clearly tried to convey that it respects "our Native Americans" in a way that could help to deflect any concerns to the effect that its celebration of Anthony Wayne elides the ways Wayne's actions negatively affected Native American groups.

Beyond such efforts to deflect criticism with positive statements about Native American groups, the organization also used Facebook to criticize Native concerns about Anthony Wayne Day. The organization's lengthiest engagement with concerns raised by the Miami Tribe of Oklahoma came in a July 17, 2021, post that linked to a 2019 report from *Indian Country Today* (and reposted on Indianz.com).[56] The report as initially posted is entitled "Celebrating (Not) Mad Wayne Day," but the repost (a day later) gives it a different title: "Miami Tribe Excluded from Event on Own Homelands." It is the latter that the organization posted to its Facebook page. The story begins as follows (Pember 2019):

> In case you missed it: Tuesday July 16, was the first General Mad Anthony Day in Fort Wayne, Indiana. Not everyone was celebrating. Members of the General Mad Anthony Wayne Organization joined the Daughters of the Revolution in a wreath laying ceremony at the foot of Wayne's statue in the city's Friemann [sic] Square, according to news reports. Reenactors Robert Jones and Andi Hahn portrayed Wayne and his wife Mary Penrose during the day's celebration. Absent were members of the Miami Tribe of Oklahoma who consider the area to be their heartlands. The Miami and other tribes were pushed out of the region by treaties and federal removal policies designed to steal lands in Ohio and Indiana for American settlers. It was General Mad Anthony Wayne who led the first wave of these actions.

The article details much of the narrative already recounted above surrounding the initial city council proposal for an Anthony Wayne Day, criticism of that resolution, and rejoinders from Arp.

The organization posted its response on Facebook exactly two years after the initial report was published. The rejoinder is lengthy and defensive: It has the tone of a statement that is meant to be the definitive response to any criticism of Wayne's treatment of Native American groups:

We'd like to set the record straight about something, and this is very troubling to the Chairman of this Organization. In 2019, I tried to reach Chief Douglas Lankford of the Miami Tribe of Oklahoma in three (3) separate telephone calls. I left messages with a live person each time. He did not return them.[57]

I called the Cultural Affairs Director, Julie Olds, on April 1, 2019, and I spoke with her for nearly 45 minutes. We had a very nice conversation, although she failed to mention to me that she is the twin sister of the Chief. Still, it was a good exchange.

I also sent a letter to the Chief, inviting him to send a representative to Fort Wayne on July 16, 2019 for a panel discussion about General Wayne at the ACPL [Allen County Public Library] (we had reserved an hour for the Miami Tribe), but he failed to reply. I sent a certified letter to the Chief, offering to bring a delegation from Fort Wayne to the tribal headquarters in Oklahoma, so that we could have a discussion about history, and determine if the Miami Tribe of Oklahoma might be interested in being a part of the curriculum that we would be introducing to the general public, so that the Tribe's perspective would be included. The Chief did not respond; the Tribe did not participate in our events. This, despite the fact that our first General "Mad" Anthony Wayne Day was all about teaching the general public about Wayne's role at the Battle of Stony Point, NY, on July 16, 1779.[58] There were no Native Americans, and no members of the Miami Tribe of Oklahoma, involved in that skirmish. It was a battle of the American Revolution.

Instead, the Miami Tribe lied in its Tribal Newsletter, indicating that they were not permitted to be a part of the 2019 festivities.[59] I am truly sorry that we could not have found common ground between us. Our Organization was formed on March 19, 2019, nearly 3 weeks after the Resolution that I suggested was passed by City Council. Our Organization was not part of the presentation of the resolution on February 26, 2019. It is apparently that presentation with which the Tribe disagrees.[60]

Ironically, our Organization was not invited to address City Council about the resolution about six (6) months later that recognized October as "Native American Heritage Month".[61] We had publicly expressed our support of the resolution.

We will not apologize for the history of our City, nor for the acts of our City's namesake. History is history, and we are not going to change it, nor will we shy away from presenting it. We will always welcome a different point of view, but we are not "revisionists".

Please also note that the Miami Tribe of Oklahoma did not have a written language during the times that General Wayne lived. Its history was passed down through the spoken word; in other words, its history is "folklore". There is no documentation, about which we are aware, that supports some of the ridiculous assertions that have been made about General Wayne's actions.[62]

Let the record stand "corrected".

Chief Douglas Lankford: you know how to find me.

J. Michael Loomis

In short, the organization's chairman has argued that Native critique of Wayne is invalid. The Miami Tribe of Oklahoma and some of its officials are represented here as having been deceptive, stubborn, opposed to "teaching," and perhaps even misinformed. Native critique is labeled a "perspective"—perhaps "a different point of view" to be offered—in the same way that Arp described such critique as a "point of view" in the televised interview described earlier. On the other hand, Loomis presents the organization as having been forthcoming, open-minded, and ultimately interested in history—not in being "revisionists" who (in this pejorative connotation of the word) might distort history to advance a political agenda.

This response by Loomis also serves as an affirmation of the legitimacy of Wayne's actions. Saying that they "will not apologize . . . for the acts of our City's namesake" clearly indicates that they will say that the American victory in the Northwest Indian War was a good thing regardless of whatever harm it wrought on Native American groups. Amid early backlash to the resolution, Arp similarly defended Wayne by saying that (quoted in Savage 2020):

For us, we're very happy to live in Fort Wayne and that the United States of America exists. I would not call those negative impacts. Maybe other people see those as negatives. As being a patriotic American, I think having the United States be a place is a good thing.

To question the legitimacy of the Northwest Indian War, Arp would seem to be suggesting, is to question the legitimacy of the United States itself, and to do so would be bad and unpatriotic in his telling.

The organization continued to press its case in the comments on this post.[63] The comments are largely a back-and-forth between the organization itself (it seems to be Loomis still writing) and a user who is somewhat critical of the organization. The user, Keenan Salla, is identified in their profile as an archivist at the Indiana Archives and Records Administration.[64] Salla begins:

> Seems to me that the text of the initial resolution is what pushed the tribe out, not a lack of subsequent invitations. The spokesperson in the article made it clear that they felt their participation would be an endorsement they didn't want to give.
>
> It's also both incorrect and seemingly in bad faith to refer to oral history as folklore in an attempt to diminish it's [sic] authority.[65]

The response from the organization begins by tagging Salla:

> Keenan Salla ". . . pushed the tribe out . . ."? Of what? We would have talked with them about their concerns, even those regarding the resolution. They sent a representative in May 2019 to talk to a member of City Council or two, but did not contact us. I merely proposed a resolution honoring General Wayne. Councilman Arp wrote it. The resolution, and the day honoring him with events planned by our Organization, are two separate matters.
>
> From Oxford Languages-
>
> "Folklore: the traditional beliefs, customs, and stories of a community, passed through the generation by word of mouth."
>
> ". . . incorrect and seemingly in bad faith"? You are clearly wrong in your effort to diminish the authority of my statement of fact.[66]

The organization (again, seemingly Loomis) then adds a second comment:

> The comments in the story, implying that the tribe was "not permitted" to participate were inaccurate; their representatives did lie to the author of the article.[67]
>
> The Tribe's purported "history" is less reliable, because it isn't documented. And as I said, I didn't write the resolution.
>
> You seem to be taking the position that their allegations about General Wayne are accurate, and that's fine; you're entitled to your opinion. But you're painting everything in a broad swath, without reference to specific facts. That is foolhardy, because history requires specific facts.
>
> The problem is that many people, perhaps including yourself, disagree now, in the context of today's history, about our Nation's domestic policy toward Native Americans. That brings its own problems, looking backwards through a contemporary lens, and blaming the General for following lawful orders. That is an affront to every Veteran who ever served this country.[68] You have no documentation to support your arguments that General Wayne was a "conquering General", whatever that is, or that he wasn't merciful.

In any event, as I said, I proposed a resolution, I didn't write it. And we made numerous invitations to the Miami Tribe of Oklahoma to be a part of our events, and to offer their perspective. For whatever their reasons, they didn't participate; but they were NOT excluded.[69]

You have an obvious agenda, and you are clearly unfamiliar with the events that have transpired in this matter. I'm happy to debate you, but you have no objectivity.

Salla then responds to those two comments as follows:

I am referring to your accusation that the tribe lied. I assume that is refer-ring to their claim in the article that it was pushed out. I read their state-ments as feeling as though their participation was entirely precluded by the text of the resolution and the presentation done by the Councilman Arp. No subsequent efforts on your organization's part were going to get results; the die was cast.

And your statement reads as implying that their history is inherently less accurate and reliable than that written by Europeans by casting it as folklore. These are events that happened a handful of generations ago, not legends. History passed through oral tradition. Personally, I think any-thing casting a conquering general as merciful deserves a healthy dose of skepticism, and the context doesn't help in this situation.[70]

This back-and-forth evinces many of the same rhetorical maneuvers that we have seen elsewhere in the organization's public messaging. They have "objectivity"; their critics do not. In a new twist on their framing of this argument, the organization claims historical objectivity because they are working with written records; the oral history of the Miami Tribe of Oklahoma is presented as less reliable "folklore." The Northwest Indian War is presented as a just war for which the British were largely to blame, not as a war of conquest; Wayne himself thus ought not to be thought of as a "conquering General." Furthermore, the organization presents itself as apolitical; their opponents allegedly are political, and Councilman Arp may be, but Arp and his resolution purportedly have nothing to do with their celebrations (despite the many points of connection between them). The organization, in short, denies that they are engaging in hegemonic mne-monical practices even while doing exactly that.

While the organization publicly represents itself as apolitical and objec-tive, its Facebook page offers clear indications that at least some of its key members share rather conservative political views of the sort associated with Donald Trump and that their activism is oriented toward political ends (Hopkins and Noel 2022). Some signs of the group's politics are relatively subtle. On October 2, 2020, for example, the organization wrote a short post about a British Army officer, John André, who "was executed by the Americans as a spy [in 1780], after conducting secret meetings with American General Benedict Arnold." Another Facebook user, Davy Macy Deppisch (who has no apparent affiliation with the organization), commented on the post, "The Deep State had a very early start!"[71] The organization "liked" the comment but did not otherwise reply. Similarly, just a couple weeks earlier, on September 22, the organization wrote a post about the executed American spy, Nathan Hale, whose last words were (recounted but not confirmed as being), "I only regret that I have but one life to lose for my country." As the organization notes, "Whether he actually made the above statement is unproven, but by all reports he did conduct himself with dignity and resolution at the time of his execution." Deppisch again comments, "Dignity and patriotism—wow the NFL and NBA and NHL could use some of that right now!"[72] This is likely a reference to protests or statements of sympathy that various professional athletes have made with reference to Black Lives Matter and related social justice movements. Once again, the organization liked the comment without replying, but that a user felt comfortable expressing such sentiments on the organization's posts and that the organization "liked" them suggests an alignment with conservative politics.

A series of posts—two on June 28, two on June 30, and one on July 1—further highlights partisan divides between those in the organization and some in Fort Wayne who would prefer that the city not honor Wayne by maintaining a statue of him. These posts came amid many protests around the country—generally framed as being about social justice and in response to police killings of black men—in which activists targeted statues of prominent Confederate leaders, slave owners, or otherwise controversial figures for removal (Benjamin et al. 2020). The organization stood squarely on the side of maintaining the statue of Wayne, and they praised then-President Trump's efforts to protect such statues. Their first post on the matter targeted a Change.org petition started by Jacob Ferris on June 20, 2020.[73] The petition, "Remove the statue of 'Mad Anthony' Wayne from Freimann Square," received 110 signatures and reads as follows:

Mad Anthony slaughtered thousands of local Native Americans in order to gain territory in the Midwest. A murderer should not be idolized as a war hero for committing atrocities against my or anyone's ancestors.

The organization's first response to this petition generated by far the most engagement they ever received on Facebook—177 "likes" (including some "loves"), 150 comments, and 463 shares—and is indicative of their conservative politics. The post reads as follows:

> We are aware that a person identifying himself as Jacob Ferris submitted a petition to Fort Wayne Mayor Tom Henry approximately 6 days ago, demanding that the statue of General Anthony Wayne in Freimann Square be removed. The reasons stated for this petition are ludicrous. Our organization will take all necessary legal action to preserve and protect this bit of history. We will pursue civil and/or criminal action against anyone vandalizing the statue or vandalizing the Old Fort. We will also be assisting in the effort to increase security at both locations. Protest in peace within the law as you desire, but do no damage to this community's historic landmarks, or we will pursue you relentlessly.

The comments are generally supportive of the organization. Those associated with and sympathetic to the organization frequently cast their opponents in the terms that Trump and other Republican elites used to excoriate those who would remove such statues. Those who wanted the statue of Wayne removed were repeatedly criticized for being ignorant of history, for not being patriotic, and for undermining what America was built on.[74]

Subsequent posts continued in that same way. Later on June 28, the organization posted a sort of counter-offer to those who wanted the statue of Wayne removed:

> Our organization suggested in an editorial published last August that the memorial to this leader, the great Miami Chief Little Turtle, be moved to a more prominent place in Fort Wayne's Headwaters Park. Perhaps those signing a petition to Mayor Tom Henry demanding that the statue of General Anthony Wayne be removed could instead use their time, talents and treasure by helping with a constructive project, instead of a destructive one.

Two days later, on June 30, the organization posted a follow-up to the discussion on their first post:

Our recent post about protecting the statue of General Anthony Wayne has, as of this writing, reached 10,023 people. While it is difficult to discern because this message was shared so widely on many different pages, it appears that we've had 67 responses on our main page alone, 66 of which were positive. Only 1, to date, was negative. Ashton Marie Martin: I would like to invite you to have a civil and friendly dialogue with us. Are you willing to sit down and discuss your differences with our desire to protect a community asset?[75]

Later that same day, the organization posted approvingly about an executive order issued by President Trump that aimed to protect public statues, including federal, state, and local properties alike.[76] Their final post on the matter came a day later on July 1:

While we very much appreciate the many offers from our followers to assist in providing security this weekend for the GMAW statue in Freimann Square, and for the Old Fort, we will defer for the time being. We are in frequent contact with local law enforcement agencies. Our best counsel is for everyone to stay out of the downtown area on Saturday, July 4, and let the police handle any threatening situations. Let's be part of the solution, and not part of the problem. We support FWPD, ACSD, and other agencies that will be involved, and, we'll be pursuing legal action against those who would damage our community assets. Thank you.[77]

The only comment was from Zachary A. Williams, whose Facebook profile identifies him as a resident of Fort Wayne: "Wouldn't want somebody making Anthony Wayne move. You can only make people move if they're native Americans and were here first and if you threaten to murder them all if they don't [pensive emoji]."

In all these Facebook posts and comments concerning Fort Wayne's statue of Anthony Wayne, the organization frames itself as the good guy in this public debate. They support "peaceful protest" and simply want to protect "community assets" from those who might engage in political violence. Their opponents are "destructive," "ludicrous," and "part of the problem"; those associated with the organization are "constructive" protectors of "history" and "part of the solution." While those associated with the organization may indeed see themselves as neutral arbiters of an "objective" history, their consistent alignment with conservative Republicans in rhetoric and in practice belies the notion that this is a wholly apolitical organization.

Finally, the organization's Facebook page also offers observers the best source for what the celebration of Anthony Wayne Day entails, and this too suggests an alignment with conservative politics. Two recorded videos of the 2023 celebrations on the organization's Facebook page help further this case and demonstrate that the organization runs its events in ways that align with a specifically Christian sort of conservativism.[78]

The recording of the 2023 Anthony Wayne Day begins with living historians David Rousculp and Carolynn Stouder (dressed as Anthony and Mary Penrose Wayne) arriving at Freimann Square in a white horse-drawn carriage. Two men associated with the Sons of the American Revolution and dressed in Revolutionary military garb carry American flags and walk ahead of Rousculp and Stouder as they make the brief walk to the area where Wayne's statue stands. The group's veneration of Wayne is in this way cast within a broader veneration of the American founders and the United States.

Judi Loomis, now the president of the organization and wife of chairman Mike Loomis, then offers a brief introduction before inviting Dennis Kruse, a member of the Indiana Senate from 2004 to 2022 and the Indiana House of Representatives from 1989 to 2004, to say a prayer. His prayer is specifically Christian rather than being generically ecumenical or otherwise pluralistic. This is perhaps unsurprising given his efforts to create a state constitutional amendment defining marriage as "one man and one woman," to require the teaching of "creation science" in public schools, to permit school districts "to start each day by reciting 'The Lord's Prayer'," and to bar public schools from providing sex education without a parent's prior written consent.[79] He prays as follows:

> Let us pray. Father, we thank you for our gathering here today in Freimann Square in Fort Wayne in celebration of General Anthony Wayne. We thank you for the Sons of the American Revolution and their participation here today, and I pray, God, that we will remember our past—we will remember the patriots who helped found our country and fought for our country and the freedoms that we have today. I pray that you be with our ceremony here today and with each one who is participating. We place this into your hands, and we ask that your presence be with us. We pray this in Christ's name. Amen.[80]

Judi Loomis then invites Alan Gaff (the organization's aforementioned historian) to lead the small crowd in the Pledge of Allegiance. He walks up to the podium and informs the crowd that "The pledge of allegiance today is going to be the traditional one—it includes the word 'God'." He then removes his hat, places it over his heart, and leads the crowd in the pledge before again taking his seat. With both a pointedly Christian prayer and pledge, the organization suggests its alignment with America's Christian right (Leege 1992).

Like much of the organization's work, the ceremony also emphasizes Wayne's actions in the Revolutionary War rather than his connection to Fort Wayne. David Rousculp, the living historian, speaks in the third person: "Anthony Wayne was a decorated military officer who served in the both the war of the American Revolution and the campaigns during George Washington's presidential administration." He speaks for about five minutes and focuses almost entirely on Wayne's actions during the Revolutionary War, especially the Battle of Stony Point. Beyond his initial reference to "the campaigns during George Washington's presidential administration," the only reference to the Northwest Indian War comes in a quotation attributed to Major William Eaton, who served under Wayne and who refers to Wayne's steadfastness on even "his most severe night of the winter of 1794." Rousculp concludes, "Let us not forget."[81] The selective description of Anthony Wayne, however, encourages the audience to remember Wayne as a Revolutionary War hero and to forget his perhaps more controversial deeds in the Northwest Indian War.[82]

Throughout this chapter, I have catalogued the ways in which the General "Mad" Anthony Wayne Organization has engaged in hegemonic mnemonical practices. These practices seek to establish one interpretation of the past as *the* interpretation of the past, and if it was not already obvious from its other public activities, content on the group's Facebook page makes especially clear that the organization's interpretation of the past comes from and is in furtherance of a conservative politics. In this view, Anthony Wayne was a virtuous patriot, military man, and Christian to be celebrated as a role model for today's Americans. To do anything less—to perhaps question Wayne's virtues or the legitimacy of his military actions—would be to besmirch all American veterans and to undermine the legitimacy of American claims to territory it has long claimed as its own.

DISCUSSION

The case study in this chapter is meant to demonstrate what hegemonic mnemonical practices might look like in practice but also to help answer two linked questions. Why would anyone pursue hegemonic rather than reflective mnemonical practices? And why did hegemonic mnemonical practices arise in this particular context?

To take the latter question first, it is notable that Fort Wayne was not already commemorating Wayne with an annual day in his honor. Why now? The hegemonic mnemonical practices on display in Fort Wayne, I argue, seem to be not just the product of local particularities but also two ongoing phenomena in American politics: polarization and nationalization. Polarization, or the widening of the ideological distance between the average Republican and the average Democrat, may give politicians incentive to stake out more extreme positions (Hare and Poole 2014). Indeed, Arp exemplifies the sort of increasingly conservative Republican that has emerged as a force within the party over the past couple decades—the "Tea Party" or "Freedom Caucus" Republican who sees more centrist Republicans as insufficiently conservative (e.g., as "RINOs," or "Republicans in name only") (Blum 2020).[83] In this political context—and given the presence of primary elections—taking more ideologically extreme positions may ensure that office-seekers cannot be out-flanked by more extreme co-partisans.

Similarly, nationalization, or the extent to which people are increasingly paying attention to national politics at the expense of state and local politics, gives local politicians incentives to link themselves to national-level political issues (Hopkins 2018). Indeed, Councilman Arp successfully couched his pitch for an Anthony Wayne Day in highly localized terms while also connecting to broader themes associated with the Republican Party. The 2016 Republican Party Platform (which was reaffirmed in 2020), for example, begins with a statement of principles, and the first three in particular find echoes in Arp's rhetoric:

We believe in American exceptionalism.

We believe the United States of America is unlike any other nation on earth.

We believe America is exceptional because of our historic role—first as refuge, then as defender, and now as exemplar of liberty for the world to see.[84]

The 2024 Republican Party Platform opens with a statement that echoes the way Arp talks about the United States, Anthony Wayne, and the role of American citizens:

> Our Nation's History is filled with the stories of brave men and women who gave everything they had to build America into the Greatest Nation in the History of the World. Generations of American Patriots have summoned the American Spirit of Strength, Determination, and Love of Country to overcome seemingly insurmountable challenges. The American People have proven time and again that we can overcome any obstacle and any force pitted against us.
>
> In the early days of our Republic, the Founding Generation defeated what was then the most powerful Empire the World had ever seen. In the 20th Century, America vanquished Nazism and Fascism, and then triumphed over Soviet Communism after forty-four years of the Cold War.
>
> But now we are a Nation in SERIOUS DECLINE. Our future, our identity, and our very way of life are under threat like never before. Today we must once again call upon the same American Spirit that led us to prevail through every challenge of the past if we are going to lead our Nation to a brighter future.

Such principles find an affirmation in Arp's telling of the reason to celebrate Wayne—as already quoted above, "I think having the United States be a place is a good thing" (Savage 2020). To affirm the goodness of Wayne is to affirm the goodness of America, and to the extent that it is the Republican Party that seeks to affirm that the United States is now and always has been fundamentally good—rather than, for example, needing to be made "more perfect" over time—Arp links his local politics to broader currents of national political discourse.[85]

Returning to the first question I posed, why would anyone pursue hegemonic mnemonical practices and oppose reflective mnemonical practices? In answering this question, I would first return to my position that while the valence of these two terms may suggest a value judgment—that being reflective is good and that being hegemonic is bad—I do not necessarily take that to be the case. Still, it may seem puzzling why someone would object to the seemingly benign "remembering by thinking through" (Mälksoo 2023, 3).

The case of Anthony Wayne Day suggests some different potential motivations. For office-seekers, they may believe there is political gain to be had. Indeed, Arp continued to seek reelection to the Fort Wayne City Council until seeking higher office by running for mayor of Fort Wayne in 2023. He may have overestimated his ability to gain support: He lost in the Republican primary to Thomas Didier, 64.1 percent to 33.3 percent, to one of his fellow council members who supported the Anthony Wayne Day resolution.[86] Nevertheless, the simplifying assumption that policymakers are "single-minded reelection seekers" seems helpful in understanding Arp's initial proposal for Anthony Wayne Day even if changes in the political environment help to demonstrate why that might have been seen as a winning issue (Mayhew 2004, 17).

Beyond the electoral incentive, this case suggests that hegemonic mnemonical practices might indeed be oriented toward "mnemonical security" (Mälksoo 2023, 3). In this case, however, the pursuit of mnemonical security seems to be about more than avoiding "the unpleasant and ontologically disturbing interpretations of the past" that reflection might produce (Mälksoo 2023, 3). It is also—to be somewhat speculative—about ensuring that no one else comes to conclusions that might disturb the material comfort of those satisfied with the status quo.[87]

Here reflective mnemonical practices are seen as being a potentially enormous threat to the United States itself and to the material benefits individual citizens might gain from being Americans. If we refuse to affirm the goodness of Anthony Wayne, we perhaps undermine the legitimacy of American claims to the territory that Wayne helped acquire, and perhaps the daily buy-in that the continued existence of any state requires dissolves. This sort of insistence on the notion that US claims to its territory are legitimate and ought not to be questioned—lest they lead to undesirable consequences—was similarly expressed by Senator Ted Cruz, a Texas Republican. After the Supreme Court held in 2020 that "much of Tulsa and eastern Oklahoma had long been a reservation of the Muscogee (Creek) Nation" because it was never explicitly disestablished by Congress, Cruz tweeted that, "Neil Gorsuch & the four liberal Justices just gave away half of Oklahoma, literally. Manhattan is next" (Healy 2020). Surely, for Arp, Cruz, and their co-partisans, there is no reason to "give away" US territory. To do so would be both an admission of some sort of guilt and a potential threat to a political order that provides material comforts to them and their constituents.

In short, for Jason Arp, Ted Cruz, and other like-minded conservatives, hegemonic mnemonical practices work to maintain the perceived material benefits provided by the continued existence of the United States. Reflective mnemonical practices are dangerous; their open-ended nature might allow people to conclude that American claims to at least some of its currently claimed territory are illegitimate. For Arp, such views would surely be erroneous, but worse, they might make him less ontologically and materially secure. He and many others reap substantial benefits from the United States "be[ing] a place," and anything that threatens to undo that should be avoided (Savage 2020). If American claims to its territory are as solid as such individuals suggest, however, one wonders why more reflective mnemonical practices would be so threatening to the continued existence of the United States.

CODA: AFTERLIVES OF THE NORTHWEST INDIAN WAR

The General "Mad" Anthony Wayne Organization's celebrations of Anthony Wayne Day now take place every year in Freimann Square. This downtown square is situated between various city government offices, a county courthouse, and multiple arts centers—as close as one can get to markers of power and prestige in Indiana's second-largest city. The statue of Wayne on horseback stands in the square's southwest corner. A historical marker in front of the statue provides extensive detail on Wayne's military activities during the 1790s.[88]

A little over a mile north of Freimann Square, across the St. Mary's River, a much more modest memorial to Little Turtle stands between two houses.[89] In 1912, construction workers building a house on the site uncovered Little Turtle's remains. Undeterred, they looted the grave and continued with construction. The memorial only exists now because a retired high school history teacher bought the house in 1959 and donated it to the city, which demolished the house and maintains the site as a small park. A plaque simply informs visitors that Little Turtle's "endeavors toward peace should serve as an inspiration for future generations." But it was not just Little Turtle's remains that were found there—dozens of others were buried alongside him (Savage 2020). The houses on either side of this memorial stand on a large grave.

The Northwest Indian War is not a major fixture in American public memory, but to the extent that the local politics of Fort Wayne have sought to entrench Anthony Wayne's role in the war in localized public memory, conservative policymakers and activists have used hegemonic mnemonical practices to valorize Wayne and to elide the suffering of Little Turtle and other Native Americans. This peculiar series of events in a relatively small American city are reflective of broader debates about how exactly the United States ought to memorialize the aspects of its past that entailed Native dispossession. At local, state, or federal levels, for example, should we be celebrating Columbus Day or Indigenous Peoples' Day (Hitchmough 2013)? What does the US government owe to Native American groups who suffered violent dispossession at the hands of settlers? Those who enact hegemonic mnemonical practices in Fort Wayne and elsewhere answer such questions by denying their legitimacy. For them, the consequences of even engaging with such questions as if they contain valid premises could be disastrous, and that is reason enough to refuse such reflection. Those who seek to establish reflective mnemonical practices will face stiff opposition from such individuals, and compelling arguments backed by vigorous, well-resourced organizing would help in such mnemonical battles.

Extending this analysis to the international sphere, it is perhaps not surprising that the United States and other relatively young settler states such as Canada, Australia, and New Zealand have resisted any serious recognition of Indigenous claims to territory and self-determination. The passage of the United Nations Declaration on the Rights of Indigenous Peoples (UNDRIP) may have been a win for many Indigenous peoples, for example, but where its principles and recommendations are ignored, there is little that Indigenous peoples can do to make states comply. To be sure, Indigenous peoples in the United States and elsewhere have consistently challenged setter state claims that are at odds with their own self-determination. The Haudenosaunee (Iroquois), for example, have long made use of passports issued by their tribal government; the US government has often tacitly allowed this, but it does not officially do so because it claims the singular sovereign authority to issue passports for US citizens (Lightfoot 2021). Whether this is indicative of or portends a sort of "hybrid sovereignty" in which Indigenous peoples are allowed to more genuinely govern themselves is unclear (Srivastava 2022).

Ultimately, my reading of the history of US foreign policy—including

US relations with Native American groups—gives me little reason to believe that the United States and other settler states will make substantive concessions to Indigenous peoples in the foreseeable future. Those who seek such concessions will find themselves hard-pressed to combat the interests underlying Arp's contention that "having the United States be a place is a good thing" (Savage 2020).

Six

CONCLUSION

Through an engagement with the Northwest Indian War, I have argued in this book that early US foreign policy was constituted in part by relations with Native American groups, that understanding these relations can thus help us understand US foreign policy, and that attending to these relations illuminates the ongoing processes by which America's conquest of Native lands is legitimized. Chapter 2's examination of the origins of the war demonstrates the extent to which relations with Native American groups were constitutive of early US foreign policy, undermines narratives of early US isolationism, and demonstrate the influence of settlers in shaping American expansion through their activation of social ties to political elites. Moreover, as I discussed in Chapters 3 and 4, the extent to which the experience of the Northwest Indian War served as a model for the effective use of a network of military bases and for a sort of informal counterinsurgency doctrine helps to demonstrate how relations with Native Americans informed—and continues to inform—important practices and debates in the conduct of US foreign policy. Finally, Chapter 5's engagement with recent commemorations of the Northwest Indian War and local political debate on this topic demonstrate one important way in which American conquest of Native lands continues to be legitimized. In short, the Northwest Indian War lingers today in debates about how we ought to think about the United States itself, its relations with Native American groups, and its role in the world.

In this concluding chapter, I suggest avenues for future research with a particular focus on work being done to bring Indigenous experiences into IR. Here I also consider what the future might hold in US relations with Native American groups, and I ultimately argue that different potential futures deserve more scholarly engagement from political scientists who might make any given future more or less likely.

DIRECTIONS FOR FUTURE RESEARCH

Political scientists across subfields still often overlook Native American groups as political actors (Ferguson 2016). While one can find the occasional article to demonstrate that Native American groups have not been completely ignored by political scientists generally or IR scholars specifically, it is relatively new to see a burgeoning literature within political science that takes Indigenous experiences seriously and that receives attention in mainstream rather than marginal venues.[1]

I have already made the case that Indigenous experiences can and should be studied as IR where there is something plausibly "international" happening. Given how little there is examining settler–Native relations as IR, there is surely much more work to be done (but see Mowatt et al. 2024 for emerging trends in this space). In the remainder of this section, I discuss a number of issues relevant to IR scholars in which Indigenous experiences could indeed provide useful experiences with which to make sense of international political phenomena. First, however, I outline a brief vignette that serves to provide an example of the experiences that scholars might examine. This vignette moves us from the late eighteenth century and into the early nineteenth century to focus on Tecumseh's War (1810 to 1813), but it keeps our focus on the Old Northwest. Indeed, Tecumseh was a Shawnee leader who had fought in the Northwest Indian War as a young man and who had engaged in some of the pre-war violence that ultimately led to US military intervention. After providing this vignette, I discuss two issue areas within IR that this conflict might illuminate. I then turn to two broader issues on which further research is warranted.

In Tecumseh's War, a division emerged among the tribes of the Northwest Territory (which by then had been broken into smaller states, including Ohio, and territories, such as Indiana and Michigan). Some felt that security could best be attained by accommodating US settlers and adopting some of their cultural practices. Others, including Tecumseh's brother, Tenskwatawa, began to articulate anti-assimilationist arguments focusing especially on the preservation of Native religious practices (Saler 2015, 79–81). Tecumseh, who had fought at the stinging loss of the Battle of Fallen Timbers, sided with Tenskwatawa. While other nearby groups began to sell lands or otherwise provide US persons with settlement rights, Tecumseh sought to craft alliances, especially with members of tribes that had fought against the United States in the Northwest Indian War. Constructing an effective coalition in such conditions was perhaps an impossible task—the choices facing Native Americans were existential and were ultimately not going to be answered in the same way by all Native individuals or groups. The eventual military confrontation would cost Tecumseh his life, and the loose confederation he built would not survive his loss. If there remained any hope of effective Native resistance to US expansion after the Northwest Indian War, the failure of Tecumseh's War dashed such hopes and led tribes of the Old Northwest to more readily accept US territorial demands.

At least two directions for future research emerge from a consideration of Tecumseh's War. First, this is a case of alliance building and failures thereof. Tecumseh and his brother crafted a modest coalition, but they were unable to get much support from other tribes. Surely, there were obstacles to such alliance formation, such as historical rivalries and technological limits on individual tribes' abilities to assess the capabilities and intentions of an expanding United States. But given what would seem to be a clear and existential threat, more research is warranted on alliance formation in this crucial period for Native nations. Why did some choose to offer military resistance to US expansion while others did not? How did Native nations assess the threat presented by the United States? Were some of Tecumseh's rhetorical appeals to potential allies more effective than others? Examining such questions could yield novel insights into debates about the conditions that yield different alliance patterns in world politics.[2]

Second, it is separately worth noting that the impetus for Tecumseh's War came when Tecumseh's brother, who became widely known as the Prophet, initiated a religious movement premised in part on an anti-assimilationist view toward the United States. Balancing and bandwagoning in modern IR literature tends to focus on military aspects of such practices (Parent and Rosato 2015). But when we survey the historical record for such instances, we should perhaps be looking beyond specifically military actions and toward prophecies, conversions, and the like—toward religious symbols and their role in world politics (Henne 2023; Nexon 2011). Religious movements such as the Prophet's were often seen as a threat by the United States.[3] On the other hand, promises to convert to one form or another of Christianity often sufficed to assuage policymakers of any such concerns and even to win alliances, both with the United States and with earlier colonial powers such as Spain. Indeed, Apaches swore to join Spanish missions if the Spaniards would help to defend them against Comanches (Hämäläinen 2008, 36). In short, US relations with Native American groups—and Indigenous experiences more broadly—could likely teach us much about the ways that actors use religion in international politics as, among other things, a source of symbols with which to signal one's intentions.

Third, to depart from the Indian Wars and speak more generally about US relations with Native American groups, securitization theory might benefit from engagement with settler–Native interactions. For early US political elites, Indian Affairs was considered to be a foreign policy issue of paramount importance; Tecumseh's War offered a hint of their worst-case scenario insofar as they worried about a broader-reaching, genuinely pan-Indian resistance movement. By the late 1840s, however, the policymaking apparatus for this issue area was transferred from the Department of War to the newly created Department of the Interior, and Indian Affairs is typically discussed today as a domestic issue. I have already argued elsewhere that this slow process of "domesticating" Indian Affairs contributed to the "desecuritization" of this issue area (Szarejko 2022).[4] Further study is warranted, however, on the processes by which such domesticity is disrupted. Scholars have examined, for example, Indigenous activism that is meant to disrupt existing patterns of oppression, but what is necessary is more comparative research that could help demonstrate what actions are more or less effective at doing so. Laura Evans (2011) offers an exemplar on which other scholars might build in considering different methods by which Native American groups carve out space for themselves in the US political system.

Fourth and finally, as suggested in my discussion of local politics in Fort Wayne, to the extent that political science engages with Indigenous politics today, there is much work that valorizes Indigenous resistance to settlers, but the potential for settler backlash is an important dynamic that merits further attention. That is, if it is worth examining how Indigenous groups might disrupt the status quo, it is also worth considering how others seek to reinscribe the status quo. This sort of "backlash politics" has been observed in other domains—often in racialized, gendered forms—and scholars ought to consider the conditions that make a settler backlash against Indigenous rights claims more or less likely (Alter and Zürn 2020).[5] The likelihood of backlash to "policy gains by marginalized groups" may be overstated, but further research is necessary to understand whether that is the case in Indigenous politics (Bishin et al. 2016). On the other hand, even when such policies do not trigger any backlash, apparent policy gains may not produce the intended liberatory effects (Bauer 2021).

VISIONS OF POTENTIAL FUTURES

There are surely many fruitful avenues for research at the intersection of international relations and Indigenous politics, but one of the more pressing practical questions one might ask of this book is what the future looks like for relations between Native American groups and the US government. Beyond that, if there are multiple potential futures, what conditions or actions make it more or less likely that one or another might be realized?

When IR scholars consider potential futures in world politics, key points of debate are often about the long-term durability of the state as a political form and the expected frequency of violent conflict. Here the question of the state is more relevant. Are we heading toward a future of less state-centric sovereignty that allows for more genuine self-determination of Indigenous peoples? Those who focus on Indigenous activism often position their subjects as presaging exactly such a post-Westphalian future (Lightfoot 2021).[6] Across political science, moreover, scholars approaching the field from various perspectives see the dominance of the state being slowly overturned by a variety of private, corporate, nongovernmental, and intergovernmental actors (see, e.g., El Amine 2023; Spalińska 2022).

On the other hand, we might be heading toward a hardening of state sovereignty—one that would provide Indigenous peoples with less room to maneuver than they might like. In general terms, this would be a world of more tightly regulated borders, less delegation of state authority to non-state actors, and fewer practices that even tacitly suggest that the state does not maintain complete sovereignty within its claimed territory (such as the aforementioned passport-related practices noted in Lightfoot 2021). This looks most like the sort of world that some of today's right-wing movements and autocracies seek—a world in which state sovereignty is vigorously protected and in which norms of non-interference prevent democracies from pursuing regime change or otherwise disrupting the status quo (Cooley and Nexon 2020). Whether we ultimately see a world of this sort or the less state-centric world imagined above thus depends partly on the nature of global competition between the United States, China, and those who align with these two states, but the resistance of the United States, Canada, Australia, and New Zealand to Indigenous rights claims to date cuts against any notion that democracies and autocracies are unambiguously "good" and "bad" for Indigenous rights.

The trajectory of state sovereignty, moreover, will be shaped by action at the domestic level. In the United States, for example, the question of whether to allow tribes more or less freedom of action may become more or less politicized over time, and this will have consequences for tribal governments. Ned Blackhawk's (2023) overview of the history of federal Indian policy, for example, suggests that policy in this domain oscillates between more restrictive and more permissive environments for Native American groups, and we may be trending toward a more restrictive environment. As suggested in Chapter 5, partisan polarization may be a decisive factor at the domestic level, and if Indian Affairs is becoming more politicized—in part by becoming racialized—we are likely to see significant swings in policy as the parties trade wins and losses in elections.[7]

If the future of Native American relations with the US government depends on political action—explicitly partisan or otherwise—an important question is what will make any given policy proposal more or less likely to succeed. The extent to which tribal interests align with the interests of non-Native Republicans and Democrats will be perhaps the key factor, but there is little that tribes can do to change those interests (Evans 2023). At least one thing that tribes can control, however, is their messaging, and that might make a difference. As David Temin and Adam Dahl (2017) argue, different ways of narrating Native history might predispose listeners to react in different ways. For example, a tragic narrative—one in which Native Americans were sadly fated to be displaced by European settlers—lends itself to a fatalistic reaction. Similarly, a romantic narrative—one in which "we" wronged Native Americans in the past but have since heroically atoned for past sins in some way—is exculpatory. By contrast, they offer a reading of Vine Deloria, Jr.'s *Custer Died for Your Sins: An Indian Manifesto* (1969), which uses irony-laden satire to espouse a "politics of postcolonial responsibility" that "strikes a balance between making claims on the collective responsibility of settler nationhood and promoting native self-determination and indigenous agency in pursuit of decolonization" (Temin and Dahl 2017, 913). In their telling, situating Indigenous rights claims within such a narrative would perhaps be the best way to narrate Indigenous histories and to thereby push for "collective responsibility" in Indian Affairs.

This injunction—that one should be attentive to the political implications of the ways one talks about Indigenous histories—applies just as much to scholarly work. As political scientists and international relations scholars work to bring these histories more fully into our scholarship, it is incumbent on us to relay these histories in a way that does justice to the past while keeping ourselves intellectually open to the many possible Native futures.

NOTES

Chapter 1

1. The so-called Indian Wars, conflicts between the United States and various Native American groups, included roughly fifty conflicts between 1790 and 1890 substantial enough for the US government to refer to them as wars. For further discussion of the monetary and human costs of these conflicts and of their place in the study of conflict, see Szarejko (2021) and Urlacher (2021).

2. I thank an anonymous reviewer for suggestions that led to this formulation of the contributions I am making.

3. Mandelbaum (2022, 86) writes that, "Cooperation and coexistence ultimately failed because at the heart of the encounter between the two groups lay an irreconcilable conflict. The European settlers wanted land . . . at the expense of the Indians, whose way of life depended on unfettered access to that land, which the European settlers were bent on denying them." While conflict over land was indeed central to settler-Native conflict, I would maintain—drawing on Wendt (1992), Fearon (1995), and Fearon and Wendt (2002)—that most (if not all) conflicts are in principle reconcilable, that the presence of competing land claims did not necessitate any specific way of settling such disputes, and that interests (in land or otherwise) are neither fixed nor endogenous. That is, the fact of US conquest and the form it took was not "predetermined" but was instead the contingent product of myriad interactions and choices.

4. In describing interactions with Native American groups as constitutive of early US foreign policy, I draw on Wendt's (1998, 103) discussion of "constitutive" questions as being concerned with "how are things in the world put together so that

they have the properties that they do?" Here I am concerned with how US foreign policy was "put together" in ways that yielded and legitimized the conquest of Native American lands. For a similar argument, see Maass (2024) on the ways in which the "racialized processes" of "Native American removal and African slavery" shaped developing ideas of American exceptionalism.

5. As I discuss in Chapter 2, this process has received more attention from scholars of history and Indigenous studies, but as one might expect, this work has not always engaged with debates especially relevant to IR (international relations) scholars.

6. As I detail in the rest of this section and at greater length in the next chapter, an approach couched in relational theory helps to decenter political elites and to frame the making of US foreign policy as an ongoing process rather than a discrete thing to which we can attribute essential characteristics. On the state, see Vergerio (2021) on the extent to which the state would only "triumph" over other modes of political organization in the latter half of the twentieth century.

7. As Beier (2005, 15) notes, "[T]he simple fact of our neglect of Indigenous peoples reflects an enduring deference to one of the most fundamental notions of settler states colonialism: the idea that Indigenous peoples do not constitute authentic political communities. By way of their omissions as much as their claims, scholars of International Relations, like those working in other disciplines, unwittingly participate in the (re)production of the enabling narratives of advanced colonialism."

8. While legal regimes vary across states, I would generally say the same of relations between other Indigenous peoples and the states in which they reside.

9. I am not the first to make this scholarly move, but I approach this goal in ways that differ from, e.g., Beier (2005) and Lightfoot (2016). While Beier and Lightfoot aim to show how Indigenous beliefs and activist practices show the limits of traditionally state-centric theories of IR, I focus more on what US relations with Native American groups can tell us about the historical and ongoing practice of US foreign policy.

10. Drawing on Hacking (1999, 6–7), I take the same position in Szarejko (2022)—that "the existence or character of *X*," in this case relations between Native American groups and the US government, "is not determined by the nature of things."

11. For one reason or another—whether, e.g., the seemingly abstract nature of foreign policy when compared to pocketbook issues or the extent of executive powers in foreign policy—public opinion is widely believed to have less weight in the calculations of policymakers in foreign policy than it does in other issue areas. See, e.g., Baum and Potter (2015, 2), who summarize the conventional wisdom as follows: "Nowhere is the gap between elected representatives and the public larger than in the 'high politics' of international affairs, particularly in matters of war and peace."

12. As suggested above, I would maintain the non-inevitability of conflict between the United States and Native American tribes even if it was highly likely given conditions at the time. For such an argument, see Morrissey (2015, 10), whose depic-

tion of French collaboration with the Illinois nation speaks to the possibility of "informed, purposeful collaboration" between settler and Indigenous members of an "intercultural community."

13. The relational sociology on which this builds is most often identified with Emirbayer's (1997) programmatic statement. Emirbayer, who taught at the New School in the late 1990s and early 2000s, has come to be identified with the New York School of relationalism alongside others at Columbia University (where Charles Tilly and Harrison White taught and where Ann Mische, after receiving her PhD at the New School, managed the Workgroup on Networks, Culture, and Social Dynamics). On this intellectual history, see Jackson and Nexon (2019). Whether relationalism ought to be labeled a "constructivist" approach is debated (McCourt 2022).

14. See also Abbott (2016). To the extent that my arguments focus on social ties, this ought not to be taken as a broader privileging of social or ideational factors as the decisive variables in world politics, nor am I seeking to make nomothetic (i.e., law-like) generalizations about causal relationships. As I detail further below, this skepticism of nomothetic generalization about the social world might be taken to put this book in a more critical disciplinary space—critical as in possessing emancipatory intent—but I see my purpose here as being explanatory. Much work that focuses on Indigenous polities does come from a more critical standpoint and often draws on the language of decoloniality, in which the goal of scholarship is to "advance the undoing of Eurocentrism's totalizing claim and frame" and to thereby create "paths and praxis" beyond the "colonial matrix of power" and "toward an otherwise of thinking, sensing, believing, doing, and living" (Mignolo and Walsh 2018, 2, 4). That my argument is oriented toward explanation rather than a more critical crafting of a decolonized future ought not to be taken as a dismissal of the value of such arguments. Rather, drawing on Sondarjee's (2022) conceptualization of feminist IR as an inclusive "community of practice" with "mainstream" and "critical" scholars, I would argue for a similar view of those doing work in IR on Indigenous politics (though I would hesitate to adopt the mainstream label given the extent to which my work is positioned as a corrective to much work I would think of as mainstream US foreign policy research).

15. Following Jackson (2011, 34), I use the term "ontological wager" rather than something with a more definitive connotation to indicate the uncertainty inherent in any such effort to make sense of the world. See also Nordin et al. (2019, 573): "[R]ather than a single coherent theory, 'relational theorizing' here denotes a set of approaches united by a broad sensibility that foregrounds concrete connections and ties, and their different functions, rather than individual characteristics or general categories."

16. See Hafner-Burton, Kahler, and Montgomery (2009, 568–572) for an overview of this previous research. Among the four empirical chapters here, Chapter 2 is most directly situated in the context of network analytic literature. The most salient examples thereof for my purposes are MacDonald (2014) and Grynaviski (2018).

17. McNamee (2023, 4) uses the terms "colonialism" and "settler colonialism" interchangeably to refer to "a process of state building involving the displacement of indigenous peoples by settlers," a definition that suffices for my purposes as well. As a concept, "settler colonialism" is often associated with Wolfe (1999, 2), whose formulation thereof as "a structure, not an event" aligns with a processual-relational approach, but Wolfe uses this topic to enter debates in anthropology that are not my concern here.

18. See, e.g., Jackson (2003, 224) on "rhetorical commonplaces."

19. Jackson (2011, 147–148) distinguishes this from "the causal logic at the core of regression analysis: take an event, decompose it into causal factors by expressing it as a function of some set of independent variables, and then—by examining multiple cases—estimate the coefficients for each independent variable, with each coefficient capturing the independent impact that the particular causal factor has on the outcome."

20. This chapter is also a response to calls within political science for more emphasis on the task of description. See, e.g., Gerring (2012, 722), in which description "aims to answer *what* questions (e.g., *when, whom, out of what, in what manner*)," and Holmes et al. (2024, 54), in which, at its best, description can help to "develop concepts, manage and leverage data, speak to policy makers and the public, and challenge inherited biases."

21. From anthropology (and similar work in political science), I draw on Geertz's (1973, 311) notion that "man is an animal suspended in webs of significance he himself has spun," the analysis thereof being "an interpretive one in search of meaning." In describing the various ways that associates of the General "Mad" Anthony Wayne Organization articulate their reasons for celebrating Wayne, I am indeed seeking their meaning. As I discuss at greater length in Chapter 5, my approach there is also informed by work in game studies that is similarly ethnographic and situated in online spaces.

22. While I use Kupchan's definition of isolationism here, I believe my argument against conceptualizing early US grand strategy as isolationist would hold even given another reasonable definition. See, e.g., Holsti (2006, 274): "*Isolationism* refers to policies that seek to limit or reduce the country's international engagements to the extent that it is possible to do so" (emphasis in original). By contrast, Narizny (2007, 11) seeks a definition of isolationism that could potentially be applied outside the American context, and he defines it as "a strategy of inactivity in which the executive decision maker chooses not to devote resources to expanding and protecting the influence of the state outside of its borders." Braumoeller (2010, 354) takes a similar approach in defining isolationism "as the voluntary and general abstention by a state from security-related activity in an area of the international system in which it is capable of action."

23. Maass's critique here is aimed primarily at the Wisconsin School of diplomatic history (2020, 219, n. 64, 65). Both Maass (2020, 10–11) and Grynaviski (2018, 282) draw on Doyle (1986) in discussing empire.

24. This sort of argument is relatively common in the historiography of American expansion. See, e.g., Weinberg (1935, 454): "Expansionism, seemingly a reaching toward the outside world, really was long a major expression of isolationism. Almost from the beginning the Americans adopted expansion as a means of freeing the United States from the entanglements threatened by European neighborhood."

25. The phrase "savage tribes" is Alexander Hamilton's from *Federalist* No. 24.

26. Historians have noted the need for caution in delineating the domestic and the foreign in early US history. Weeks (2013, xx), for example, offers a broad statement to this effect: "More generally it can be said that the boundary between the 'domestic' and the 'foreign' is itself an evolving, semipermeable barrier with political, economic, and psychological components."

27. Indeed, US expansion is often assessed with reference to the proliferation of US military posts and government-subsidized transportation and communication infrastructure across the continent. See, e.g., Sparrow (2018/2019) and Adler (2021).

28. One might argue that what I have depicted as "enduring strategic commitments" were not strategic commitments as Kupchan would define them insofar as they were not lasting military alliances. However, Kupchan (2020, 31) seems to acknowledge that expansion—the acquisition of new territory and its incorporation into the polity—constitutes an enduring strategic commitment in its own right. "What the United States did not do—and what qualifies it as an isolationist nation par excellence—was take on enduring strategic commitments beyond its immediate neighborhood. Until 1898," he continues, "Americans repeatedly turned their backs on opportunities to expand beyond North America." Alternatively, one might argue that these commitments were more incidental than part of a self-consciously expansive grand strategy. Kupchan (2020, 136–137) notes of the US acquisition of the Midway Atoll, for example, that the island "ended up in U.S. hands more by accident than by design" when an American ship's captain "obtained the island for the United States under the Guano Islands Act of 1856." But to treat this acquisition as an accident is to overlook the fact that the federal government had already provided a legal framework for such acquisitions to ease the process of expansion, a process that led to many other such acquisitions in the Pacific and in the Caribbean.

29. See also Immerwahr (2019), for whom the "guano islands" constitute an important part of his case for discussing the United States as an empire.

30. I am not convinced that we need an alternative metanarrative that can encapsulate US foreign policy in one word. In an analogous debate about the origins of sovereignty and the modern state, scholars have moved past the metanarrative of the 1648 Peace of Westphalia as denoting the supposed origins thereof without coalescing around a similarly tidy alternative metanarrative, and that is perhaps simply because the historical record does not present one. See De Carvalho et al. (2011) and Vergerio (2021).

31. I prefer the term "domination" to "dominance" here insofar as it suggests an ongoing, active effort to retain one's superordinate status in relations to others

rather than a more static situation. As noted above, I am not otherwise interested in trying to craft a simplifying label such as isolationist or internationalist for early US foreign policy.

32. Saler (2015, 43) uses the term "intertribal" rather than "multiethnic" to describe such communities, and beyond the Shawnee and Miami to which I give the most attention here, Saler lists Wea, Piankashaw, Kickapoo, Mascouten, Delaware, Munsee, Ottawa, Ojibwe, and Abenaki peoples as those who settled in the Old Northwest. (Some of these groups, as noted below, are considered bands of a broader Miami people.) Saler also notes—as suggested above—that at least some members from the six Iroquois nations remained in the area.

33. The war is named for Pontiac, a leader of the Ottawa (or Odawa) people, an Algonquian group that resided primarily in the Great Lakes region at the time, in modern-day Michigan and Ontario, though there is ongoing debate about just how large a role Pontiac played in inspiring the war effort.

34. Posited start and end dates for this conflict vary, but it is widely agreed to have been comprised of intermittent conflict lasting nearly the entirety of the seventeenth century.

Chapter 2

1. Today, Filson is perhaps best known through the Filson Historical Society, a private organization based in Louisville, Kentucky, that was founded in 1884—on the centenary of the publication of *The Discovery, Settlement, and Present State of Kentucke.* Among other things, the society publishes a peer-reviewed journal, *Ohio Valley History.*

2. Questions of whether the so-called frontier fostered and/or attracted those with a sense of "rugged individualism" are tangential to my own inquiry, but as this anecdote suggests, settlers often sought and received federal assistance in ways that complicate any such narrative. For an economistic argument to the effect that the frontier did indeed have such effects, see Bazzi et al. (2020), but I would note my skepticism of the proxy measure of "rugged individualism" that relies on "individualistic" names. For research that instead emphasizes the dependence of settlers on the state, see Rockwell (2010). I lean more toward the latter than the former, but I do not think these ideas are mutually exclusive—the frontier might have attracted or fostered a rugged individualism even as those rugged individuals frequently turned to the state for assistance in ways that belied their self-presentation, and the belief that one is characterized by rugged individualism might have effects of its own even if behavior belies the belief. I posit no particular causal effect of "rugged individualism" here.

3. DuVal (2006, 11) makes a similar argument with respect to the ways that American settlers resisted incorporation into Indigenous political networks: "They came seeking individual and family independence, but it was their ties to the East that granted them the military and economic power to reject the earlier patterns of cross-cultural relationships."

4. I use the term "political elites" to refer generally to officeholders at the local, state, and/or federal level, but I am most often focused on federal officeholders here.

5. My argument here is similar to those that argue for the non-automaticity of other such political phenomena like democratization (Carothers 2002). More relevant to IR scholars are long-running debates about how balancing occurs (Schweller 2004; Waltz 1979). For example, see Parent and Rosato (2015, 56) for an argument that balancing, defined as "a state's efforts to amass military might so as to deter another's aggression or prevail in a conflict should deterrence fail," is generally prompt and focused on the "internal" generation of military capabilities rather than the "external" formation of alliances. Even there, however, balancing is not automatic (Parent and Rosato 2015, 53):

> Great powers have routinely engaged in internal balancing since 1816, arming and imitating the successful military practices of others to counter the capabilities of their rivals. In approximately 80 percent of the cases we examined, they achieved an effective balance in military capabilities with relevant competitors and promptly copied the major military innovations of the period (the Prussian system, battlefleet warfare, blitzkrieg, carrier warfare, strategic bombing, and nuclear weapons).

6. For an interesting case in which settlers engaged in conflict with Native American groups but did not request federal assistance, consider the members of the Church of Jesus Christ of Latter-day Saints who settled in Utah and who were often unwilling to request federal assistance given federal hostility to this heterodox religious movement (Peterson 1998).

7. Thus, while it may seem clear in hindsight that the United States "faced virtually no opposition" to its expansion and eventual attainment of "regional hegemony" (Elman 2004, 563), political elites certainly feared the potential opposition from Native nations, European powers, secessionist movements, and alliances between such groups.

8. My view of intentions is closer to Goddard (2018b) and Edelstein (2017) than to Mearsheimer (2001) and Rosato (2021), the former being more optimistic about the abilities of polities to probabilistically assess the intentions of other polities.

9. In a fine study of expansionist foreign policies, for example, Anderson (2022/2023, 137), makes a distinction between "centrally driven 'strategic expansion' and peripherally driven 'inadvertent expansion,'" the latter of which, he argues, characterized US expansion into at least Florida and Texas. In a manner similar to my emphasis on settlers in the initiation of the Northwest Indian War, Anderson makes the case that settlers pushed policymakers to expand into areas where they would not otherwise have done so. While I agree on the importance of settlers in shaping early US foreign policy, I am less inclined to describe US expansion as "inadvertent" for reasons I describe throughout this chapter. That is, in many such cases (as in the Northwest Indian War), it is not so much that settlers directed fed-

eral officials to acquire territory they did not already want to acquire; rather, settlers pushed federal officials to commit to territorial acquisition sooner and by different means than the officials wanted.

10. Expansion, however, was not an end in itself. "American leaders" of the time "had different visions of future economic growth—the Federalists anticipating the emergence of domestic industry while Republicans looked to agriculture and trade—but all conceptions presupposed the westward movement of population and a widening scope for domestic commerce as well as international trade" (Adler 2021, 8).

11. I thank an anonymous reviewer for this point.

12. IR scholars have paid increasing attention to race and processes of racialization in world politics in recent years. Within IR, this is an area of inquiry in which much of the most prominent early work is of a critical theoretical sort. My reading of ongoing trends in the discipline is that the increasing attention to race in recent years has been driven largely by increased attention in positivist scholarship. For overviews of more critical and positivistic clusters in this literature, see, e.g., Barder (2017) and Freeman (2024).

13. The origins of "red" as a descriptor for Native Americans is unclear; as Shoemaker (1997) notes, there is some reason to believe that the term may have originated with Native tribes either as a self-description, as a description of other tribes, or as a kind of response to settler descriptions of "white" and "black" populations. Whatever the origins, as she notes, settlers would nonetheless use the term pejoratively.

14. As Maass (2023, 96) argues, IR scholars should perhaps focus less on "race" per se and more on "racialization," "the processes that infuse social and political phenomena with racial identities and implications."

15. For general sources on the balance between elite desires to expand and to avoid militarized conflict with Native Nations in particular, see, e.g., Banner (2005, 26–29, 114–115), Rockwell (2010, 23–25), and Guyatt (2016, 48–60).

16. Similar concerns arose in the Revolutionary War and were sustained for as long as European powers retained claims on the North American continent: "Indians who were not accorded the respect to which they believed they were entitled did not fight as allies and were likely to appear in battle on the other side of the line" (Deloria and Wilkins 1999, 6).

17. On the costs of war, the conventional wisdom in IR is best represented by Fearon's (1995) argument to the effect that rational policymakers should try to avoid war given the costs it always imposes beyond what one would incur in a negotiated settlement.

18. Here Stephanson (1995) is not making an argument that purchase was indeed "morally correct" but was seen by policymakers as the "morally correct" way to expand. I take a similarly agnostic view here as to whether there was any such way for the United States to acquire Native territory, and I suggest that purchase may well have been the "preferred . . . way of expansion" prior to 1803.

19. The Spanish–American War is often treated as an especially important point in US foreign policy. As discussed in Chapter 1, some see the war as marking a transition from isolationism to internationalism or imperialism (see, e.g., Kupchan 2020). For others, it clarifies a consistent impulse toward expansion in US foreign policy—it was simply going from continental to overseas expansion (see, e.g., LaFeber 1989). As I discuss below, my interpretation of the Spanish–American War is closer to the latter interpretation, though Maass's (2020) examination of the domestic politics of US expansion cautions against a portrayal of the United States as unrelentingly expansionist (the sort of portrayal one might assume based on Mearsheimer [2001]).

20. See also Prucha (2000, 3, 7, 13). Because this Prucha volume is a reader, I cite document numbers rather than page numbers.

21. I cite Flint (1833, 8), a copy of which I first encountered at the Seminole Tribe of Florida's Ah-Tah-Thi-Ki Museum, for its early description of settler emigration patterns:

> In 1790 the population of this [Ohio] valley, exclusive of the country west of the Mississippi and of Florida, which were not then within our territorial limits, was estimated by enumeration, at little more than one hundred thousand. In 1800 it was something short of three hundred and eighty thousand. In 1810 it was short of one million. In 1820, including the population west of the Mississippi, rating the population of Florida at twenty thousand, and that of the parts of Virginia and Pennsylvania included in this valley at three hundred thousand. The present population may be rated at four millions.

22. See the description of the Indian Wars in the United States Census Bureau (1890).

23. On matters of war, presidents were quite powerful vis-à-vis Congress in the early republic (Adler 2013). I thus emphasize presidents and their appointees here.

24. If a relational approach can draw our attention to networks, those networks present opportunity structures that channel behavior in different directions, and the most salient features of the opportunity structure facing settlers in the 1780s were the availability of relatively cheap land and the size and distribution of the early US military. Given that available land was sufficiently desirable to drive a massive settler movement, I focus more here on the character of the early US military.

25. Whether those ideas were the product of constrained material circumstances is a question I cannot answer here.

26. Here "the public lands" refers to those lands claimed by both the United States and Native nations.

27. The respective quotes come from his third and sixth annual addresses to Congress (Washington 1791, 1794).

28. For more detail on one such congressional authorization of expenditures

related to "promoting a friendly intercourse, and preserving peace with the Indian tribes," see United States Congress (1790, 2241).

29. Relevant archival documents available from the Indiana Historical Society are as follows: Josiah Harmar to Henry Knox, June 1, 1785, in SCP, 6–7; Henry Knox to Josiah Harmar, May 12, 1786, #38, vol. 3, JHP; Josiah Harmar to Henry Knox, August 4, 1786, Harmar Papers, pp. 144–145, Letterbook A, vol. 28, JHP. The documents are available upon request from the Indian Historical Society.

30. The first United States Congress reaffirmed the ordinance in 1789.

31. By contrast, throughout the Revolutionary War, Britain encouraged some of the worst violence between settlers and Native American groups that the region had seen to that point. Moreover, it continued to do so even after the Treaty of Paris ended the Revolutionary War (Hurt 1996; Sword 1985, 98–99).

32. I first accessed the report by O'Malley cited here at the Shawnee Tribe Cultural Center in June 2019.

33. See also the discussion of Lockean ideals above.

34. The quotation is an excerpt from Genesis 1:28 in the King James Version of the Bible.

35. Ostler notes that the settler population of Kentucky grew from 12,000 in 1783 to 74,000 in 1790, and other frontier territories saw similar growth in the same time period.

36. As Gailmard (2024, 14) notes, the early American political system built on the legacy of British colonial institutions, and this favored property-holders, land speculators included.

37. Note that this is not the same entity as the Ohio Company, which was organized primarily by wealthy Virginians under the British Crown in the mid-1700s (Saler 2015, 52–55).

38. In describing the purchase in question, a delegate of the Confederation Congress, Nathan Dane of Massachusetts (quoted in Hall 1905, 497), noted that, "If the lands can be immediately purchased on the terms the Company propose, we have the fullest assurance that the subscription for one million dollars well be completed in a short time. Many of the subscribers are men of very considerable property, who intend to become residents of that country." Some of the land being purchased was meant for immediate settlement; some of the land was meant for speculative purposes. Manasseh Cutler, a minister who had served as an occasional military chaplain during the Revolutionary War and who worked with Parsons on this new venture, noted in correspondence that their purchase would be amenable to "private speculation in which many of the principal characters of America are concerned" (Hall 1905, 509).

39. Interview with author, May 31, 2019. I received approval from the Georgetown University Institutional Review Board (IRB study number: 2018–0630) to make audio recordings of interviews with tribal citizens that I arranged through the Shawnee Tribe Cultural Center. While I did interview others for their perspectives on the

onset of the war, Barnes is the only interviewee I find it necessary to cite here. Five other interviewees were largely in agreement that settlers and speculators were to blame for the war and helped me determine whether my proposed explanation for the war had face validity in their eyes.

40. As McNamee (2023, 10–11) puts it, "American officials, facing a relentless emigration to the backcountry, feared that without any formal incorporation settlers would soon found independent republics." He then quotes a letter from George Washington to Henry Lee, the president of the Confederation Congress, in which Washington evinces a concern that, "People have got impatient and, though you cannot stop the road it is yet in your power to mark the way; a little while later and you will not be able to do either."

41. As Grynaviski (2018) shows, for example, the presence of an intermediary with substantive ties to both US and Native American communities often facilitated cooperation.

42. As Grenier (2005, 194) puts it, "The government's conciliatory messages to the Indians—diluted by settlers' murders of peaceful Indians and attacks on Indian villages—had failed miserably."

43. Indeed, as McNamee (2023, 34–35) notes, a common issue in settler-driven colonization is that it is not clear if the metropole has the ability to contain settlement even if it wants to do so. Tribes of the Ohio River Valley, for instance, might have thought that federal officials had good intentions but lacked the ability to realize their goals.

44. Congress did not declare war. Rather, "President Washington allowed Secretary of War Henry Knox to order Josiah Harmar to begin a 'punitive expedition' against the Indians, a federal response to the raids of approximately 200 'renegade' Indian warriors," and he justified this decision to Congress in a December 1790 address arguing that Native "provocations rendered it essential to the safety of the Western settlements, that the aggressors should be made sensible that the Government is not less capable of punishing their crimes, than it is disposed to respect their rights and reward their attachments" (Mendel 2016, 1321, 1333).

45. One exchange of speeches between US and Native officials is recorded in George Washington's papers. See Putnam et al. (1792).

46. As noted in the report itself, Knox wrote in response to a January 16, 1792, request by President Washington that he "prepare and publish, from authentic documents, a statement of those circumstances [that led to the war], as well as of the measures which have been taken, from time to time, for the re-establishment of peace and friendship."

47. In recent years, advocates of restraint or retrenchment have been particularly vocal in arguing that US foreign policy has become dangerously detached from public sentiments; these critics are essentially testing one plausible theory of change now: that a more restrained, less militarized foreign policy can be articulated and perhaps eventually implemented by vigorously promoting such proposals in the

public sphere through a well-funded think tank, the Quincy Institute for Responsible Statecraft (Bender 2019). The institute is named for John Quincy Adams, whose famous statement that America "goes not abroad, in search of monsters to destroy" is now being used as an aspirational statement.

48 See, e.g., Anderson (2022/2023) on settlers and Evers and Grynaviski (2024) on entrepreneurs.

Chapter 3

1. More than that, Hamilton (1787) saw it as necessary to staff those garrisons with professionalized, federal military personnel rather than state or local militiamen, a controversial position at the time. As he stated in *Federalist* No. 24:

> These garrisons must either be furnished by occasional detachments from the militia, or by permanent corps in the pay of the government. . . . The latter resource of permanent corps in the pay of government amounts to a standing army in time of peace; a small one, indeed, but not the less real for being small. Here is a simple view of the subject, that shows us at once the impropriety of a constitutional interdiction of such establishments, and the necessity of leaving the matter to the discretion and prudence of the legislature.

2. I generally use the terms "base," "facility," "fortification," and "installation" interchangeably. Others have argued for a distinction among these terms; "base," for Harkavy (1989, 7–8):

> has come to define a situation in which the user nation (i.e., the foreign presence) has unrestricted access and freedom to operate. 'Facility,' meanwhile, has come to be the preferred term where the host nation exerts ultimate sovereignty and where the user nation's access is contingent, restricted and subject to ad hoc decisions about use in given situations.

3. Scholars associated with the Wisconsin School of American diplomatic history (Priest 2021, 5):

> used the terms *empire* and *imperialism* to describe the American trajectory from continental to extracontinental nation. . . . Wisconsin scholars counteracted the idea that the United States was an exceptional nation that had arisen largely because of the unusual circumstances in which the founders conceived it and the pathbreaking nature of its political settlement.

Rather than thinking of the United States as fundamentally different from "imperial" powers of the "Old World," scholars of the Wisconsin School therefore suggest that "the United States was an empire in how it imposed its will on territories and peoples—including with violence—regardless of whether they were part of the American continent or lived beyond its shores" (Priest 2021, 5). Scholars associated with the Wisconsin School often locate the source of this imperialism in economic incentives; see Schlesinger (1999, 128–148) for a critique of this position that instead frames this imperialism as driven by a desire for security. I am not concerned with settling that dispute here, but I would align myself with arguments to the effect that notions of American isolationism have been exaggerated (Braumoeller 2010), including arguments made by Wisconsin School scholars (Williams 1954). "[K]eeping out of the squabbles of the European Powers," as Morgenthau (1969, 116) puts it, was an indeed important aspect of early US foreign policy, but this treats US relations with Native nations as either trivial or as something other than "foreign" relations from the start. On the legal and bureaucratic evolution of these relations over time, see Deloria and Wilkins (1999) and Szarejko (2022).

4. The scope of any given study of US military basing practices might justifiably start in 1898, 1945, or in some other year. Kim's (2023) study of contestation over US military bases in South Korea and Japan, for example, would not have any data to consider from before 1945. My argument does not imply that all studies of US military basing need to start in 1783 or 1789. My argument is more limited: There is more continuity in the history of US military basing policy than is typically assumed, so studies of contemporary US military bases might draw more frequently on earlier basing histories.

5. Joyce and Blankenship (2024) similarly describe at least "foreign bases" as being oriented toward "power projection."

6. See, e.g., Blankenship and Lin-Greenberg (2022) on "tripwires."

7. The construction of forts in the Northwest Indian War was thus not a revolutionary military innovation, but it did offer US policymakers a sort of proof of concept in showing after early losses in the war that a sufficiently well-trained and well-resourced fighting force could effectively project power along an expanding frontier if it could rely on a robust basing network.

8. Much of the literature on anti-base protest movements focuses on overseas bases, but even domestic bases sometimes provoke backlash. Such protests are often couched in a broader anti-militarism or in the context of specific local grievances such as environmental degradation (see, e.g., Alfonseca and Carr 2022; Zak 2014). On the "politics of sight" more generally, see Pachirat (2011).

9. The extent to which military bases can become taken-for-granted objects in a given community, Enloe (1990, 67) argues, "rests on ideas about masculinity and femininity. A foreign base requires especially delicate adjustment of relations between men and women, for if the fit between local and foreign men and local and foreign women breaks down, the base may lose its protective cover."

10. US policymakers continue to work toward a global environment more conducive to the pursuit of perceived US interests, so this is not to say that the United States does not now have any revisionist objectives. I would argue, however, that we might conceptualize "revisionist" and "status quo" in ideal typical terms and place the United States closer to being a status quo power today than it was in 1783. Much of the research on revisionism today suggests that the United States is more of a

status quo power than the rising China that has prompted various typologies of revisionism aimed at explaining how China or others might try to revise the "liberal international order" and whether it is likely to succeed in doing so. See, e.g., Goddard (2018a), Cooley et al. (2019), and Kustermans et al. (2023).

11. The omitted portion of the text reads as follows (Allens et al. 2022, 10):

> The US gained control and access in perpetuity to its first permanent base in Guantánamo Bay, Cuba. The conclusion of the war with Spain also brought the Philippines, Guam, and Puerto Rico under US control. However, the US base in Cuba proved unique in that the US only sought direct territorial possession of the base at Guantánamo Bay rather than the entire island.

12. Similarly, in explaining why overseas basing (or, "sovereign basing") expanded after World War II, Schmidt (2020, 4) writes that, "Two major developments in security politics threw the accepted relationship between military presence and territorial authority into question: the radically increased speed and scale of warfare and the emergence of the Cold War with its overtones of transnational ideological threat." Yeo and Pettyjohn (2021, 27) quote then-Assistant Secretary of Defense Frank Nash's 1957 rationale for the maintenance of "overseas" bases, which speaks to the perceived necessities of the Cold War:

> (a) to maintain a deterrent to general war by assuring our capability to deliver a strategic counteroffensive . . . ; (b) to assure that we can maintain tactical forces in being at or close to potential trouble spots . . . so that a potential aggressor knows that we are determined to assist indigenous forces in defending themselves . . . ; and (c) [to] promote US political objectives, giving tangible evidence of political solidarity with our friends and our intention to honor our various defense alliances.

13. Cooley (2008, 5) similarly describes the purposes of US military bases as follows:

> Overseas bases in countries such as Spain and Uzbekistan act as "force multipliers" and enable U.S. planners to rapidly project power both within and across regions. . . . Even when not used for combat purposes, bases are significant when they guarantee U.S. access to neighboring assets, territories, or resources that are of critical importance. Beyond their military roles and strategic functions, bases also provide service and repair facilities, storage, training facilities, and logistical staging posts. Bases can also be used to conduct surveillance, coordinate tasks, collect intelligence, and facilitate command, control, and communications (C3).

14. Ninety-eight, three, and fifteen installations in those respective categories were classified as large installations—that is, as having a total "plant replacement value" of at least $1.61 billion.

15. Downloadable copies of the reports are available at the following web address: https://www.basenation.us/bsr.html.

16. Debates on expansion of coastal fortifications continued for decades. The War of 1812 was particularly important in convincing political elites that more coastal fortifications could be useful. President James Madison established the Board of Engineers and Fortifications to study a more expansive system of coastal fortification that would remain manned during peacetime, the first report from which was produced in 1821 (Maslowski 1994, 227). As President James Monroe described the proposed fortifications in 1824, they would "retard the movement of the enemy into the country, and give time for the collection of our regular troops, militia, and volunteers" (quoted in Maslowski 1994, 214). The results of this program were mixed. "The board recommended fortifying fifty positions at a cost of almost $18,000,000. . . . The program went forward, but slowly and beset by difficulties; yet by the 1850s a substantial system was nearing completion, although the works remained inadequately armed and garrisoned" (Maslowski 1994, 228).

17. On this point, see also Weeks (1996, ix): "An expansionist consensus unified the nation and provided the ultimately rationale for its existence."

18. See Maulden (2016) on the desire to "awe" Native Americans into submission with the mere presence of the US military.

19. "As late as 1899, the Secretary of War referred to the army's 'police duty against Indians'" (Maslowski 1994, 212, n. 13).

20. Here Vine (2019) cites Lutz (2009, 10), from which the most relevant passage is:

> [T]he early U.S. military became entwined with the frontier project of removing Indians from the land and protecting colonists who settled there. In this sense, every Western fort—and there were 255 of them—was a foreign military base, established on native land during the Indian campaigns and the Mexican-American War.

Lutz (2009, 11), however, still creates an analytic separation between pre- and post-1898 periods of US foreign policy, and military bases are central in making this separation: "After consolidation of its continental dominance, there were three periods of global ambition in U.S. history beginning in 1898, 1945, and 2001, and each is associated with the acquisition of significant numbers of new overseas military bases."

21. Italics in original.

22. Harmar reported that between 1783 and his arrival at Fort McIntosh in early 1785, settlers had "destroyed the gates, drawn all the nails from the roofs, taken off all the boards, and plundered it of every article" (quoted in Prucha 1969, 7).

23. As noted in Chapter 2, Knox was conscious of the limited resources for a small military and therefore wrote to Washington in December of 1790 to make the case for concentrating settlements such that they would be easier to defend:

It will be our true wisdom to condense our population instead of dispersing it. Besides the expense of protecting such distant settlements greatly exceeds the value of them, whether considered as purchases of the land, as consumers of articles contributing to the revenue, or as constituting a strength of any real use to the empire.

24. While Harmar's losses had been blamed on undisciplined militiamen, St. Clair's loss was blamed more narrowly on the lack of time St. Clair had been given to organize and drill his troops.

25. Secretary of War Henry Knox seemed particularly intent on trying to negotiate a settlement at this point. "We shall always possess the power of rejecting all unreasonable propositions," he wrote to Wayne on January 5, 1793 (quoted in Prucha 1969, 33):

But the sentiments of the great mass of the Citizens of the United States are adverse in the extreme to an Indian War and although these sentiments would not be considered as sufficient cause for the Government to conclude an infamous peace, yet they are of such a nature as to render it adviseable to embrace every expedient which may honorably terminate the conflict.

26. This failure led some Native groups to abandon the coalition (Fernandes 2015, 175).

27. I thank an anonymous reviewer for suggesting further theoretical development on this point.

28. We might think similarly about naval fortifications that allowed for power projection while also providing a robust coastal defense.

29. As noted in Chapter 2 with reference to (dis)trust on the frontier, Grynaviski (2018) suggests that the presence of "middlemen"—individuals with strong ties to both American and Native societies who could act as mediators—was a moderating factor on the frontier, but there may well have been other components at work alongside countervailing, aggravating factors.

Chapter 4

1. Alfred Thayer Mahan became famous in the late nineteenth century in part by applying this same sort of thinking to naval warfare, and Mahan would become one of the most influential strategists of his day (Breemer 1994, 48).

2. Learning, as I discuss below, does not necessarily indicate that there was a correct, beneficial, or morally praiseworthy lesson to be learned.

3. I provide more detail on *habitus* below, but the concept comes from Bourdieu's (1990) work in sociology, and as Leander (2011) and Nair (2024) detail, the concept has been brought into international relations scholarship largely through variants of constructivist thought.

4. As Khong (1992) has shown, political leaders frequently rely on analogies to guide their actions in new situations even as analogies vary in their resonance

among groups of policymakers and advisors. Analogies, as he notes, can deceive just as easily as they can inform.

5. On the Dawes Act of 1887 and the often-disastrous ways in which it broke communally owned reservation lands into individualized plots of land—while making some former reservation land available to settlers—see Cotroneo and Dozier (1974).

6. Then-Secretary of War Elihu Root similarly drew on *Cherokee Nation v. Georgia* in a 1902 address justifying US policy in the Philippines. He anticipated a similar ruling that would legitimize American claims to the Philippines; "in the meantime the close general analogy to the relations of the North American Indians indicates a duty, for the present at least, of limited supervision and control" (quoted in Williams 1980, 829).

7. The political scientist in question is Harry Pratt Judson, who initially taught history at the University of Minnesota and later taught political science at the University of Chicago (of which he would become the second president in 1907).

8. These two quotes are attributed to Colonel Jacob Smith and General James Parker, respectively.

9. After serving in the Civil War, Merritt "had further distinguished himself campaigning against the Indians"; Otis "had served with distinction in the Civil War and in several Indian campaigns"; Chaffee was "a cavalryman and veteran of the Civil War, Indian campaigns, and Boxer Rebellion" (Linn 1989, 2, 10, 26). General Douglas MacArthur (1964, 12–13), Arthur's son, would later detail his father's experiences in the Indian Wars in his memoir: "He engaged in the Indian wars around Fort Rawlins in Utah Territory. He served at Fort Bridges and Camp Stanbough, at Fort Fred Steele and Camp Robinson in Wyoming Territory, where life was governed by the rifle and pistol. . . . He was present when General Sheridan met with the Indian chiefs in an effort to stop hostilities."

10. I use the term "Napoleonic" here in the sense that Biddle (2021, 12–13) uses it to describe one pole on a spectrum of military behavior. That is, Napoleonic military behavior is "a pure version of the popular intuition of 'conventional' war fighting" that stands in contrast with irregular (or "Fabian") war fighting. "The characteristics of pure *Napoleonic* methods," he continues,

> include an insistence on decisive engagement to defend or seize ground that will not be voluntarily relinquished; local concentration to shoulder-to-shoulder densities at a point of attack where ground is contested; use of uniformed forces on battlefields removed from urban population centers; exclusive reliance on brute force rather than coercion; and preferential employment of the heaviest weapons available to maximize firepower and armor protection.

11. The Indian Wars, as others have noted, also have more diffuse legacies in the practices of the US military. "Military personnel invoke symbols from the 'wild west' while deployed in 'Injun Country,' all the while, Tomahawk missiles and Apache helicopter gunships fly overhead" (Crane-Seeber 2011, 452).

12. We need not, however, assume that organizations possess the sort of consciousness that we would associate with individuals. Assumptions of metaphorical or literal organizational consciousness—as applied to states by, e.g., Lerner (2021), Mitzen (2006), and Steele (2008)—may be helpful in some contexts, but I do not believe any such assumptions are necessary here. That is, the notion of organizational learning need not be built on an anthropomorphized organization. We might instead see organizations not as conscious agents who learn in their own right but as systems constituted by individuals; these systems can change over time as their constitutive individuals change due to endogenous and/or exogenous processes—in line, as I see it, with traditions of systemic and relational theorizing. While I have discussed relational theory largely by way of Jackson and Nexon (1999) earlier in this book, I am here putting that alongside systemic theorizing that crosses theoretical and methodological divides—see, e.g., Waltz (1979), Wendt (1992), Jervis (1997), and Braumoeller (2012). Relational theory, I would argue, tends toward a focus on systems insofar as relationality of any kind takes place in (or perhaps creates) some broader system that is often of interest to individual researchers.

13. MacKay (2023) places a similar emphasis on formal doctrinal statements, especially military manuals, in his intellectual history of counterinsurgency.

14. One military officer-turned-theorist of the late nineteenth century, John Bigelow, Jr., provided intellectual support for such a policy in his 1891 text, *Principles of Strategy* (Gates 1973, 83), but this process of bringing noncombatant civilians onto one's side as an occupier is a more complicated process than simply offering a metaphorical carrot given the difficult of legitimizing foreign rule (Pampinella 2012). Miller (1982, 2) cites Gates (1973) in noting that some maintain or have tried to salvage a "patriotic interpretation" of the Philippine–American War in which "the Yankee presence was bloody initially" but ultimately "ephemeral and supposedly most beneficial to the Filipinos." The citation to Gates here should not be taken as an endorsement of his broader interpretation of war.

15. See Lyall (2010) on the use of "coethnics" as aids in counterinsurgency.

16. Such practices were applied in later Indian Wars as well. See, e.g., Ostler (2019, 161) and Wooster (2009, 159).

17. I emphasize US agency here in denying Filipinos a chance to govern themselves in part because early narratives of the war sometimes make it sound like the United States came to govern the Philippines by accident or against its will. Early work in the *American Political Science Review*—the flagship journal of the American Political Science Association—exhibits that trend. Story (1909, 30) writes that, "The close of the war with Spain in 1898 and the cession of the Philippines to the United States brought to this country a number of serious and difficult problems in the islands other than those immediately connected with the exercise of governmental control over them." Cunningham (1916, 465) writes that, "When the American government found itself in possession of the newly acquired portions of Spain's colonial empire, and particularly of the Philippines, it was forced to deal with many new and

hitherto unfamiliar problems." Finally, Jones (1924, 287) expresses that the fundamental problem allegedly facing the United States in 1898 was that the Filipinos did
not know how to govern themselves; thus, "The key to the local government policy
followed is that we tried to teach the Filipinos to run their local affairs, at the same
time that we were modifying the form of the local government so that they could
run it." At least some contemporaries had a higher opinion of Filipino capabilities:
"Without belittling what America has done for the Philippines, it must be recognized
that the progress towards democracy in the Philippines has been due mainly to the
materials that America found there" (Kalaw 1919, 416).

18. Such a gap in active hostilities is not unique. Indeed, this is similar to the
period in the Northwest Indian War after St. Clair's Defeat in 1791 during which
Anthony Wayne spent almost two years training a new federal force to defeat the
Native coalition; this was in part due to halting efforts at negotiations, but in many
such contexts, there is a "fighting season" that slows or pauses during the winter.

19. Here "European nations" are Young's own words as quoted by Linn (1989). The
subsequent quoted material is Linn's summary of Young's recommendations.

20. This amnesty did not have as significant an effect as MacArthur hoped; only
5,022 purported insurgents accepted the amnesty offer, and many of those individuals had already been captured or were not in areas of significant guerrilla activity
(Linn 1989, 22).

21. The remainder of this paragraph draws on the same source: Linn 1989, 42–43.

22. As Go (2024, 112) puts it, the US military employed such detachments in
conflicts with "the Sioux, Kiowa, Arapaho, Comanche, Cheyenne, and Apache" because of the necessity to "move columns through rugged terrain and operate deftly,
swiftly, and flexibly."

23. The final campaigns in the war were marked by a flurry of war crimes (which
is not to say that war crimes did not happen earlier in the war), including the use of
the "water cure" (a euphemistic term for the torture technique described above;
today's readers might know it as waterboarding). Brigadier General Jacob H. Smith,
then the commander of the Sixth Separate Brigade for example, oversaw one of the
final major campaigns in the war and provided orders that would later result in a
court-martial: "I want no prisoners. I wish you to kill and burn, the more you kill
and burn the better it will please me." For Smith, all Filipinos at or above "ten years
of age" were to be treated as a legitimate target (Miller 1982, 220). At Smith's court-
martial, however, he was tried not specifically for war crimes but for "conduct to the
prejudice of good order and military discipline," a charge of which he was found
guilty. To spare him any further punishment, however, Secretary of War Elihu Root
recommended that President Theodore Roosevelt order Smith's retirement. Roosevelt, who had taken office after McKinley's assassination in September 1901, accepted the recommendation (Miller 1982, 236–238, 255).

24. "Success in counterinsurgency," for Hazelton (2021, 1, 5) entails "defeating
armed, organized, persistent political challengers to the government," and this re-

quires both military and political measures, especially "alliance building" with local elites and the application of "brute force" to degrade the insurgency's capacity to acquire necessary resources and to fight. Notably, however, Hazelton (2021, 2) hastens to distinguish between analysis and prescription: "This book is not a prescription of counterinsurgent success. I do not advocate implementation of my findings." Rather, she suggests, the significant costs associated with successful counterinsurgency caution against such efforts. MacKay (2023, 36) similarly reads the intellectual history of counterinsurgency and arrives at a cautionary note: "even in the ashes of the global war on terror, the counterinsurgent imagination is still with us, shaping how great powers envision their capacity to remake the world in their own image, even as they often fail to do so."

25. Both Flyvbjerg (2001, 57) and Brown (2012) note that *phronesis* has no clearly analogous term in modern English in the way that *episteme* and *techne* do; prudence and practical wisdom are close to its meaning but require further elaboration. See Gould (2015) for a discussion of *phronesis* and the similar concept of *prudentia*.

26. As Brown (2012) argues, it is this sort of "prudence" that can be identified in the prescriptions of classical realists such as Hans Morgenthau. Nardin (1989, 212) does not use the language of *phronesis*, but he similarly divides realist ethics into two schools of thought—"moral realism" and "prudential realism"—in which either "there are moral reasons for [the leader's] departing from ordinary moral standards" or "public officials must sometimes act immorally if they are to protect the community." The place of *phronesis* in realist thought, however, is not my central concern here.

27. *Phronesis* has a moral quality for Aristotle: Good character is required to make the right choice, and consistently making the right choices improves one's character (Emery 2021, 17). Another definition describes *phronesis* as "a person's skill to deliberate about what, in concrete situations, will advance the common good" (Kustermans 2016, 184).

28. I am less concerned here with Aristotle's conception of *praxis* and the ways this has been used to analyze human "practices," a concept that, as Frost and Lechner (2016, 341–342) contend, Aristotle individualizes such that a more relational, rule-bound conception of practices ought to be used for the study of social practices, something that they argue can be found in Ludwig Wittgenstein's "language-games."

29. "In International Relations, and in social theory more generally," Kustermans (2016, 185–186) argues,

> practical knowledge has come to mean the ability to navigate a social milieu successfully, to secure one's position of power, to manage one's social image, or even to work the bureaucracy skillfully. . . . Practical knowledge hovers somewhere between tactical and strategic skill. It is prudence for modern man.

30. Discourse, which shapes *habitus*, has been defined in the context of IR scholarship as "the representation and constitution of the 'real'" (Campbell 1998, 6–7)

and as "framings of meaning and lenses of interpretation" (Hansen 2006, 7). For scholars who foreground discourse, "politics is the process through which identities are constructed, deconstructed, and reconstructed and through which discourses struggle against other discourses to achieve dominance," and narratives are a key vehicle through which discourse circulates (Krebs 2015, 9–15; Solomon 2015, 27).

31. Miller (1982, 179) quotes Private Samuel Hays as opposing the annexation of the Philippines because "we have negroes enough in the country without hunting more trouble," and he likewise quotes an unnamed Kansas veteran as stating to a reporter that, "The country [of the Philippines] won't be pacified until the n——s are killed off like the Indians." The omitted portion of the latter quotation indicates a racial slur in the original text. Silbey (2007, 62, 68) similarly quotes a California soldier as referring to Filipinos as "sassy n——s" and a Nebraska soldier as saying before the initiation of hostilities that, "If they would turn the boys loose, there wouldn't be a n—— left in Manila twelve hours after."

32. See Aune (2023, 18) on "civilized war" and "savage war."

33. As noted in Chapter 2, IR scholarship has paid increasing attention to race in recent years, and my own interpretation of the events I survey here is shaped by that literature. On counterinsurgency and race, see, e.g., Goddard and MacDonald (2023).

34. To the extent that any "lessons" of the Philippine–American War would be transmitted to future soldiers, Aune (2021, 442) argues, they would come primarily in the form of literature for children and adolescents, a format in which authors could easily elide the actual treatment of Filipinos in favor of sanitized, heroic narratives. Such popular cultural artifacts can indeed shape behavior. As Jutta Weldes (1999, 119) notes, "Popular culture . . . helps to construct the reality of international politics for officials and non-officials alike and, to the extent that it reproduces the content and structure of the dominant foreign policy discourse, it helps to produce consent for foreign policy and state action." Romantic narratives of the sort found in early children's and teen literature about the Philippine–American War often have a "politics of exculpation" that allows those telling the stories to deny or excuse any alleged wrongdoing (Temin and Dahl 2017, 909).

35. On civil-military relations in the United States, see Brooks (2020), which suggests that while civilian control of the military is relatively well-entrenched in the United States, there are patterns of behavior among both civilians and the military that undermine norms of civilian control and that require ways of rethinking military professionalism.

36. A notable exception is a white paper by Kori Schake (2013) that looks to recent counterinsurgency campaigns in Iraq and Afghanistan to argue that the US military would be more effective if only it was more willing to "get its hands dirty." (This is less about a reticence among military officers for Schake than it is about a reticence among policymakers and the general public.) Schake (2013) explicitly engages with the Indian Wars at length and takes the lesson of those conflicts to be that

The United States wins war when it decides to stop losing wars. . . . In the case of the Indian Wars, that meant "simplifying our objectives"—relinquishing any pretense at justice in our dealing with Indians and fighting a war of imperial consolidation that would win control of the territory in question.

The implication for contemporary conflicts, Schake (2013) argues, is clear: "In wondering why we don't win our current wars, we ought perhaps to reflect that we as a society have not wanted that outcome enough to commit ourselves to the gritty and awful business of destruction." As Aune (2023, see esp. ch. 7) details, Schake is not alone in this return to the Indian Wars; it has been a frequent reference point for those interested in prosecuting recent counterinsurgencies.

37. The "idealistic philosopher" seems to be Emer de Vattel, an international lawyer who serves as Colby's first quoted source espousing such a view.

38. This sweeping generalization is false. Even solely within the domain of Native North America, practices of warfare do not fit Colby's characterization. See, e.g., Lee (2023).

39. This is similar to typical scholarly perspectives on these matters; that is, despite any tactical or strategic genius among Native leaders, the US military's quantitative and qualitative edge—combined with the effects of disease and ecological devastation that weakened many tribes—would ultimately negate any Native advantages. See, e.g., Richter (2001) and Immerwahr (2022).

Chapter 5

1. A sign at the Fort Crawford Museum in Prairie du Chien, Wisconsin, for example, contains only a terse reference to the US victory in the brief Black Hawk War. "In 1825, 1829, and 1830 important Indian treaties were negotiated at the first and second Fort Crawford. Here, on August 27, 1832, Sauk Indian leader Black Hawk surrendered, ending the Black Hawk War." See Szarejko (2021) for more on the Black Hawk War.

2. Indeed, while some academics, policymakers, and activists have urged the use of certain kinds of mnemonical practices with the stated goal of enabling post-conflict reconciliation (or other similarly justice-oriented goals), it is not actually clear that any particular mnemonical practice is universally "good." The standardization of such mnemonical practices, as David (2020) argues, entails a shift away from more contextual interventions in ways that might exacerbate existing mnemonical conflicts.

3. Partisan self-identification does not wholly overlap with ideological self-identification (that is, "Republican" does not always mean "conservative," and what such terms mean can shift over time in the minds of those who claim such affiliations). See, e.g., Hopkins and Noel (2022) on the process by which many self-described conservatives have come to use that label to refer simply to an affinity for Donald Trump.

4. Indeed, Bruyneel (2021, 138–139) posits that there are distinct conservative and liberal variants of "settler memory":

> While they all have consistent and notable tendencies toward disavowing Indigeneity, they do not do so in the same way and for the same reason. Liberals and leftists . . . often acknowledge the history of Indigenous peoples and anti-Indigenous actions by white settlers and the U.S. state but then refuse or do not know how precisely to attend to the contemporary politics and persistence of Indigenous political life and of settler colonialism. On the other hand, the views of white nationalists are shaped by their righteous settler claims to authority over territory in order to define who belongs on these lands and who does not, and what can and should be the proper uses of the land as a secure site of settler domesticity and as a resource.

As discussed below, in contrast with the hegemonic mnemonical practices conservatives enacted in Fort Wayne, liberals offered a more reflective approach, but the latter had little to offer beyond a vague sense that memorializing Anthony Wayne with an annual commemoration would be uncouth.

5. In the British context, Bentley (2023, 334) notes, the country's history of colonialism presents "conservative columnists, academics, and politicians . . . invested in a patriotic national past" with a "conundrum": "how can they harness the British Empire to emplot a desirable national past?" See also Subotić (2013) on state use of hegemonic mnemonical practices in the Balkans.

6. Linkage to war seems to be a frequent feature of hegemonic mnemonical practices. In seeking more federal recognition for settler graves along the Overland Trail, one early twentieth-century activist, Ezra Meeker, "began likening the Trail to a battlefield," one that he compared to Gettysburg (quoted in Keyes 2023, 156–157).

7. Memory, for Bruyneel (2021, 9), "plays a key role in the reproduction and securing of white settler status, land dispossession, and 'hierarchies of Otherness.'" Here Bruyneel is quoting Dhamoon (2015, 32), for whom

> settler colonialism is not only a structure but also a process, an activity for assigning political meanings and organizing material structures driven by forces of power. This process-oriented approach emphasizes that the productive capacities of settler colonialism function to make and consolidate hierarchies of Otherness (e.g., among gendered people of colour, among Indigenous people, and between people of colour and Indigenous people across borders of the nation-state).

8. In this chapter especially, I would align myself with DeLucia's (2018, 4) statement: "The insistent refrain of this project is that localization is crucial to understanding historical and memorial developments."

9. As Murthy (2008, 845) notes, some of the virtues of social networking sites for academic research are that "they contain vast stores of multimedia material regard-

ing even the most marginal social movements or groups" and that "ethnographers can 'invisibly' observe the social interactions of page members, gleaning a previously unavailable type of ethnographic data."

10. My approach is inspired especially by work in game studies that analyzes how video gamers interact with one another—often by enacting various forms of racialized, gendered, and/or sexualized harassment (Cote 2020; Gray 2012; Healey 2016). I am not, however, engaged here in participant observation as such work often is.

11. Henry was first elected to this position in 2008. As of this writing, Tom Henry had recently passed away—on March 28, 2024. Deputy Mayor Karl Bandemer served as acting mayor until April 2024, when Sharon Tucker, a Democrat, was elected mayor by the Allen County Democratic Party caucus. Tucker will serve as mayor for the remainder of Henry's term, until January 2028. See Brown (2024).

12. See here for data on Fort Wayne City Council elections going back to 2015: https://ballotpedia.org/Fort_Wayne,_Indiana#City_council

13. As discussed below (and reproduced as is, without correction), Arp eventually made an unsuccessful bid for the Republican nomination in Fort Wayne's mayoral race. His online website makes a pitch for his candidacy by noting that

> Jason Arp was elected to Fort Wayne City Council in November 2015, where is has been advocate for free enterprise, private property rights and individual liberty. He has authored legislation to remove meddlesome regulations and onerous taxes for both business and individuals. His dogged pursuit of ending cronyism has earned him the right enemies.

In his first year on the council, for example, Arp proposed voiding a city law that banned the carrying of firearms in city parks (a city law that was by then void due to Indiana state law), proposed eliminating the city business personal property tax, and asked the Indiana state legislature to consider giving city council the ability to reduce the salary of elected city officials (such as Fort Wayne's Democratic mayor). See his website https://jasonarp.com/bio/ as well as Blakeslee (2016) and Wright (2016a, 2016b).

14. I will occasionally refer to this day as "Anthony Wayne Day." I have aimed to reproduce the text of the resolution as it is styled in the original resolution, including the use of indentation, all capital letters for some words, bold text, and line breaks. The resolution does not conclude with a period.

15. In the title of the resolution and in much public reference to it, "Mad" Anthony Wayne Day is often stylized with quotation marks around "Mad" to denote that this was a nickname. Those quotation marks do not appear in the text of the resolution.

16. Native forces might more accurately be described as having been "aligned" with Britain. The British received Native requests for military aid early in this conflict, and while they did initially provide some military equipment, they only authorized the use of a small contingent of British troops at the Battle of Fallen Timbers, and those troops tried to disguise themselves as Native Americans and

did not command Native troops (Sword 1985, 297–298). The British ultimately did not want to spark a broader war with the United States and sought to avoid escalation (on the use of covert action as a means of limiting escalation, see Carson 2016). As the conflict turned in America's favor, the British refused further requests for military aid.

17. I have transcribed this text based on my viewing of a recording of the Fort Wayne City Council meeting of February 26, 2019. The video is available at: https://acpl.viebit.com/player.php?hash=0sODf2ov8CIN. I have sought to faithfully represent Arp's language while omitting filler language like "uh" or "um," and I have reproduced the errors and inconsistencies in the slides as shown.

18. This is false, and in short, the portrayal of Washington's escape may have come from a fictionalized account of these events prepared for a television series. As Savage's (2020) journalistic recounting of Arp's proposal and the subsequent contestation of it notes,

> The resolution's dramatic selling point was the claim that by capturing Stony Point, Anthony Wayne had foiled a bold British attempt to capture General George Washington, whose location they had learned as part of Benedict Arnold's treason. I had scoured books and consulted historians for any support for Arp's tale, but every source portrayed the battle as a strategically minor morale booster, with no mention of Arnold or any risk that Washington might have been captured. Where had that come from? . . . I had a theory. One day, I had tried an Internet search for keywords from Arp's version of Stony Point but without Wayne's name. The query returned recaps for an episode from the AMC television series *Turn: Washington's Spies*. Although it had no Wayne character, the episode's fictionalized version of Stony Point lined up with the dramatic version put forward by Arp—who had even told the city council that Washington ordered the attack after learning of a British plan to surround his encampment "from his own spies." The AMC show contained that exact plot point. A call to Craig Silverstein, *Turn*'s executive producer and showrunner, confirmed that they had made all this up. "Stony Point in history has nothing to do with Benedict Arnold," Silverstein added. "We connected that for dramatic license." I asked Arp whether he had watched the series, and he had. I asked if this episode was the origin. "I don't know," he replied curtly. "I guess anything's possible."

19. Many reviewers found Gaff's book to be overly credulous of American accounts of the "savagery" of the Native nations involved in the Northwest Indian War. "In many ways," for Parmenter (2005, 133), "Gaff's monograph mirrors aspects of his protagonist's [i.e., Wayne's] character; it is methodical, possessed of an eye for symbolism, and ultimately unable to view Native Americans as anything other than savage obstacles to the advancing tide of American civilization." Another reviewer notes that Gaff's narrative adopts an American point of view by largely ignoring British records and dismissing Native American oral histories as not "objective . . .

by any definition" (Gaff, xiii, quoted in Nelson 2005, 205). As Gooding (2005, 79–80) notes of Gaff's account,

> With a few exceptions, the Indians appear in this work as the stock "vicious savage' character, capable only of brutality and cruelty. They are described as "blood thirsty" and "butchers" (7), and their army as a "ravenous multitude" (242). Following the defeat of St. Clair's army, Gaff notes that "whooping with laughter, grinning warriors swiftly scalped those corpses that had thus far escaped ritual mutilation" (7).

20. I have reproduced the text as it appears on his slides; the variation in spelling, dashes, and styling of dates is Arp's.

21. Without assessing the fairness of this comparison, St. Clair's Defeat did come as a shock to many political elites. It would remain the most significant defeat of US forces by Native American groups (in terms of casualty percentages), and it resulted in Congress's first formal investigation of executive branch operations. The investigation cleared St. Clair of any personal failings and blamed the loss more on the ability to field only a small military force, many members of which were poorly trained, undisciplined militiamen rather than federal regulars (Waxman 2018). Arp's rhetorical move, however, seems less about the quality of the comparison and more about telling the audience that there is a thread that connects today's Americans to the founding generation; they were just like us.

22. References to St. Clair's Defeat as a "mass execution" (or otherwise indicating that it was an indiscriminate slaughter) often cite the fact that the American dead included many women and children, perhaps in the range of forty to sixty killed. It is likely that, like other camp followers of that era, many of the women were married or related to men in the force, and they may have performed various forms of labor for the force (see, e.g., Skalenko 2022). What can be said is that the American forces were thoroughly defeated by a large, well-organized Native force that caught them by surprise, that women and children with the force were among those killed, and that there was "extra-lethal violence" practiced on the American dead (Calloway 2014; Fujii 2013). Upwards of 600 Americans were killed with nearly 300 wounded.

23. Didier, for example, notes that "I knew a little bit about Anthony Wayne, but with this little thing, I felt like I was back in school again, learning. . . . I love US history. It's just phenomenal. I don't have any issues with this particular, you know, resolution, or whatever." Another Republican councilman, Tom Freistroffer, says that, "I think it's important for all of us in Fort Wayne to identify with our identity, our character, and the integrity of Fort Wayne. . . . This is gonna bring more people into the context of studying that, and I'll back it, I think it's great."

24. No one else in the meeting mentioned having been a history major at Manchester University, but Didier mentioned having enjoyed US history as a high school class, and Freistroffer mentioned having been a US history teacher.

25. Republican Paul Ensley spoke in favor of the resolution:

I would just warn against the folly, in my opinion, of viewing historical events through a lens of modern morality. . . . [C]ertainly, for the overwhelming majority of human history, the right of conquest has been certainly an acceptable form of acquiring land. With regards to the Native Americans, obviously, Anthony Wayne—as Councilman Arp has recounted to us—was very merciful and sought a less violent solution, a less violent means than what the Native Americans had shown the Europeans before that. And so, again, I will look forward to supporting this and honoring General Wayne July 16th.

Republican Michael Barranda also spoke in favor:

[T]his is a resolution, so I don't really know the effect of council signing a resolution to declare July 16th as "Mad" Anthony Wayne Day other than, it is a recognition and an opportunity to have a discussion. Things that I learned tonight were both good and bad about General "Mad" Anthony Wayne, and I think that's what these things do—is start a discussion and allow us to talk about our history so that we can learn from it.

26. Paddock, upon hearing critique of his vote from at least one constituent and then doing further research and consultation with the city's History Center, later introduced resolution R-76–19: "A Resolution Celebrating National Native American Heritage Month in the City of Fort Wayne and Providing a Historical Perspective on Past Events." On the same council (with seven Republicans and two Democrats), the resolution passed 8–1. Only Arp voted nay. Beyond being a statement that the "Fort Wayne City Council acknowledges and honors National Native American Heritage Month," the resolution was also a sharp critique of Arp's original resolution. Its text notes that shortly after the passage of Arp's R-5–19, "representatives from the Miami Tribe of Oklahoma contacted members of the Fort Wayne City Council about factual inaccuracies in the resolution as passed, as well as in the presentation provided at the Fort Wayne City Council meeting on February 26, 2019," and it therefore resolves that, "The Fort Wayne City Council acknowledges that R-19-02-12 did not provide a complete telling of certain historical aspects of the establishment of Fort Wayne." It is not immediately clear why the same resolution is referred to first as R-5–19 and then as R-19-02-12; it may be that the latter becomes the former upon adoption, but that was not immediately clear. R-19-02-12 and R-76–19 are available here: https://www.cityoffortwayne.org/custom/council_documents/documents/download/2019-02-22/R-19-02-12.pdf; https://www.cityoffortwayne.org/custom/ordinance_view/files/R-19-11-14.pdf

27. Hereafter, I will often refer to the General "Mad" Anthony Wayne Organization as "the organization."

28. Among the individuals associated with the organization, Loomis appears to have the most clearly political background. The website for Loomis Law Office advertises that "Mike served as an aide to U.S. Senators Richard G. Lugar and Danforth

J. Quayle from 1981–1983" and that "Mike served as a Marion County (Indianapolis) Deputy Prosecutor" starting in 1984 and ending in 1991. He later served in the Allen County Prosecuting Attorney's Office in various roles. See here: https://loomislaw .net/about-us

29. Loomis has tried to distance himself from Arp's resolution to some extent. Savage (2020), for example, reports that "Loomis said he found out what Arp was doing two hours before the meeting and did not see the resolution's text in advance." Similarly, Savage reports that Loomis was watching the city council meeting during which the resolution was being debated on television, and when Arp noted that there might be some "unpatriotic" detractors of the resolution, Loomis told Savage, "I remember thinking 'oh boy.'" When the organization was founded, however, Loomis served as chairman and Arp as chief executive officer (Savage 2020). They soon had a falling out, seemingly over just how overtly political to make the celebratory events. Arp invited then-Vice President Mike Pence, a Republican with a long track record in Indiana politics, but Loomis "did not want to politicize our event. . . . I did not want to turn it over to the Secret Service. I did not want to have criticism of the Trump administration to become the centerpiece of our first General Wayne Day. And I didn't want protesters" (Savage 2020).

30 I discuss the website material that was available as of November 2024. Some of the information discussed here is no longer presented on the website, as of this writing in February 2025. There have also been times in the past few years when the website has not been online. For older versions of the organization's website, please see the Internet Archive Wayback Machine: https://web.archive.org/web/ 20231201000000*/https://madanthonywayne.org/

31 See Jackson (2025, 3) on the "impersonally true" character that most would attribute to their factual claims.

32. This is not to say, however, that those associated with this organization are being intentionally deceptive. They may indeed see their work as apolitical even as I argue that their actions are ultimately political.

33. Here I have reproduced capital and lowercase letters exactly as they appear on the website.

34. As of this writing in February 2025, the QUEST Tournament no longer appears on the organization's website, but it does have a functioning Facebook page (which I discuss at length below); a photograph posted on May 26, 2021, identifies David Rousculp, the living historian who has portrayed Anthony Wayne for the organization, as the host of the show: https://www.facebook.com/QUESTquizshow /photos/pb.100068716457934.-2207520000/102513978712800/?type=3 In short, this is a trivia show for high school students that is televised locally, and it appears largely dependent on local businesses to serve as sponsors. An announcement on the Facebook page dated March 12, 2023 https://www.facebook.com/photo?fbid= 521419830158561&set=pb.100068716457934.-2207520000 indicates that Season 2 was postponed until 2024. As of this writing in February 2025, there has been no further update on this topic, and the posts linked above had been deleted or made private.

The tournament was discussed on the local news segment and on a separate Facebook page that remains online: https://www.21alivenews.com/2022/10/13/quest-tournament/; https://www.facebook.com/QUESTquizshow/

35 As of this writing in February 2025, the organization lists the following offices and officers: Chairman (J. Michael Loomis), President (Judi Loomis), Vice President/Treasurer (Jeffrey W. Jones), Secretary (vacant), National Award Co-Chairs (Alan D. Gaff and Maureen Gaff), Finance Sub-Committee Chair (vacant), Event Planning Sub-Committee Chair (vacant), Liaison to Educators (vacant), Official Historian (Alan D. Gaff), and Researcher (Maureen Gaff), President Emeritus (Michael Skeens). It is not clear whether Rousculp still serves as the organization's living historian. Text advertising his availability for personal appearances that once appeared on the website has since been removed. As his biography on the website once noted, he has a day job in the area—he serves as general manager, director, and embalmer at Harper's Community Funeral Home in New Haven, Indiana.

36. Auditions were apparently held on May 20, 2023. Up through at least June 2024 (when this manuscript was first submitted for publication), no update on the website had been posted, but as is apparent from coverage of the 2023 celebrations, they did indeed hire someone for this role. The most detailed reporting surrounding Mary Penrose Wayne to have come out of the organization's recent activities appears in a report for the *Greater Fort Wayne Business Weekly* on the forthcoming debut of a new Mary Penrose Wayne reenactor who would appear at the 2023 Anthony Wayne Day celebrations (Hawkins 2023):

> As the wife of a soldier, and a very important one, his wife's life would not have been easy. In the 1700s women had a different role in family life, following their husbands, raising their children, and holding down the homestead while their husbands fought in the war. Penrose was originally born in Pennsylvania and had two children with Gen. Wayne. Despite a marriage of 17 years, she had to be brave during the war as well as her husband. She was known to be mild in nature and very much a homebody, but actively supported her husband in his occupation. She died at [the] age of 44 years old. [The age given is incorrect; Mary Penrose Wayne lived from 1746 to 1793 and died at the age of 47.]

> As of this writing in February 2025, the page had been updated to highlight a new actress who would be portraying Mary Penrose Wayne going forward (and who is described as both an "actress" and a "living historian."

37. The organization's use of Mary Penrose Wayne speaks to its selective use of history to positively portray Anthony Wayne in that the organization depicts their marriage as a loving one between two virtuous patriots. In a lengthy post published on their Facebook page on March 25, 2023, for example, the organization notes that,

> Today, we congratulate General "Mad" Anthony Wayne (1745–1796), and his bride, Mary "Polly" Penrose (1746–1793), on the occasion of the couple's 257th Anniversary of their wedding. The couple met at a military ball in Philadelphia,

and they were married on March 25, 1776 at Christ's Church, Pennsylvania. The couple settled on Wayne's family estate in Eastown, located in Chester County, PA. They remained married for 17 years until Mary's death at the age of 47, three years before the General's death at the age of 51.

The post continues at length and concludes with a caption for an associated photograph:

The couple had two children, Margaretta Wayne Atlee (1770–1810); and, Isaac Wayne (1772–1852). The remains of both Anthony Wayne and Mary Penrose Wayne rest in peace at St. David's Episcopal Church, Radnor Township, Delaware County, PA. Interestingly, the Allen County Public Library Genealogy Center has an artifact of that marriage, being the Anthony and Mary (Penrose) Wayne Family Bible. It was published in 1788, and presented by Wayne's wife, Mary, to their son, Isaac Wayne. It is believed that this occurred relatively soon after the book was published, and it contains Mary Wayne's inscription to Isaac. The family's events were recorded in the Bible, with more than sixty years of family information contained in it. The Bible was acquired approximately twenty years ago, at auction, to the chagrin of other Wayne fans around the country. Our friend, Curt B. Witcher, Director of Special Collections at the Genealogy Center, Allen County Public Library, Fort Wayne, IN, showed General "Mad" Anthony Wayne (living historian David Rousculp) the Wayne Family Bible on Friday, March 24, 2023 at the library, and they're both seen in the photo on this post. "We think that it is both notable and significant that the actual Wayne Family Bible, being such an important item in history, is located at the public library in the city named for General Wayne," Rousculp stated. "It creates a physical bond with the namesake of our city that cannot be denied." Curt B. Witcher with General Wayne at the Allen County Public Library, Genealogy Center.

The post is online here: https://www.facebook.com/photo?fbid=1386761005425 116&set=a.478295762938316

Despite the organization's relatively positive depiction of the couple's marriage, Mary had become estranged from her husband by the time of her death; their relationship had "lapsed into a sort of distant and businesslike formality" (Nelson 1985, 19). This likely had something to do with the relationships Anthony Wayne had with other women. The historical record is not clear on the intimacy of these relationships, but at least as early as 1780, Wayne appeared to have developed a close relationship with a Miss Mary Vining—to the extent that he sought to purchase and have some "fine English cloth . . . made up into clothes for 'the very amiable—but too *fascinating* Miss V——g'" (Nelson 1985, 104, emphasis in original).

Mary Penrose Wayne died on April 19, 1793, in Waynesborough, Pennsylvania, after an extended (unknown) illness. Anthony learned on April 28 through a letter sent by William R. Atlee, Anthony's son-in-law, at which point Anthony wrote that he was "in such a state of torture for the recent loss of my long loved & very esteemed

Maria" that he could hardly manage his military duties (quoted in Nelson 1985, 239). Afterwards and until Anthony's own death in 1796, he would enjoy a more public relationship with Mary Vining to the point that it was widely rumored (but never publicly confirmed or denied) that they were engaged (Nelson 1985, 289). The organization does not draw attention to these tensions in the Waynes' marriage and instead suggests that they had a happy marriage.

38. As I have suggested above, assessments of the significance of the Battle of Stony Point vary. A National Park Service biography of Wayne describes the battle and its importance as follows (https://www.nps.gov/people/anthony-wayne.htm):

> In 1779, as the northern theater settled into stalemate, Wayne led a surprise assault on a British garrison at Stony Point, along the Hudson River in New York, inflicting over 100 British casualties and capturing over 400 prisoners. Wayne was briefly stunned by a musket ball to the head during the battle, but he was able to provide the Americans with a tactical victory critical for raising morale.

39. A nomination form at the bottom of the page indicates that, "Nominees must be American citizens who consistently display excellence in enhancing education about local, regional, and national history, and who: [d]emonstrates a passion for local, regional, and national history; [l]eads by example with integrity, respect, and professionalism; [e]xhibits a positive attitude; [e]ngages in community service; [i]dentifies and promotes opportunities to educate others about history; [c]ommunicates effectively; and, [m]entors others." The list of items following the colon is presented as a list of bullet points in the original document.

40. The 2021 award, which was given on December 31, 2020, is described as follows:

> That date was chosen for the presentation because General Wayne was born on January 1, 1745, and we celebrated the 276th anniversary of his birthday. The first winner was local living historian and frequent volunteer Robert Jones, a retired educator who is active in supporting activities at The Historic Old Fort. He also portrayed our General Wayne at countless events. After winning the first award, Bob Jones also chaired the Committee that found our next living historian to portray General Wayne. Robert Jones will continue to portray General and President George Washington. (See Bob, at right, receiving first Legion of the United States Award.) The 2022 Legion of the United States Award was presented to Dr. Jerome Adams, former Surgeon General of the United States.

The subsequent living historian to portray Anthony Wayne for the organization, David Rousculp, was introduced at a press conference on March 5, 2021, a video recording of which was posted on their Facebook page: https://www.facebook.com/share/v/1AG3tiq6R1/?mibextid=wwXIfr. Jones introduces Rousculp first as someone with "an extensive career in theater and in film," then as someone who "is a member of the Sons of the American Revolution" and as "an avid eighteenth-century American history aficionado." Jones then briefly talks about how Wayne's soldiers saw him:

> There's an inscription chiseled in stone on a monument in Pennsylvania that was placed there by men he served with prior to his death, and it was constructed in 1809. And at the very bottom it simply says this—and I think this is how we should remember General Wayne—"An American soldier and patriot."

Jones then reveals Rousculp as the next living historian to take on the role of Wayne and gives Rousculp a rolled-up piece of paper with his "orders" before Rousculp speaks. In his remarks, Rousculp notes that his family came to the United States on a ship called *The King of Prussia* in 1764 and that when Wayne created the Fourth Battalion in Pennsylvania, his great-great-great-great-great-great-grandfather, John Phillip Rousculp, enlisted in 1776. Rousculp also notes that,

> The focus of "Mad" Anthony Wayne with this organization is to focus on him being an American Revolutionary hero. His achievements during the campaign played a huge role in the United States in defeating Britain. Many would argue that his win at Battle of Stony Point was the victory that restored the hope to the military to push on for the win. Another point of interest is the relationship of Mad Anthony Wayne with George Washington. There are many letters that are shared—a common bond that he had.

The page includes a picture of Jones in costume accepting the award alongside a cake with a picture of Wayne on it and with icing spelling out "Happy 276th Birthday." The second award winner, Dr. Jerome Adams, served as surgeon general under President Donald Trump and had previously served as health commissioner of Indiana from 2014 to 2017, a position to which he was appointed by then-Governor Mike Pence, who would later serve as Trump's vice president. After resigning at the request of Trump's Democratic successor, President Joseph Biden, Adams took a position at Purdue University as a presidential fellow and the executive director of Purdue's Health Equity Initiatives on October 1, 2021.

41. See here for the announcement on the organization's Facebook page: https://www.facebook.com/photo/?fbid=1446896399411576&set=a.478295762938316. The 122nd Fighter Wing is nicknamed "Blacksnakes," which Command Chief Master Sergeant Kyle Hoopingarner says "is absolutely an homage to Gen. Wayne himself, who was called 'Blacksnake' by the Native Americans at that time." For local coverage of the 2023 award, see Sloboda (2023).

42. The description appears as is, with mistakes, inconsistencies, and punctuation errors in place.

43. Assessments of Wayne's abilities as a military officer vary—most notably, George Washington himself had mixed opinions of the man to whom he eventually entrusted command of the military. In a 1792 memorandum (quoted in Prucha 1969, 28–29), Washington noted that Wayne was

More active and enterprising than judicious & cautious. No œconomist it is feared. Open to flattery; vain; easily imposed upon; and liable to be drawn into scrapes. Too indulgent (the effect perhaps of some of the causes just mentioned) to his Officers and men. Whether sober, or a little addicted to the bottle, I know not.

44. I describe only the most salient interviews here; those interviewed held these positions at the time of the interviews.

45. As with most YouTube videos posted by local news stations in the United States, this video did not reach many viewers. As of January 7, 2025, the WANE 15 News You-Tube channel has about 46,500 subscribers, but this interview has received only 317 views since it was posted on July 13, 2019. Comments were allowed on the video, but there was no sign of controversy there. Only one user (@chrisjoy439) posted a comment: "I was born and raised in Fort Wayne!!" The permanent link is as follows: https://youtu.be/SfqOcV2Cx1g?si=Mbd39bGVs_hwVwTD. The title of the video is "First-Ever 'Mad' Anthony Wayne Day Set to Honor Fort Wayne's Namesake."

46. At about this point in the video, footage plays to show a man in a Revolutionary War uniform and otherwise dressed to resemble Anthony Wayne. Footage also shows a hanging dress that one assumes "his wife" will be wearing for the festivities. Mike Loomis is also shown (but not identified) speaking to an audience at what appears to be the public library; he wears a tie that alternates between red and white stripes and a blue field with white stars (an evocation but not a direct representation of the American flag).

47. As of January 7, 2025, the video on YouTube has 137 views and two "likes." The video is entitled, "Councilman Stands by 'Anthony Wayne Day' Resolution Despite Opposition from Tribe," and there is one comment on the video. The user "@JOHN-MARCEY" writes simply, "Good lord." The permanent link is here: https://youtu.be/mOcSiXVo9Ow?si=bJeRCidrUr3i_WfC.

48. As per the city's website, "In 1824, the Indiana General Assembly established Allen County, and the 1830s brought about the construction of the Wabash and Erie Canal in Fort Wayne. This famous canal earned Fort Wayne the nickname 'Summit City' because it was the highest point above sea level along the entire canal route." The permanent link is here: https://www.visitfortwayne.com/about-us/about-fort-wayne-indiana/history/

49. As noted above, the British were only minimally involved in the Northwest Indian War. For example, early in the war the United States informed the British at Detroit (where they continued to inhabit a fort) that the United States was going to wage war on the Native coalition; this was to avoid any British perception that the United States sought conflict with them. The British passed this word along to British traders who did business with the Native groups in question, which gave the Native population advance warning of the American military. Many Native groups in the region also traded with the British to acquire firearms. The British were not in command of Native forces, however, and when Native emissaries went to Detroit

to request British military assistance early in the war, the British offered only some supplies. As the Native coalition began to suffer losses later in the war and as Britain became preoccupied with events unfolding amid the French Revolution, the British would refuse to provide any additional support (Calloway 2014, 66, 105).

50. The video, "General 'Mad' Anthony Wayne Day," did not list viewer statistics alongside it. This video is available at: https://www.wane.com/video/general-mad -anthony-wayne-day/7841057/

51. Facebook has been one of the most popular social media websites for over a decade at this point, but its user base has become older on average over time. Facebook may thus be a relatively good place for an organization such as this to promote its work.

52. The other person was of no immediately clear connection to the organization. As has been noted at multiple points already, the organization sometimes seeks to distance itself from Arp and the resolution he introduced, but connections between the two are readily apparent in various places.

53. The post was once available at the following link but has since been removed or made private: https://www.facebook.com/photo?fbid=731437945694372&set=a.65 8955942942573

54. Available at: https://www.facebook.com/photo/?fbid=1307419946692556&set =a.493895751378317

55. The original sources of the images the organization used are not entirely clear, but a Google search for "Native American heritage" returned results that included these two images. The image associated with the 2023 post is attributed to Adobe Stock here: https://nativenewsonline.net/currents/november-is-native-amer ican-heritage-month-here-s-how-that-happened-2; the image associated with the 2022 post is used but not properly cited here: https://nationaltoday.com/native -american-heritage-day/

56. The reason for the delayed response is unclear to this reader. I would speculate that the article circulated again around the 2021 Wayne Day celebrations. See https://ictnews.org/news/celebrating-not-mad-wayne-day?redir=1 and https:// indianz.com/News/2019/07/18/indian-country-today-miami-tribe-exclude.asp

57. I cannot independently verify this recounting of events. This statement is reproduced as is.

58. As the Gaffs noted in the televised interview quoted above, the first celebration included an event held at the Old Fort. This tourist attraction is a recreation of a fort that was constructed in 1815; that fort was constructed near the site of the original Fort Wayne that Lieutenant Colonel Commandant John Hamtramck (having since been promoted from major) had built on Wayne's orders in 1794. This belies the notion that the event was purely about Wayne's actions during the Revolutionary War. For more on the Old Fort, see here: https://www.fortwayneparks.org /facilities/historic-old-fort.html

59. It is not clear if there was a tribal newsletter in which this story appeared or

if this conflates the reporting in *Indian Country Today* or the repost on Indianz.com with a tribal newsletter. Regardless, the rephrased title on Indianz.com, "Miami Tribe Excluded from Event on Own Homelands," is the only part of the article that could be taken to convey that the tribe was "not permitted" to partake in the festivities. That was not the original title, and there is no further content in the article that communicates that the tribe was not permitted to take part in the events. Rather, there is simply criticism of the original resolution, the celebrations, and the organization's attempts to engage in outreach only after the fact. For example, the article notes that, "Since passing the resolution, city council has reached out to tribal leaders seeking their input in planning celebrations for Mad Anthony Day." It then quotes George Ironstrack, then-assistant director of education for the Myaamia Center at Miami University, as follows: "They're not interested in our genuine input; they want us to offer up language in support of their resolution as a means to fix their mess" (Pember 2019).

60. As noted above, the attempt to separate the organization from the presentation of the original resolution is difficult to maintain given that Loomis was the one who suggested such a resolution. Moreover, after Arp's presentation and before turning to other members of the council for discussion, the councilman asked Robert "Bob" Jones—the organization's first living historian to take on the role of Wayne and the first recipient of their Legion of the United States Award—to contribute to the discussion. Arp notes after his own presentation that

> When I first talked about this a couple years ago, I had a few people reach out to me, and Mr. Bob Jones from the Fort Wayne Historical Society was kind enough to reach out to me. [Arp then looks and gestures in Jones's direction.] Do you mind coming up and telling us a little bit about your organization and the opportunities that Anthony Wayne presents?

Jones then joined the council members while expressing surprise. "Oh, really? Okay, wow. First time ever coming to a meeting and I find myself at the table—that was unexpected. Well, thank you for a wonderful, excellent presentation of history that is very near and dear to my heart having been a fourth grade history [teacher] teaching Indiana history." He later continues, "That's why I'm involved—keeping the 'Fort' in 'Fort Wayne.' We do all we can to maintain the structure." He later gives his opinion on the resolution:

> I speak in favor of having an Anthony Wayne Day. Just a brief check—I found a lot of cities that have a special day to honor their founder, whoever that may be, or founders day, because it may not have been one individual. And I met [inaudible] tonight, I'm sitting with him, and he's got a Marine jacket on. My dad's a Marine, and when I meet a veteran, I thank them for their service because I know that it meant personal sacrifice. And I began thinking, Anthony Wayne was a veteran—we should thank him if we could. He would have—as you [Arp]

pointed out—received the Purple Heart had that been in place at the time. . . .
I think it's fitting to have a day to honor our founder. He's not "Anthony Wayne
the Great," but he sure did a lot of great things, and I think it's a great idea. . . .
As long as we're Americans, I think we should honor those who did sacrifice
personally and had some contribution to make.

61. November was eventually recognized by the Fort Wayne City Council as
Native American Heritage Month. It is not clear if October was ever considered as
the month to be recognized as such or if this is simply a mistake.

62. It is not clear which assertions are being labeled ridiculous here. This could
refer to the statement by Diane Hunter, the tribe's Tribal Historic Preservation Officer, to the effect that, "He destroyed our villages and food supplies; it was his intention to wipe us out." As I noted in Chapter 4, however, Wayne did indeed ensure
Native villages and food supplies were destroyed; whether that and Wayne's other
military actions suffice to establish that it was Wayne's "intention to wipe us out"
(or whether that was a "ridiculous assertion") is a judgment I leave to the reader.

63. The post by Loomis seems to have received more engagement than their average post—it generated nine "likes," six shares, and six comments.

64. A brief online search suggests that this is true.

65. This seems to me to be a reasonable reading of the article and the broader
situation.

66. The idea that the resolution and the annual events celebrating Wayne "are
two separate matters," as I have already suggested at numerous points, is belied by
the frequency with which the resolution is used to specify why those annual celebrations are happening. They do so, for example, in a July 16, 2020, Facebook post:

Happy General "Mad" Anthony Wayne Day! This is the second annual day hon-
oring General Wayne for his victory with and for the Continental Army against
the British at Stony Point (NY). While activities this year were cancelled due to
COVID-19, we have already begun planning for next year! (The Fort Wayne City
Council passed a resolution on February 26, 2019 setting aside this day for the
General.)

The organization's 2022 celebration is similarly framed with reference to the
resolution: "Today, July 16, pursuant to a resolution passed by City Council on February 26, 2019, we honor General Anthony Wayne." Similarly, as noted above, the
fact that Arp gave the keynote address at the inaugural celebration in July 2019
suggests a stronger connection between Arp's resolution and the organization's celebration than Loomis acknowledges.

67. As noted above, only Indianz.com's rephrased title of the original article
could be taken to indicate that the tribe was not permitted to participate in the
commemoration.

68. The emphasis on "blaming the General for following lawful orders" and the
notion that this is "an affront to every Veteran who ever served this country" is

noteworthy in that it affirms the legitimacy of Wayne's actions while eliding the discretion Wayne was allowed in accomplishing his objective. This also constructs veterans as a category whose actions—so long as they are following orders—ought not to be questioned and, indeed, ought to be celebrated.

69. Here it becomes clear that Loomis is indeed reacting to Indianz.com's rephrased title.

70. The exchange concludes with a new user entering the conversation—Paul Calloway, whose Facebook profile identifies him as a senior account manager at Dynatronics, an electrotherapy and light therapy equipment manufacturer (with no clear connection to the General "Mad" Anthony Wayne Organization). His response to Salla, which received no reply, is as follows:

> Keenan Salla what you may not realize is that Wayne was actively trying the win the Confederated tribes over as they were being heavily influenced by British. It was in Britain's interest to manipulate the Miami etc against the Americans—in doing so they denied the Americans access to the Great Lakes. Wayne had attempted to make a peace at Fort Defiance and allowed the native army to retreat under the watchful eyes of the British at Fort Miami. Wayne allowed the natives to run straight to the British fort—and as he suspected, the British turned their native "allies" away and would not let them enter the fort for protection against Wayne's army. The point of all this was to illustrate to the natives how impotent the British were . . . and how they were being manipulated in bad faith into a war with the United States. To drive that point home, Wayne surrounded Fort Miami well within range of British artillery and rode up by himself within pistol shot of the walls. He rode the entire perimeter of the fort—BY HIMSELF. The officers within pleaded for permission to shoot Wayne but Wayne correctly surmised that the British didn't want another all-out-war with the US. These are just a few examples, but Wayne was clearly did not mistreat the native combatants as he was attempting to win peace with them.

71. Trump frequently complains about the alleged Deep State, which he presented as unelected bureaucrats who worked to illegitimately thwart his (and in his telling, the American people's) will (Moynihan 2022).

72. In the face of such critique, Trump and other conservatives have often offered variations on a theme: "stick to sports" (Peterson and Muñoz 2022).

73. The organization's posts on the topic are available here: https://www.facebook .com/photo/?fbid=725620911539132&set=a.493895751378317; https://www.facebook .com/photo/?fbid=725630014871555&set=a.493895751378317; https://www.facebook .com/GenAnthonyWayne/posts/pfbidoUjn4H5RfTuKrEtZ61VxW2WyNkpiLd1A5ER T83PmANLsgyKvgWm4ix58UvGdnqjdYl. As of January 7, 2025, the petition is viewable online here: https://www.change.org/p/mayor-tom-henry-remove-the-statue -of-mad-anthony-wayne-from-freimann-square

74. The publicly viewable shares generally did not add any further comment to

the post or noted the user's agreement with the post. One user, Mark Rudolph, shared the post without adding any text, but the comments on his shared post are indicative of the sort of sentiment seen on many of the other shared posts. (Harsh language follows.) Another user, Kevin Kunberger, comments first: "If it gets taking down might as well rename our city to while you're at it. Fucking assholes. I just want to punch people like that right in the fucking face." Rudolph responds: "I looked up the ass hat that started the petition and he doesn't even live here." Kunberger then responds: "I would love to meet that guy face to face. I can tell you he wouldn't have a face for very long not one you would recognize anyway." After Rudolph concurs with "no doubt," another user, Ronnie Rudolph (who may or may not be related to Mark), adds that, "They better not take down any of our history or vandalize it. Dumb ass people doing that is retarded." In a second comment (to which there were no further replies), Ronnie writes as follows: "And he doesn't live here. Mind your own business bitch." (I have reported their comments exactly as written.)

Few users add criticism of the post. At least one presumably pseudonymous user, Comrade Bumblejack, adds a note of critique: "Open comments. Please have at them. Mad Anthony was a genocidal maniac and shouldn't have a statue where kekionga, the heart of the Miami tribe and native resistance in the area, once was." Loomis himself appears to have debated Wayne's merits with a more critical user, Gwen Williams, but Loomis has since deleted his comments in that exchange (they are not visible, but Loomis is tagged in Williams's comments as if they were replies directly to Loomis). In Williams's initial comment on the post, she writes that, "If you want to commemorate history put a statue up of the native victims of this man and his contribution to white supremacy and genocide. Let's not honor racists by having big ol statues of them. His name is in a history book somewhere can we melt his face please." Her next comment tags the organization itself at the beginning and starts as if it were a direct reply: "yeah, he didnt though. In fact, he and his wife kept slaves until the moment the civil war started pretty much." (It is unclear who "he" is in this case.) Another critical user received a reply from the organization that remains public. Kay Harrington wrote that, "Y'all are about to die mad [crying laughing emoji] That statue is coming the fuck down [yelling emoji, double exclamation point emoji]." Harrington adds in a follow-up comment, "By legal means of course. Wouldn't want anyone to try and accuse me." The organization then responds as follows: "Kayla Harrington That little disclaimer will not protect you. You'll now be one of the first people we'll talk to, if anything happens to that statue. 'That statue is coming the fuck down' sure doesn't sound like a peaceful protest to us."

When sorting comments by "most relevant," the top comment (by a Daniel O'Donnell) offers a mixed but ultimately positive assessment of Wayne:

> He was a tax evader whom was whipped bye the Brits. But he was kick as as a leader. Further more in the West Indian war he popped of the heads of recalcitrant Brits whom formed alliance with Ohio Indians and would not leave the

Continental US as stipulated as treaty. If there is one character whom should not be toppled it's general Wayne.

The second "most relevant" comment similarly expresses agreement with the organization—user Dax Thomas writes as follows: "Idiots unbelievable that they are allowed to take down what America was built on." There are, on the other hand, some comments that urge a more reflective approach to historical memory. The presumably pseudonymous user Bizzy Bee, for example, writes that,

> Taking down a statue of someone we are collectively coming to realize shouldn't be celebrated is not erasing history. If you actually listened to the folks who want to remove it you would realize that is not the case, that we understand it's important to know history as it informs our current socio-political context. I would ask you why [you] think removing a statue that celebrates a perpetrator of genocide is going to somehow erase him or ask you why you want to celebrate a perpetrator of genocide but you seem confused as to how genocide is defined and how it functions. You deny that there is a cultural aspect to genocide even though any community that has faced genocide as well as scholars on the subject disagree with you and literally mention cultural aspects of genocide in how it is defined. All of that said, why [not] just support a memorial to natives in the area? Why not contact tribes and do it yourself if you believe that public statues are the only way not to erase history?

75. This post received only eleven "likes," two "laughs," one "love," and two (private) shares. Comments were largely negative in response to this post. The first commenter, Justin TheTactictionist Thomas, provides the only positive or perhaps neutral response: "I pm'd [private messaged] you with useful information." The remaining comments were more negative. Charissa O'Quinn commented next: "Yet AGAIN irresponsibly using people's full name. If you wanted an open dialog might I suggest Private Message. Or is your intent to cause your followers to find and bully these individuals [pensive emoji]." The aforementioned Kay Harrington and Bizzy Bee then return to the page to comment. Harrington writes that, "We will get it down [shrug emoji]," whereas Bizzy succinctly comments, "Go fuck yourselves." Bizzy then adds a more detailed reply to their own comment:

> Either you don't know his history or you are cool with it. Given you seem to be all about him, you seem cool with it. I which case, fuck you, there is no point in civil discussion. It needs to be taken the fuck down and dumb fucks like you need to shut the ever living hell up bc his history isn't something to be proud of. Your casual white supremacy is sickening.

The comments here received no public reply from the organization.

76. The post received thirteen "likes," two "loves," and one "shocked" reaction, but it received no comments and only two (private) shares. The text of the post is as follows and is broken into four paragraphs in the original post (represented with

line breaks here): "Much to our amazement, the recent Executive Order issued by the President on June 26, 2020, has verbiage that will extend protection to State and local statues and memorials, and not just those owned by the federal government. See Section 2, Policy:

(d) It is the policy of the United States, as appropriate and consistent with applicable law, to withhold Federal support tied to public spaces from State and local governments that have failed to protect public monuments, memorials, and statues from destruction or vandalism. These jurisdictions' recent abandonment of their law enforcement responsibilities with respect to public monuments, memorials, and statues casts doubt on their willingness to protect other public spaces and maintain the peace within them. These jurisdictions are not appropriate candidates for limited Federal funds that support public spaces.

(e) It is the policy of the United States, as appropriate and consistent with applicable law, to withhold Federal support from State and local law enforcement agencies that have failed to protect public monuments, memorials, and statues from destruction or vandalism. Unwillingness to enforce State and local laws in the face of attacks on our history, whether because of sympathy for the extremists behind this violence or some other improper reason, casts doubt on the management of these law enforcement agencies. These law enforcement agencies are not appropriate candidates for limited Federal funds that support State and local police.

77. The post received sixteen "likes" and one (private) share.

78. The videos are available here: https://www.facebook.com/GenAnthonyWayne /videos/251734197641258/; https://www.facebook.com/GenAnthonyWayne/videos/ 2229058680816297

79. See Kurtz (2021), Lindsay (2018), and NCSE (2012).

80. The camera pans across the crowd after the prayer. Other than a reporter and those who have some formal role in the ceremony, there are ten people shown on camera.

81. Rousculp then shifts to the first person and introduces "my wife, Mary Penrose Wayne." "Mary" approaches the podium and simply says, "Hello—thank you so much for coming today," before turning around and returning to her seat, accompanied by Rousculp.

82. Any representation of a person's life will inevitably be selective, so selectivity in itself does not necessarily suggest a hegemonic mnemonical project. Rather, the nature of the selectivity—what is and is not being presented about Anthony Wayne—indicates that the organization's goal is to affirm its interpretation of history as *the* proper interpretation.

83. Those associated with the Tea Party use the term both in reference to frame themselves as patriots akin to participants in the Boston Tea Party of 1773 but also

as an acronym—TEA representing that they are "taxed enough already." Such conservatives have generally positioned themselves as more conservative than "mainstream" Republicans. Arp, as Savage (2020) notes, even produced a scorecard rating of his fellow council members that assessed "whether a councilman favors more government interference or less," with a 100 percent score indicating a perfect "liberty" score and 0 percent indicating a wholly "authoritarian" score. Arp's own system puts him at 93 percent, one fellow Republican (Ensley) at 80 percent, and every other council member at or below 32 percent. Democrats Hines and Paddock received ratings of 3 percent and 0 percent, respectively (Gong 2018).

84. For a collection of party platforms, see: https://www.presidency.ucsb.edu/documents/app-categories/elections-and-transitions/party-platforms

85. A narrative of the United States as always having been fundamentally good would contrast with a reading of American history as either having been deficient at some point in the past or as still being deficient (due to illiberal aspects of national politics, such as, e.g., slavery or continued limitations on civil rights). Such narratives often identify within the United States the potential to overcome those deficiencies and to create "a more perfect Union" (though these narratives diverge on whether those deficiencies have already been overcome).

86. Didier lost in the general election to the Democratic nominee, Tom Henry, 51.9 percent to 48.1 percent.

87. I am ambivalent about whether to think of "mnemonical security" as a subset of ontological security or as a kind of security that includes an ontological dimension among others. Here, "mnemonical security" will suffice. See Ejdus (2023) for a fuller discussion of this relationship.

88. The marker reads as follows:

In the early 1790s, the United States Army suffered two serious defeats at the hands of Indians under the leadership of Little Turtle, war chief of the Miami nation. In response, President George Washington sent Revolutionary War hero Gen. "Mad" Anthony Wayne into the western frontier. He had earned the nickname "Mad" for his reckless daring in a spectacular attack on the British at Stoney Point, New York, during the Revolution. A stern disciplinarian, Wayne rigorously trained his troops before he took his "Legion of the United States" into Miami territory in 1794. His forces defeated the Indian confederacy at the battle of Fort Recovery, Ohio (July 2, 1794) and then again at the battle of Fallen Timbers, near Toledo (August 20, 1794). Wayne next moved his "Legion" up the Maumee River to the large Native American settlement of Kekionga at the confluence of the Three Rivers. He chose a site across the Maumee River from Kekionga to build the first American fort and then handed over command to Col. John Hamtramck. On October 22, 1794, the fourth anniversary of the defeat of the United States at the Battle of Kekionga, Hamtramck called together a parade of the garrison, fired 15 rounds of cannon (in honor of each of the fifteen states of the Union), and formally announced that this place was henceforth to be called Fort Wayne. Anthony Wayne left Fort Wayne four days later, never to return. After inspecting other U.S. garrisons and successfully negotiating the Treaty of Greenville in 1795 with the Indians of the region, Wayne returned to Pennsylvania where he died in 1796.

The transcription is available here: https://www.hmdb.org/m.asp?m=119973

89. Between Wayne's statue in Freimann Square and the Little Turtle Memorial described in this paragraph, there is also a statue of Little Turtle. The statue, farther from the city center, stands along the eastern edge of Headwaters Park, a city park along the St. Mary's River. Besides inhabiting a less conspicuous place in the city than Wayne's statue, the plaque on Little Turtle's statue offers far less information than the historical marker in front of Wayne's statue. It simply reads, "Little Turtle / Me-She-Kin-No-Quah, Chief of Miami Indian Nation / In commemoration of our nation's bicentennial" (slashes indicate line breaks). It then lists donors who helped fund the sculpture, and it names Hector Garcia as the sculptor and 1976 as the date of the sculpture's creation.

Chapter 6

1. Prominent journals in political science and (more narrowly) international relations, for example, include relatively little content on Native American groups or Indigenous peoples. A search for relevant key terms such as "Native American," "American Indian," "Indigenous People(s)," and "Indian Affairs," for example, returns very few results in journals such as *International Security, International Organization, International Studies Quarterly*, and the *American Political Science Review*. Few of the results that do appear indicate a substantive engagement with such groups as political actors. This has improved to some extent in the past decade or so, but much of the work on Indigenous politics in IR continues to be published in journals that are known for publishing more critical work and that are, by most metrics, less prominent than those noted above; see, e.g., Szarejko (2022) and Mowatt et al. (2024).

2. See, e.g., Davidson (2020) for an overview of literature on alliances that is nested in an examination of US foreign policy

3. See, e.g., later fears surrounding the so-called Ghost Dance (Blackhawk 2006, 270).

4. There I critiqued the normative assumptions that tend to be built into securitization theory, which would suggest that "desecuritization" is generally a good thing; rather, I argue, we need not assume that either securitization or desecuritization has any intrinsic moral valence. I instead draw on Levine (2012) to make the case that we ought to think of securitization theory as a "chastening" tool—one that allows for the critique of any given (de)securitizing move.

5. For an argument to the effect that the likelihood of backlash to "policy gains by marginalized groups" may be overstated, however, see Bishin et al. (2016).

6. This is not to say, however, that the state has always been effective in realizing its claims to sovereignty. As Srivastava (2022) shows, the practice of sovereignty has always been messier than states would like to publicly acknowledge insofar as state sovereignty has coexisted and overlapped with other claimants to sovereignty.

7. See Musgrave (2019) for a discussion of a similar dynamic on the domestic political incentives that have led to increasingly significant changes on foreign policy from one administration to the next. See Evans (2023) for a discussion of how Native American groups have aligned with different partisans over time. My reference to racialization concerns the fundamentally political process of federal recognition of tribal sovereignty. As has occurred in litigation regarding the Indian Child Welfare Act of 1978, some seek to remove legal protections that tribe members receive due to their political relationship with the US government by claiming that such protections are inappropriately racially discriminatory against non-tribe members.

BIBLIOGRAPHY

Abbott, Andrew. *Processual Sociology*. Chicago: University of Chicago Press, 2016.

Ablavsky, Gregory. "The Adjudicatory State: Sovereignty, Property, and Law in the U.S. Territories, 1783–1802." PhD dissertation, University of Pennsylvania, 2016.

Adler, William D. *Engineering Expansion: The U.S. Army and Economic Development, 1787–1860*. Philadelphia: University of Pennsylvania Press, 2021.

———. "'Generalissimo of the Nation': War Making and the Presidency in the Early Republic." *Presidential Studies Quarterly* 43, no. 2 (2013): 412–426.

Alfonseca, Kiara, and Will Carr. "Hawaii Residents Call on Navy to Address Jet Fuel Water Contamination." *ABC News*, August 31, 2022. https://abcnews.go.com/US/hawaii-residents-call-navy-address-jet-fuel-water/story?id=89045641

Alker, Hayward. "Emancipation in the Critical Security Studies Project." In *Critical Security Studies and World Politics*, edited by Ken Booth, 189–214. Boulder: Lynne Rienner Publishers, 2005.

Allen, Michael A., Michael E. Flynn, Carla Martínez Machain, and Andrew Stravers. *Beyond the Wire: US Military Deployments and Host Country Public Opinion*. Oxford: Oxford University Press, 2022.

Alter, Karen J., and Michael Zürn. "Conceptualising Backlash Politics: Introduction to a Special Issue on Backlash Politics in Comparison." *British Journal of Politics and International Relations* 22, no. 4 (2020): 563–584.

Anderson, Nicholas D. "Push and Pull on the Periphery." *International Security* 47, no. 3 (2022/2023): 136–173.

Andreas, Peter. *Smuggler Nation: How Illicit Trade Made America*. Oxford: Oxford University Press, 2013.

Anson, Bert. *The Miami Indians*. Norman: University of Oklahoma Press, 1970.

Ashworth, Lucian M. "Warriors, Pacifists and Empires: Race and Racism in International Thought before 1914." *International Affairs* 98, no. 1 (2022): 281–301.

Aune, Stefan. "Indian Fighters in the Philippines: Imperial Culture and Military Violence in the Philippine–American War." *Pacific Historical Review* 90, no. 4 (2021): 419–447.

———. *Indian Wars Everywhere: Colonial Violence and the Shadow Doctrines of Empire*. Oakland: University of California Press, 2023.

Banner, Stuart. *How the Indians Lost Their Land: Law and Power on the Frontier*. Cambridge, MA: Harvard University Press, 2005.

Barder, Alexander D. *Global Race War: International Politics and Racial Hierarchy*. New York: Oxford University Press, 2021.

———. "Race and International Relations." *International Studies Review* 19, no. 3 (2017): 509–516.

Bauer, Kelly. *Negotiating Autonomy: Mapuche Territorial Demands and Chilean Land Policy*. Pittsburgh: University of Pittsburgh Press, 2021.

Baum, Matthew A., and Philip B. K. Potter. *War and Democratic Constraint: How the Public Influences Foreign Policy*. Princeton: Princeton University Press, 2015.

Bazzi, Samuel, Martin Fiszbein, and Mesay Gebresilasse. "Frontier Culture: The Roots and Persistence of 'Rugged Individualism' in the United States." *Econometrica* 88, no. 6 (2020): 2329–2368.

Beier, J. Marshall. *International Relations in Uncommon Places: Indigeneity, Cosmology, and the Limits of International Theory*. New York: Palgrave Macmillan, 2005.

Bender, Bryan. "George Soros and Charles Koch Take on the 'Endless Wars.'" *Politico*, December 2, 2019. https://www.politico.com/news/2019/12/02/george-soros-and-charles-koch-take-on-the-endless-wars-074737

Benjamin, Andrea, Ray Block, Jared Clemons, Chryl Laird, and Julian Wamble. "Set in Stone? Predicting Confederate Monument Removal." *PS: Political Science and Politics* 53, no. 2 (2020): 237–242.

Bennett, Andrew. *Condemned to Repetition? The Rise, Fall, and Reprise of Soviet-Russian Military Interventionism, 1973–1996*. Cambridge, MA: MIT Press, 1999.

Bentley, Tom. "'Culture War': The Contradictions of Conservative Representations in the Mnemonic Battle over the British Empire." In *Handbook on the Politics of Memory*, edited by Maria Mälksoo, 334–348. Cheltenham: Edward Elgar, 2023.

Biddle, Stephen. *Nonstate Warfare: The Military Methods of Guerrillas, Warlords, and Militias*. Princeton: Princeton University Press, 2021.

Bishin, Benjamin G., Thomas J. Hayes, Matthew B. Incantalupo, and Charles Anthony Smith. "Opinion Backlash and Public Attitudes: Are Political Advances in Gay Rights Counterproductive?" *American Journal of Political Science* 60, no. 3 (2016): 625–648.

Blackhawk, Ned. *The Rediscovery of America: Native Peoples and the Unmaking of US History*. New Haven: Yale University Press, 2023.

———. *Violence over the Land: Indians and Empires in the Early American West*. Cambridge, MA: Harvard University Press, 2006.

Blakeslee, Kayla. "Councilman Arp Responds to Business Personal Property Tax Outcome." *WOWO Radio* (blog), September 29, 2016. https://wowo.com/council man-arp-responds-business-personal-property-tax-outcome/

Blankenship, Brian, and Erik Lin-Greenberg. "Trivial Tripwires?: Military Capabilities and Alliance Reassurance." *Security Studies* 31, no. 1 (2022): 92–117.

Blum, Rachel M. *How the Tea Party Captured the GOP: Insurgent Factions in American Politics*. Chicago: University of Chicago Press, 2020.

Booth, Ken. "Security and Emancipation." *Review of International Studies* 17, no. 4 (1991): 313–326.

Bourdieu, Pierre. *The Logic of Practice*. Translated by Richard Nice. Stanford: Stanford University Press, 1990.

Braumoeller, Bear F. *The Great Powers and the International System: Systemic Theory in Empirical Perspective*. Cambridge, UK: Cambridge University Press, 2012.

———. "The Myth of American Isolationism." *Foreign Policy Analysis* 6, no. 4 (2010): 349–371.

Breemer, Jan S. "The Burden of Trafalgar: Decisive Battle and Naval Strategic Expectations on the Eve of World War I." *Journal of Strategic Studies* 17, no. 1 (1994): 33–62.

Brooks, Risa. "Paradoxes of Professionalism: Rethinking Civil-Military Relations in the United States." *International Security* 44, no. 4 (2020): 7–44.

Brown, Alex. "Fort Wayne Mayor Tom Henry Dies After Cancer Battle." *Indianapolis Business Journal*, March 28, 2024. https://www.ibj.com/articles/fort-wayne -mayor-tom-henry-dies-after-cancer-battle

Brown, Chris. "The 'Practice Turn,' Phronesis and Classical Realism: Towards a Phronetic International Political Theory?" *Millennium* 40, no. 3 (2012): 439–456.

Bruyneel, Kevin. *Settler Memory: The Disavowal of Indigeneity and the Politics of Race in the United States*. Chapel Hill: University of North Carolina Press, 2021.

Calloway, Colin G. *The American Revolution in Indian Country: Crisis and Diversity in Native American Communities*. Cambridge, UK: Cambridge University Press, 1995.

———. *The Shawnees and the War for America*. New York: Penguin, 2007.

———. *The Victory with No Name: The Native American Defeat of the First American Army*. Oxford: Oxford University Press, 2014.

Campbell, Arthur. "Arthur Campbell to George Washington." National Archives. *Founders Online*, May 10, 1789. https://founders.archives.gov/documents/Wash ington/05-02-02-0185

———. "Arthur Campbell to Governor Beverley Randolph." In *Calendar of Virginia State Papers and Other Manuscripts*, vol. 4, edited by William P. Palmer. Richmond: Superintendent of Public Printing, 1789.

———. "Arthur Campbell to James Madison." National Archives. *Founders Online*, October 28, 1785. https://founders.archives.gov/documents/Madison/01-08-02-0201

————. "Arthur Campbell to James Madison." National Archives. *Founders Online,* January 4, 1787. https://founders.archives.gov/documents/Madison/01-09-02-0119

Campbell, David. *Writing Security: United States Foreign Policy and the Politics of Identity.* Minneapolis: University of Minnesota Press, 1998.

Carothers, Thomas. "The End of the Transition Paradigm." *Journal of Democracy* 13, no. 1 (2002): 5–21.

Carson, Austin. "Facing Off and Saving Face: Covert Intervention and Escalation Management in the Korean War." *International Organization* 70, no. 1 (2016): 103–131.

Cayton, Andrew R. L. "'Separate Interests' and the Nation-State: The Washington Administration and the Origins of Regionalism in the Trans-Appalachian West." *Journal of American History* 79, no. 1 (1992): 39–67.

Clark, Thomas D., ed. *The Voice of the Frontier: John Bradford's Notes on Kentucky.* Lexington: University Press of Kentucky, 1993.

Clausewitz, Carl von. *On War.* Edited by Michael Howard and Peter Paret. Princeton: Princeton University Press, 1976 [1832].

Clayton, Andrew R. L. "The Contours of Power in a Frontier Town: Marietta, Ohio, 1788–1803." *Journal of the Early Republic* 6, no. 2 (1986): 103–126.

Coates, Ken S. *A Global History of Indigenous Peoples: Struggle and Survival* Hampshire. Palgrave Macmillan, 2004.

Colby, Elbridge. "How to Fight Savage Tribes." *American Journal of International Law* 21, no. 2 (1927): 279–288.

————. "The Progressive Character of War." *American Political Science Review* 18, no. 2 (1924): 366–373.

Colby, Elbridge A. *The Strategy of Denial: American Defense in an Age of Great Power Conflict.* New Haven: Yale University Press, 2021.

Cooley, Alexander. *Base Politics: Democratic Change and the US Military Overseas.* Ithaca: Cornell University Press, 2008.

Cooley, Alexander, and Daniel H. Nexon. "'The Empire Will Compensate You': The Structural Dynamics of the US Overseas Basing Network." *Perspectives on Politics* 11, no. 4 (2013): 1034–1050.

————. *Exit from Hegemony: The Unraveling of the American Global Order.* New York: Oxford University Press, 2020.

Cooley, Alexander, Daniel H. Nexon, and Steven Ward. "Revising Order or Challenging the Balance of Military Power? An Alternative Typology of Revisionist and Status-Quo States." *Review of International Studies* 45, no. 4 (2019): 689–708.

Copeland, Dale C. *A World Safe for Commerce: American Foreign Policy from the Revolution to the Rise of China.* Princeton: Princeton University Press, 2024.

Cote, Amanda C. *Gaming Sexism: Gender and Identity in the Era of Casual Video Games.* New York: New York University Press, 2020.

Cotroneo, Ross R., and Jack Dozier. "A Time of Disintegration: The Coeur d'Alene and the Dawes Act." *Western Historical Quarterly* 5, no. 4 (1974): 405–419.

Crane-Seeber, Jesse. "Everyday Counterinsurgency." *International Political Sociology* 5, no. 4 (2011): 450–453.

Cunningham, Charles H. "Origin of the Friar Lands Question in the Philippines." *American Political Science Review* 10, no. 3 (1916): 465–480.

Dahl, Adam. *Empire of the People: Settler Colonialism and the Foundations of Modern Democratic Thought*. Lawrence: University Press of Kansas, 2018.

Dalton, Tristram. "Letter to John Adams." In *Papers of John Adams*, vol. 16. *Massachusetts Historical Society*, June 16, 1784. http://www.masshist.org/publications/adams-papers/index.php/view/ADMS-06-16-02-0139

David, Lea. *The Past Can't Heal Us: The Dangers of Mandating Memory in the Name of Human Rights*. Cambridge, UK: Cambridge University Press, 2020.

Davidson, Jason W. *America's Entangling Alliances, 1778 to the Present*. Washington, DC: Georgetown University Press, 2020.

De Carvalho, Benjamin, Halvard Leira, and John M. Hobson. "The Big Bangs of IR: The Myths That Your Teachers Still Tell You About 1648 and 1919." *Millennium* 39, no. 3 (2011): 735–758.

Deloria, Jr., Vine. *Custer Died for Your Sins*. New York: University of Oklahoma Press, 1969.

Deloria, Jr., Vine, and David E. Wilkins. *Tribes, Treaties, and Constitutional Tribulations*. Austin: University of Texas Press, 1999.

DeLucia, Christine M. *Memory Lands: King Philip's War and the Place of Violence in the Northeast*. New Haven: Yale University Press, 2018.

Dhamoon, Rita. "A Feminist Approach to Decolonizing Anti-Racism: Rethinking Transnationalism, Intersectionality, and Settler Colonialism." *Feral Feminisms* 4, no. 1 (2015): 20–37.

Dombrowski, Peter, and Simon Reich. "The United States of America." In *Comparative Grand Strategy: A Framework and Cases*, edited by Thierry Balzacq, Peter Dombrowski, and Simon Reich, 25–49. Oxford: Oxford University Press, 2019.

DuVal, Kathleen. *The Native Ground: Indians and Colonists in the Heart of the Continent*. Philadelphia: University of Pennsylvania Press, 2006.

Echavarria II, Antulio J. *Reconsidering the American Way of War: US Military Practices from the Revolution to Afghanistan*. Washington, DC: Georgetown University Press, 2014.

Edelstein, David M. *Over the Horizon: Time, Uncertainty, and the Rise of Great Powers*. Ithaca: Cornell University Press, 2017.

Edelstein, David M., and Joshua R. Itzkowitz Shifrinson. "It's a Trap! Security Commitments and the Risks of Entrapment." In *US Grand Strategy in the 21st Century: The Case for Restraint*, edited by A. Trevor Thrall and Benjamin H. Friedman, 19–41. London: Routledge, 2018.

Ejdus, Filip. "Ontological Security and the Politics of Memory in International Relations." In *Handbook on the Politics of Memory*, edited by Maria Mälksoo, 31–45. Cheltenham: Edward Elgar, 2023.

El Amine, Loubna. "The Nation-State 1648–2148." *Political Theory* 51, no. 1 (2023): 65–73.

Elkins, Stanley, and Eric McKitrick. "A Meaning for Turner's Frontier: Part I: Democracy in the Old Northwest." *Political Science Quarterly* 69, no. 3 (1954): 321–353.

Elman, Colin. "Extending Offensive Realism: The Louisiana Purchase and America's Rise to Regional Hegemony." *American Political Science Review* 98, no. 4 (2004): 563–576.

Emery, John R. "Moral Choices Without Moral Language: 1950s Political-Military Wargaming at the RAND Corporation." *Texas National Security Review* 4, no. 4 (2021): 11–31.

Emirbayer, Mustafa. "Manifesto for a Relational Sociology." *American Journal of Sociology* 103, no. 2 (1997): 281–317.

Enloe, Cynthia. *Bananas, Beaches, and Bases: Making Feminist Sense of International Politics.* Berkeley: University of California Press, 1990.

Evans, Laura E. *Power from Powerlessness: Tribal Governments, Institutional Niches, and American Federalism.* Oxford: Oxford University Press, 2011.

———. "The Strange Career of Federal Indian Policy: Rural Politics, Native Nations, and the Path Away from Assimilation." *Studies in American Political Development* 37, no. 2 (2023): 89–110.

Evers, Miles M., and Eric Grynaviski. *The Price of Empire: American Entrepreneurs and the Origins of America's First Pacific Empire.* Cambridge, UK: Cambridge University Press, 2024.

Fearon, James D. "Rationalist Explanations for War." *International Organization* 49, no. 3 (1995): 379–414.

Fearon, James D., and Alexander Wendt. "Rationalism v. Constructivism: A Skeptical View." In *Handbook of International Relations*, edited by Walter Carlsnaes, Thomas Risse, and Beth A. Simmons, 52–72. London: SAGE Publications, 2002.

Fenton, William N. *The Great Law and the Longhouse: A Political History of the Iroquois Confederacy.* Norman: University of Oklahoma Press, 1998.

Ferguson, Kennan. "Why Does Political Science Hate American Indians?" *Perspectives on Politics* 14, no. 4 (December 2016): 1029–1038.

Fernandes, Melanie L. "'Under the Auspices of Peace': The Northwest Indian War and Its Impact on the Early American Republic." *Gettysburg Historical Journal* 15, no. 8 (2015): 135–185.

Flaherty, Daniel. "'People to Our Selves': Chickasaw Diplomacy and Political Development in the Nineteenth Century." PhD dissertation, University of Oklahoma, 2012.

Flint, E. H. *Indian Wars of the West: Containing Bibliographical Sketches of Those Pioneers Who Headed the Western Settlers in Repelling the Attacks of the Savages, Together with a View of the Character, Manners, Monuments, and Antiquities of the Western Indians.* Cincinnati: N. & G. Guilford & Co., 1833.

Flyvbjerg, Bent. *Making Social Science Matter: Why Social Inquiry Fails and How It Can Succeed Again*. Cambridge, UK: Cambridge University Press, 2001.

Freeman, Bianca. "The Positivist Turn of Race in IR." *International Studies Review* 26, no. 3 (2024). https://doi.org/10.1093/isr/viae034.02

Friedman, B. A. *On Tactics: A Theory of Victory in Battle*. Annapolis: Naval Institute Press, 2017.

Frost, Mervyn, and Silviya Lechner. "Two Conceptions of International Practice: Aristotelian Praxis or Wittgensteinian Language-Games?" *Review of International Studies* 42, no. 2 (2016): 334–350.

Frymer, Paul. *Building an American Empire: The Era of Territorial and Political Expansion*. Princeton: Princeton University Press, 2017.

———. "'A Rush and a Push and the Land Is Ours': Territorial Expansion, Land Policy, and U.S. State Formation." *Perspectives on Politics* 12, no. 1 (March 2014): 119–144.

Fujii, Lee Ann. "The Puzzle of Extra-Lethal Violence." *Perspectives on Politics* 11, no. 2 (2013): 410–426.

Funkhouser, Anthony C. "Efficient or Effective? An Assessment of the Army Lessons Learned Program." U.S. Army War College Strategy Research Project, 2007.

Gailmard, Sean. *Agents of Empire: English Imperial Governance and the Making of American Political Institutions*. Cambridge, UK: Cambridge University Press, 2024.

Galula, David. *Counterinsurgency Warfare: Theory and Practice*. Westport: Praeger Security International, 2006 [1964].

Gates, John M. *Schoolbooks and Krags: The United States Army in the Philippines, 1898–1902*. Westport: Greenwood Press, 1973.

Geertz, Clifford. *The Interpretation of Cultures*. New York: Basic Books, 1973.

Gerring, John. "Mere Description." *British Journal of Political Science* 42, no. 4 (2012): 721–746.

Go, Julian. "Introduction: Global Perspectives on the U.S. Colonial State in the Philippines." In *The American Colonial State in the Philippines: Global Perspectives*, edited by Julian Go and Anne L. Foster, 1–42. Durham: Duke University Press, 2003.

———. *Policing Empires: Militarization, Race, and the Imperial Boomerang in Britain and the US*. Oxford: Oxford University Press, 2024.

Goddard, Stacie E. "Embedded Revisionism: Networks, Institutions, and Challenges to World Order." *International Organization* 72, no. 4 (2018a): 763–797.

———. *When Right Makes Might: Rising Powers and World Order*. Ithaca: Cornell University Press, 2018b.

Goddard, Stacie E., and Paul K. MacDonald. "From 'Butcher and Bolt' to 'Bugsplat': Race, Counterinsurgency, and International Politics." *Security Studies* 32, no. 4–5 (2023): 714–747.

Gong, Dave. "Arp Takes Shots at Republicans." *Journal Gazette*, September 5, 2018.

https://www.journalgazette.net/local/arp-takes-shots-at-republicans/article_f3db8713-96da-5faa-8752-e0d85574c816.html

Gooding, Mark. "Bayonets in the Wilderness: Anthony Wayne's Legion in the Old Northwest by Alan D. Gaff (Review)." *Ohio Valley History* 5, no. 1 (2005): 79–80.

Gould, Harry. "A Reflexive Practice of Prudence." In *Reflexivity and International Relations: Positionality, Critique, and Practice*, edited by Jack L. Amoureux and Brent J. Steele, 253–263. Abingdon: Routledge, 2015.

Gray, Kishonna L. "Intersection Oppressions and Online Communities: Examining the Experiences of Women of Color in Xbox Live." *Information, Communication and Society* 15, no. 2 (2012): 411–428.

Grenier, John. *The First Way of War: American War Making on the Frontier, 1607–1814*. Cambridge, UK: Cambridge University Press, 2005.

Greve, Charles Theodore, ed. "Letter of John Cleves Symmes to Elias Boudinot of January 12 and 15, 1792." *Quarterly Publication of the Historical and Philosophical Society of Ohio* 5, no. 3 (1910): 93–101.

Grynaviski, Eric. *America's Middlemen: Power at the Edge of Empire*. Cambridge, UK: Cambridge University Press, 2018.

Guyatt, Nicholas. *Bind Us Apart: How Enlightened Americans Invented Racial Segregation*. New York: Basic Books, 2016.

Hacking, Ian. *The Social Construction of What?* Cambridge, MA: Harvard University Press, 1999.

Hafner-Burton, Emilie M., Miles Kahler, and Alexander H. Montgomery. "Network Analysis for International Relations." *International Organization* 63, no. 3 (2009): 559–592.

Hall, Charles S. *Life and Letters of Samuel Holden Parsons: Major General in the Continental Army and Chief Judge of the Northwestern Territory, 1737–1789*. Binghamton: Otseningo Publishing Co., 1905.

Hämäläinen, Pekka. *The Comanche Empire*. New Haven: Yale University Press, 2008.

Hamilton, Alexander. "Federalist No. 24: The Powers Necessary to the Common Defense Further Considered." *Independent Journal*, December 19, 1787. https://avalon.law.yale.edu/18th_century/fed24.asp

Hansen, Lene. *Security as Practice: Discourse Analysis and the Bosnian War*. London: Routledge, 2006.

Hare, Christopher, and Keith T. Poole. "The Polarization of Contemporary American Politics." *Polity* 46, no. 3 (2014): 411–429.

Harkavy, Robert E. *Bases Abroad: The Global Foreign Military Presence*. Oxford: Oxford University Press, 1989.

Harmar, Josiah, Gayle Thornbrough, John Francis Hamtramck, and William L. Clements Library. *Outpost on the Wabash, 1787–1791: Letters of Brigadier General Josiah Harmar and Major John Francis Hamtramck, and Other Letters and Documents Selected from the Harmar Papers in the William L. Clements Library*. Indianapolis: Indiana Historical Society, 1957.

Hawkins, Emeline. "Mary Penrose Wayne to Make Her Debut July 16." *Greater Fort Wayne Business Weekly*, July 10, 2023. https://www.fwbusiness.com/news/arti cle_b525f28e-cf05-5832-abbf-2a2f18dcbcc4.html

Hazelton, Jacqueline L. *Bullets Not Ballots: Success in Counterinsurgency Warfare.* Ithaca: Cornell University Press, 2021.

Healey, Gareth. "Proving Grounds: Performing Masculine Identities in Call of Duty: Black Ops." *Game Studies* 16, no. 2 (2016). https://gamestudies.org/1602/articles/ healey

Healy, Jack. "For Oklahoma Tribe, Vindication at Long Last." *New York Times*, July 11, 2020. https://www.nytimes.com/2020/07/11/us/muscogee-creek-nation-okla homa.html

Helderman, Leonard C. "Danger on Wabash: Vincennes Letters of 1786." *Indiana Magazine of History* 34, no. 4 (1938): 455–467.

Henne, Peter. *Religious Appeals in Power Politics.* Ithaca: Cornell University Press, 2023.

Herring, George C. *From Colony to Superpower: US Foreign Relations Since 1776.* New York: Oxford University Press, 2008.

Hietala, Thomas R. *Manifest Design: American Exceptionalism and Empire.* Ithaca: Cornell University Press, 2003 [1985].

Hitchmough, Sam. "'It's Not Your Country Any More': Contested National Narratives and the Columbus Day Parade Protests in Denver." *European Journal of American Culture* 32, no. 3 (2013): 263–283.

Hixson, Walter L. *American Settler Colonialism: A History.* New York: Palgrave Macmillan, 2013.

Holmes, Carolyn E., Meg K. Guliford, Mary Anne S. Mendoza-Davé, and Michelle Jurkovich. "A Case for Description." *PS: Political Science and Politics* 57, no. 1 (2024): 51–56.

Holsti, Ole R. *Making American Foreign Policy.* New York: Routledge, 2006.

Holton, Woody. "The Ohio Indians and the Coming of the American Revolution in Virginia." *Journal of Southern History* 60, no. 3 (1994): 453–478.

Hopkins, Daniel J. *The Increasingly United States: How and Why American Political Behavior Nationalized.* Chicago: University of Chicago Press, 2018.

Hopkins, Daniel, and Hans Noel. "Trump and the Shifting Meaning of 'Conservative': Using Activists' Pairwise Comparisons to Measure Politicians' Perceived Ideologies." *American Political Science Review* 116, no. 3 (2022): 1133–1140.

Horsman, Reginald. "American Indian Policy in the Old Northwest, 1783–1812." *William and Mary Quarterly* 18, no. 1 (1961): 35–53.

Hurt, R. Douglas. "John Cleves Symmes and the Miami Purchase." In *Builders of Ohio: A Biographical History,* 14–25. Columbus: Ohio State University Press, 2003.

———. *The Ohio Frontier: Crucible of the Old Northwest, 1720–1830.* Bloomington: Indiana University Press, 1996.

Immerwahr, Daniel. "Contest or Conquest? A Provocative History of Indigenous America." *Harper's Magazine*, November 2022. https://harpers.org/archive/2022/11/contest-or-conquest-indigenous-continent-the-epic-contest-for-north-america-pekka-hamalainen-provocative-history/

———. *How to Hide an Empire: A History of the Greater United States.* New York: Farrar, Straus and Giroux, 2019.

Jackson, Patrick Thaddeus. *The Conduct of Inquiry in International Relations.* New York: Routledge, 2011.

———. "Defending the West: Occidentalism and the Formation of NATO." *Journal of Political Philosophy* 11, no. 3 (2003): 223–252.

———. *Facts and Explanations in International Studies . . . and Beyond.* Abingdon: Routledge, 2025.

Jackson, Patrick Thaddeus, and Daniel H. Nexon. "Reclaiming the Social: Relationalism in Anglophone International Studies." *Cambridge Review of International Affairs* 32, no. 5 (2019): 582–600.

———. "Relations Before States: Substance, Process and the Study of World Politics." *European Journal of International Relations* 5, no. 3 (1999): 291–332.

Jefferson, Thomas. "Letter to Governor Monroe: November 24, 1801." In *The Writings of Thomas Jefferson: Being His Autobiography, Correspondence, Reports, Messages, Addresses, and Other Writings, Official and Private,* vol. IV, edited by H. A. Washington. New York: H. W. Derby, 1861.

Jervis, Robert. *System Effects: Complexity in Political and Social Life.* Princeton: Princeton University Press, 1997.

Johnston, Josiah Stoddard. *First Explorations of Kentucky: Journals of Dr. Thomas Walker, 1750, and Christopher Gist, 1751.* Louisville: John P. Morton and Company, 1898.

Jones, O. Garfield. "Teaching Citizenship to the Filipinos by Local Self-Government." *American Political Science Review* 18, no. 2 (1924): 285–295.

Joyce, Renanah Miles, and Brian Blankenship. "The Market for Foreign Bases." *Security Studies* 33, no. 2 (2024): 194–223.

Kalaw, Maximo M. "The New Philippine Government." *American Political Science Review* 13, no. 3 (1919): 415–428.

Katznelson, Ira. "Flexible Capacity: The Military and Early American Statebuilding." In *Shaped by War and Trade: International Influences on American Political Development,* edited by Ira Katznelson and Martin Shefter, 82–110. Princeton: Princeton University Press, 2002.

Keller, Christine, Colleen Boyd, Mark Groover, and Mark Hill. "Archeology of the Battles of Fort Recovery, Mercer County, Ohio: Education and Protection." National Park Service, American Battlefield Protection Program, 2011.

Keyes, Sarah. *American Burial Ground: A New History of the Overland Trail.* Philadelphia: University of Pennsylvania Press, 2023.

Khong, Yuen Foong. *Analogies at War: Korea, Munich, Dien Bien Phu, and the Vietnam Decisions of 1965.* Princeton: Princeton University Press, 1992.

Kim, Claudia Junghyun. *Base Towns: Local Contestation of the U.S. Military in Korea and Japan.* Oxford: Oxford University Press, 2023.

Kluger, Richard. *Seizing Destiny: How America Grew from Sea to Shining Sea.* New York: Vintage, 2007.

Knopf, Richard Clark. "Anthony Wayne and the Founding of the United States Army." PhD dissertation, Ohio State University, 1960.

Knox, Henry. "The Causes of the Existing Hostilities Between the United States, and Certain Tribes of Indians North-West of the Ohio." U.S. War Department, *Library of Congress*, January 26, 1792. https://www.loc.gov/item/rbpe.21800100/

———. "Henry Knox to George Washington." National Archives. *Founders Online*, July 7, 1789. https://founders.archives.gov/documents/Washington/05-03-02-0067

———. "Indian Affairs." In *George Washington's Papers*, Series 4, General Correspondence. *Library of Congress,* 1794. https://www.loc.gov/resource/mgw4.106_0891_0896/?sp=1

———. "Land Purchase from the Wabash Indians." In *George Washington Papers,* Series 4, General Correspondence. *Library of Congress*, December 10, 1790. https://www.loc.gov/item/mgw436868/

Krebs, Ronald R. *Narrative and the Making of US National Security.* Cambridge, UK: Cambridge University Press, 2015.

Kupchan, Charles A. *Isolationism: A History of America's Efforts to Shield Itself from the World.* New York: Oxford University Press, 2020.

Kurtz, Dave. "Dennis Kruse Will Retire from Indiana Senate; Replacement to Announce Aug. 30." *Greater Fort Wayne Business Weekly*, August 27, 2021. https://www.fwbusiness.com/fwbusiness/article_fcc15a16-9374-5f42-9ef4-1dead4b29c62.html

Kustermans, Jorg. "Parsing the Practice Turn: Practice, Practical Knowledge, Practices." *Millennium* 44, no. 2 (2016): 175–196.

Kustermans, Jorg, Benjamin de Carvalho, and Paul Beaumont. "Whose Revisionism, Which International Order? Social Structure and Its Discontents." *Global Studies Quarterly* 3, no. 1 (2023). https://doi.org/10.1093/isagsq/ksad009

LaFeber, Walter. *The American Age: United States Foreign Policy at Home and Abroad, 1750 to the Present.* New York: Norton, 1989.

Larson, Edward J. *The Return of George Washington: United the States, 1783–1789.* New York: William Morrow, 2014.

Layne, Christopher. *The Peace of Illusions: American Grand Strategy from 1940 to the Present.* Ithaca: Cornell University Press, 2006.

Leadingham, Christopher L. "To Open 'the Doors of Commerce': The Mississippi River Question and the Shifting Politics of the Kentucky Statehood Movement." *Register of the Kentucky Historical Society* 114, no. 3/4 (2016): 341–369.

Leander, Anna. "The Promises, Problems, and Potentials of a Bourdieu-Inspired Staging of International Relations." *International Political Sociology* 5, no. 3 (2011): 294–313.

Lee, Jacob F. *Masters of the Middle Waters: Indian Nations and Colonial Ambitions Along the Mississippi.* Cambridge, MA: Belknap Press, 2019.

Lee, Wayne E. *The Cutting-Off Way: Indigenous Warfare in Eastern North America, 1500–1800*. Chapel Hill: University of North Carolina Press, 2023.

Leege, David C. "Coalitions, Cues, Strategic Politics, and the Staying Power of the Religious Right, or Why Political Scientists Ought to Pay Attention to Cultural Politics." *PS: Political Science and Politics* 25, no. 2 (1992): 198–204.

Lemke, Tobias, Andrew A. Szarejko, Jessica Auchter, Alexander D. Barder, Daniel Green, Stephen Pampinella, and Swati Srivastava. "Forum: Doing Historical International Relations." *Cambridge Review of International Affairs* 36, no. 1 (2023): 3–34.

Lerner, Adam B. "What's It Like to Be a State? An Argument for State Consciousness." *International Theory* 13, no. 2 (2021): 260–286.

Levine, Daniel J. *Recovering International Relations: The Promise of Sustainable Critique*. Oxford: Oxford University Press, 2012.

Lightfoot, Sheryl R. *Global Indigenous Politics: A Subtle Revolution*. London: Routledge, 2016.

———. "Decolonizing Self-Determination: Haudenosaunee Passports and Negotiated Sovereignty." *European Journal of International Relations* 27, no. 4 (2021): 971–994.

Limerick, Patricia Nelson. *The Legacy of Conquest: The Unbroken Past of the American West*. New York: Norton, 1987.

Lindberg, Timothy. "Legislating for American Empire: The U.S. Congress and Territorial Policy." PhD dissertation, State University of New York at Albany, 2015.

Lindsay, Jeanie. "Lawmakers Compromise on Sex Ed Bill, Opt-In Requirement." *WFYI Indianapolis*, March 13, 2018. https://www.wfyi.org/news/articles/lawmakers-compromise-on-sex-ed-bill-opt-in-requirement

Linklater, Andro. *An Artist in Treason: The Extraordinary Double Life of General James Wilkinson*. New York: Walker & Company, 2009.

Linn, Brian McAllister. *The U.S. Army and Counterinsurgency in the Philippine War, 1899–1902*. Chapel Hill: University of North Carolina Press, 1989.

Lutz, Catherine, ed. *The Bases of Empire: The Global Struggle Against U.S. Military Posts*. New York: New York University Press, 2009.

Lyall, Jason. "Are Coethnics More Effective Counterinsurgents? Evidence from the Second Chechen War." *American Political Science Review* 104, no. 1 (2010): 1–20.

Maass, Richard W. *The Picky Eagle: How Democracy and Xenophobia Limited U.S. Territorial Expansion*. Ithaca: Cornell University Press, 2020.

———. "Racialization and International Security." *International Security* 48, no. 2 (2023): 91–126.

———. "Whitewashing American Exceptionalism: Racialized Subject-Positioning and US Foreign Policy." *International Studies Quarterly* 68, no. 3 (2024). https://doi.org/10.1093/isq/sqae085

MacArthur, Douglas. *Reminiscences*. Annapolis: Naval Institute Press, 1964.

MacDonald, Paul K. *Networks of Domination: The Social Foundations of Peripheral Conquest in International Politics*. Oxford: Oxford University Press, 2014.

MacKay, Joseph. *The Counterinsurgent Imagination: A New Intellectual History.* Cambridge, UK: Cambridge University Press, 2023.

Mälksoo, Maria. "Politics of Memory: A Conceptual Introduction." In *Handbook on the Politics of Memory,* edited by Maria Mälksoo, 1–16. Cheltenham: Edward Elgar, 2023.

Mandelbaum, Michael. *The Four Ages of American Foreign Policy: Weak Power, Great Power, Superpower, Hyperpower.* Oxford: Oxford University Press, 2022.

Maslowski, Peter. "To the Edge of Greatness: The United States, 1783–1865." In *The Making of Strategy: Rulers, States, and War,* edited by Williamson Murray, MacGregor Knox, and Alvin Bernstein, 205–241. Cambridge, UK: Cambridge University Press, 1994.

Maulden, Kristopher. *The Federalist Frontier: Settler Politics in the Old Northwest, 1783–1840.* Columbia: University of Missouri Press, 2019.

———. "A Show of Force: The Northwest Indian War and the Early American State." *Ohio Valley History* 16, no. 4 (2016): 20–40.

Mayhew, David R. *Congress: The Electoral Connection,* 2nd ed. New Haven: Yale University Press, 2004 [1974].

McAlister, Lyle N. "William Augustus Bowles and the State of Muskogee." *Florida Historical Quarterly* 40, no. 4 (1962): 317–328.

McCourt, David M. *The New Constructivism in International Relations Theory.* Bristol: Bristol University Press, 2022.

———. "Practice Theory and Relationalism as the New Constructivism." *International Studies Quarterly* 60, no. 3 (2016): 475–485.

McDermott, John D. *A Guide to the Indian Wars of the West.* Lincoln: University of Nebraska Press, 1998.

McGlinchey, Frazer Dorian. "'A Superior Civilization': Appropriation, Negotiation, and Interaction in the Northwest Territory, 1787–1795." In *The Boundaries Between Us: Natives and Newcomers Along the Frontiers of the Old Northwest Territory, 1750–1850,* edited by Daniel P. Barr, 118–142. Kent: Kent State University Press, 2006.

McNamee, Lachlan. *Settling for Less: Why States Colonize and Why They Stop.* Princeton: Princeton University Press, 2023.

Mearsheimer, John J. *The Tragedy of Great Power Politics.* New York: Norton, 2001.

Mendel, Adam. "The First AUMF: The Northwest Indian War, 1790–1795, and the War on Terror." *University of Pennsylvania Journal of Constitutional Law* 18, no. 4 (2016): 1309–1346.

Merk, Frederick. *History of the Westward Movement.* New York: Knopf, 1978.

———. *Manifest Destiny and Mission in American History: A Reinterpretation.* Cambridge, MA: Harvard University Press, 1963.

Middleton, Richard. *Pontiac's War: Its Causes, Course and Consequences.* New York: Routledge, 2007.

Mignolo, Walter D., and Catherine E. Walsh. *On Decoloniality: Concepts, Analytics, Praxis.* Durham: Duke University Press, 2018.

Miller, Stuart Creighton. *"Benevolent Assimilation": The American Conquest of the Philippines, 1899–1903.* New Haven: Yale University Press, 1982.

Millett, Allan R., and Peter Maslowski. *For the Common Defense: A Military History of the United States of America.* New York: Free Press, 1984.

Mitzen, Jennifer. "Ontological Security in World Politics: State Identity and the Security Dilemma." *European Journal of International Relations* 12, no. 3 (2006): 341–370.

Morgenthau, Hans J. "The United States as a World Power: A Balance-Sheet." *International Studies* 11, no. 2 (1969): 111–148.

Morrissey, Robert Michael. *Empire by Collaboration: Indians, Colonists, and Governments in Colonial Illinois Country.* Philadelphia: University of Pennsylvania Press, 2015.

Mowatt, Morgan, Matthew Wildcat, and Gina Starblanket. "Indigenous Sovereignty and Political Science: Building an Indigenous Politics Subfield." *Annual Review of Political Science* 27, no. 1 (2024): 301–316.

Moynihan, Daniel. "Delegitimization, Deconstruction and Control: Undermining the Administrative State." *Annals of the American Academy of Political and Social Science* 699, no. 1 (2022): 36–49.

Murthy, Dhiraj. "Digital Ethnography: An Examination of the Use of New Technologies for Social Research." *Sociology* 42, no. 5 (2008): 837–855.

Musgrave, Paul. "International Hegemony Meets Domestic Politics: Why Liberals Can Be Pessimists." *Security Studies* 28, no. 3 (2019): 451–478.

Nagl, John A. *Counterinsurgency Lessons from Malaya and Vietnam: Learning to Eat Soup with a Knife.* Westport: Praeger, 2002.

Nair, Deepak. "Using Bourdieu's Habitus in International Relations." *International Studies Quarterly* 68, no. 2 (2024): 1–10.

Nardin, Terry. "Realism and Redistribution." *Journal of Value Inquiry* 23, no. 3 (1989): 209–225.

Narizny, Kevin. *The Political Economy of Grand Strategy.* Ithaca: Cornell University Press, 2007.

Narrett, David E. "Geopolitics and Intrigue: James Wilkinson, the Spanish Borderlands, and Mexican Independence." *William and Mary Quarterly* 69, no. 1 (2012): 101–146.

NCSE. "Mounting Opposition to Indiana's Creationist Bill." *National Center for Science Education (NCSE)* (blog), January 23, 2012. https://ncse.ngo/mounting-opposition-indianas-creationist-bill

Nelson, Larry L. "Bayonets in the Wilderness: Anthony Wayne's Legion in the Old Northwest." *Journal of American History* 92, no. 1 (2005): 204–205.

Nelson, Paul David. *Anthony Wayne, Soldier of the Early Republic.* Bloomington: Indiana University Press, 1985.

Nexon, Daniel H. "Relationalism and New Systems Theory." In *New Systems Theories of World Politics*, edited by Mathias Albert, Lars-Erik Cederman, and Alexander Wendt, 99–126. New York: Palgrave, 2010.

———. "Religion and International Relations: No Leap of Faith Required." In *Reli-*

gion and International Relations Theory, edited by Jack L. Snyder, 141–167. New York: Columbia University Press, 2011.

Nordin, Astrid H. M., et al. "Toward Global Relational Theorizing: A Dialogue Between Sinophone and Anglophone Scholarship on Relationalism." *Cambridge Review of International Affairs* 32, no. 5 (2019): 570–581.

Nordlinger, Eric. *Isolationism Reconfigured: American Foreign Policy for a New Century*. Princeton: Princeton University Press, 1996. https://www.degruyter.com/document/doi/10.1515/9781400821815/html

O'Malley, Nancy. "'Stockading Up': A Study of Pioneer Stations in the Inner Bluegrass Region of Kentucky." Kentucky Heritage Council, April 30, 1987. Accessed at the Shawnee Tribe Cultural Center.

O'Shea, Paul. "Strategic Narratives and US Military Bases in Japan: How 'Deterrence' Makes the Marine Base on Okinawa 'Indispensable.'" *Media, War and Conflict* 12, no. 4 (2019): 450–467.

Ostler, Jeffrey. *Surviving Genocide: Native Nations and the United States from the American Revolution to Bleeding Kansas*. New Haven: Yale University Press, 2019.

———. "'To Extirpate the Indians': An Indigenous Consciousness of Genocide in the Ohio Valley and Lower Great Lakes, 1750s–1810." *William and Mary Quarterly* 72, no. 4 (2015): 587–622.

Pachirat, Timothy. *Every Twelve Seconds: Industrialized Slaughter and the Politics of Sight*. New Haven: Yale University Press, 2011.

Pampinella, Stephen. "Hegemonic Competition in Intrastate War: The Social Construction of Insurgency and Counterinsurgency in Iraq's al-Anbar Province." *Studies in Conflict and Terrorism* 35, no. 2 (2012): 95–112.

———. "'The Way of Progress and Civilization': Racial Hierarchy and US State Building in Haiti and the Dominican Republic (1915–1922)." *Journal of Global Security Studies* 6, no. 3 (2021). https://doi.org/10.1093/jogss/ogaa050

Parent, Joseph M. *Uniting States: Voluntary Union in World Politics*. New York: Oxford University Press, 2011.

Parent, Joseph M., and Sebastian Rosato. "Balancing in Neorealism." *International Security* 40, no. 2 (2015): 51–86.

Parmenter, Jon. "Bayonets in the Wilderness: Anthony Wayne's Legion in the Old Northwest." *Journal of the Early Republic* 25, no. 1 (2005): 133–135.

Pawlikowski, Melissah. "The Plight and the Bounty: Squatters, War Profiteers, and the Transforming Hand of Sovereignty in Indian Country, 1750–1774." PhD dissertation, Ohio State University, 2014.

Pember, Mary Annette. "Celebrating (Not) Mad Wayne Day." *Indian Country Today*, July 17, 2019. https://ictnews.org/news/celebrating-not-mad-wayne-day

Peterson, Erik, and Manuela Muñoz. "'Stick to Sports': Evidence from Sports Media on the Origins and Consequences of Newly Politicized Attitudes." *Political Communication* 39, no. 4 (2022): 454–474.

Peterson, John Alton. *Utah's Black Hawk War*. Salt Lake City: University of Utah Press, 1998.

Priest, Andrew. *Designs on Empire: America's Rise to Power in the Age of European Imperialism.* New York: Columbia University Press, 2021.

Prior, Charles W. A. *Settlers in Indian Country: Sovereignty and Indigenous Power in Early America.* Cambridge, UK: Cambridge University Press, 2020.

Prucha, Francis Paul. *American Indian Policy in the Formative Years: The Indian Trade and Intercourse Acts, 1790–1834.* Cambridge, MA: Harvard University Press, 1962.

———. *American Indian Treaties: The History of a Political Anomaly.* Berkeley: University of California Press, 1994.

———. *Documents of United States Indian Policy,* 3rd ed. Lincoln: University of Nebraska Press, 2000.

———. *A Guide to the Military Posts of the United States, 1789–1895.* Madison: State Historical Society of Wisconsin, 1964.

———. *The Sword of the Republic: The United States Army on the Frontier, 1783–1846.* New York: Macmillan, 1969.

Putnam, Rufus, Wabash Indians, and Weya Indians. "Speech by Weya Indian, with Putnam's Reply." In *George Washington's Papers,* Series 4, General Correspondence. *Library of Congress,* 1792. https://www.loc.gov/resource/mgw4.102_0241_0243/?sp=1

Rafert, Stewart. *The Miami Indians of Indiana: A Persistent People, 1654–1994.* Indianapolis: Indiana Historical Society, 1996.

Randolph, Edmund. *The Debates in the Several State Conventions, of the Adoption of the Federal Constitution.* Philadelphia: J.B. Lippincott and Co., 1788.

Restad, Hilde Eliassen. *American Exceptionalism: An Idea That Made a Nation and Remade the World.* New York: Routledge, 2015.

Richter, Daniel K. *Facing East from Indian Country: A Native History of Early America.* Cambridge, MA: Harvard University Press, 2001.

Robertson, James Rood. *Petitions of the Early Inhabitants of Kentucky to the General Assembly of Virginia, 1769 to 1792.* Baltimore: Genealogical Publishing Co., 1998 [1914].

Robinson, Albert G. *The Philippines: The War and the People.* New York: McClure, Phillips, & Co., 1901.

Rockwell, Stephen J. *Indian Affairs and the Administrative State in the Nineteenth Century.* Cambridge, UK: Cambridge University Press, 2010.

Rodabaugh, Cathy. "Contested Patriarchy: John Cleves Symmes and the Struggle for Family Control in the Post-Revolutionary West." *Ohio History* 122, no. 1 (2015): 5–28.

Rosato, Sebastian. *Intentions in Great Power Politics: Uncertainty and the Roots of Conflict.* New Haven: Yale University Press, 2021.

Saler, Bethel. *The Settlers' Empire: Colonialism and State Formation in America's Old Northwest.* Philadelphia: University of Pennsylvania Press, 2015.

Salter, Mark B., and Can E. Mutlu. "Securitisation and Diego Garcia." *Review of International Studies* 39, no. 4 (2013): 815–834.

Savage, Charlie. "When the Culture Wars Hit Fort Wayne." *Politico*, July 31, 2020. https://www.politico.com/news/magazine/2020/07/31/culture-wars-fort-wayne -373011

Schake, Kori. "Lessons from the Indian Wars." *Hoover Institution* (blog), February 1, 2013. https://www.hoover.org/research/lessons-indian-wars

Scheerer, Hanno. "For Ten Years Past I Have Constantly Wished to Turn My Western Lands into Money: Speculator Frustration and Settlers' Bargaining Power in Ohio's Virginia Military District, 1795–1810." *Ohio Valley History* 14, no. 1 (2014): 3–27.

Schlesinger, Jr., Arthur M. *The Cycles of American History*. New York: Houghton Mifflin, 1999 [1986].

Schmidt, Sebastian. *Armed Guests: Territorial Sovereignty and Foreign Military Basing*. Oxford: Oxford University Press, 2020.

Schwartz-Shea, Peregrine, and Dvora Yanow. *Interpretive Research Design: Concepts and Processes*. Abingdon: Routledge, 2012.

Schweller, Randall L. "Unanswered Threats: A Neoclassical Realist Theory of Underbalancing." *International Security* 29, no. 2 (2004): 159–201.

Sexton, Jay. *The Monroe Doctrine: Empire and Nation in Nineteenth-Century America*. New York: Hill and Wang, 2011.

Shannon, Timothy J. "The Ohio Company and the Meaning of Opportunity in the American West, 1786–1795." *New England Quarterly* 64, no. 3 (1991): 393–413.

Shetrone, H.C., and R. B. Sherman. "Ohio Country of the Historic Indian Period." Columbus: Ohio Historical Society, 1918.

Shoemaker, Nancy. "How Indians Got to Be Red." *American Historical Review* 102, no. 3 (1997): 625–644.

SIGAR, Office of the Special Inspector General for Afghanistan Reconstruction. "What We Need to Learn: Lessons from Twenty Years of Afghanistan Reconstruction." Arlington, 2021. https://www.sigar.mil/Portals/147/Files/Reports/Lessons -Learned/SIGAR-21-46-LL-Executive-Summary.pdf

Silbey, David J. *A War of Frontier and Empire: The Philippine-American War, 1899– 1902*. New York: Hill and Wang, 2007.

Skalenko, Nicole. "Marching to the Beat of Their Own Drum: Female Camp Followers of the American Revolution." *American Philosophical Society* (blog), October 3, 2022. https://www.amphilsoc.org/blog/marching-beat-their-own-drum -female-camp-followers-american-revolution

Skogen, Larry C. *Indian Depredation Claims, 1796–1920*. Norman: University of Oklahoma Press, 1996.

Sloboda, Ashley. "122nd Fighter Wing Blacksnakes Honored for Education at General 'Mad' Anthony Wayne Day." *Journal Gazette*, July 17, 2023. https://www.jour nalgazette.net/local/122nd-fighter-wing-blacksnakes-honored-for-education -at-general-mad-anthony-wayne-day/article_09c4cf0c-2415-11ee-81de-33e195 93f621.html

Solomon, Ty. *The Politics of Subjectivity in American Foreign Policy Discourses.* Ann Arbor: University of Michigan Press, 2015.

Sondarjee, Maïka. "We Are a Community of Practice, Not a Paradigm! How to Meaningfully Integrate Gender and Feminist Approaches in IR Syllabi." *International Studies Perspectives* 23, no. 3 (2022): 229–248.

Spalińska, Aleksandra. "New Medievalism (Re)Appraised: Framing Heterarchy in World Politics." In *Heterarchy in World Politics*, edited by Philip G. Cerny, 42–53. Abingdon: Routledge, 2022.

Sparrow, Bartholomew H. "Becoming an American Empire." *Tulsa Law Review* 54, no. 2 (2018/2019): 339–352.

Srivastava, Swati. *Hybrid Sovereignty in World Politics.* Cambridge, UK: Cambridge University Press, 2022.

Steele, Brent J. *Ontological Security in International Relations: Self-Identity and the IR State.* Abingdon: Routledge, 2008.

Steele, Brent J., and Luke B. Campbell. "(Inter)National Ethics and the Politics of Memory." In *Handbook on the Politics of Memory*, edited by Maria Mälksoo, 46–64. Cheltenham: Edward Elgar, 2023.

Stephanson, Anders. *Manifest Destiny: American Expansion and the Empire of Right.* New York: Hill and Wang, 1995.

Stevenson, Jonathan. *Overseas Bases and US Strategy: Optimising America's Military Footprint.* Abingdon: Routledge, 2022.

Story, Russell M'Culloch. "The Problem of the Chinese in the Philippines." *American Political Science Review* 3, no. 1 (1909): 30–48.

Subotić, Jelena. "Stories States Tell: Identity, Narrative, and Human Rights in the Balkans." *Slavic Review* 72, no. 2 (2013): 306–326.

Sugden, John. *Blue Jacket: Warrior of the Shawnees.* Lincoln: University of Nebraska Press, 2000.

Sword, Wiley. *President Washington's Indian War: The Struggle for the Old Northwest, 1790–1795.* Norman: University of Oklahoma Press, 1985.

Szarejko, Andrew A. "Do Accidental Wars Happen? Evidence from America's Indian Wars." *Journal of Global Security Studies* 6, no. 4 (2021): 1–7.

———. "Foreign or Domestic? The Desecuritisation of Indian Affairs and Normativity in Securitisation Theory." *Millennium* 50, no. 3 (2022): 785–809.

Tate, Michael L. *The Frontier Army in the Settlement of the West.* Norman: University of Oklahoma Press, 1999.

Temin, David Myer, and Adam Dahl. "Narrating Historical Injustice: Political Responsibility and the Politics of Memory." *Political Research Quarterly* 70, no. 4 (2017): 905–917.

Tichenor, Irene. "Tracking the Mysteries: The Legacy of John Filson's 1784 Book and Map." *Ohio Valley History* 9, no. 4 (2009): 4–26.

Tilly, Charles. *Stories, Identities, and Political Change.* Lanham: Rowman & Littlefield, 2002.

Todorov, Tzvetan. *The Conquest of America: The Question of the Other.* Norman: University of Oklahoma Press, 1999 [1982].

Trubowitz, Peter. *Politics and Strategy: Partisan Ambition and American Statecraft.* Princeton: Princeton University Press, 2011.

United States Census Bureau. "Indian Wars, Their Cost, and Civil Expenditures." In *Eleventh Census,* vol. 10. 1890, last revised December 16, 2021. https://www.cen sus.gov/library/publications/1894/dec/volume-10.html

United States Congress. "An Act Providing for Holding a Treaty or Treaties to Establish Peace with Certain Indian Tribes." *Annals of Congress,* July 22, 1790. https://congressional.proquest.com/congressional/docview/t19.d20.ac-001-3 -laws?accountid=11091

Urlacher, Brian R. "Introducing Native American Conflict History (NACH) Data." *Journal of Peace Research* 58, no. 5 (2021): 1117–1125.

Utley, Robert M. *The Contribution of the Frontier to the American Military Tradition.* The Harmon Memorial Lectures in Military History. Colorado: United States Air Force Academy, 1977.

Van Evera, Stephen. *Guide to Methods for Students of Political Science.* Ithaca: Cornell University Press, 1997.

Vergerio, Claire. "Beyond the Nation-State." *Boston Review,* May 27, 2021. https://www.bostonreview.net/articles/beyond-the-nation-state/

Vine, David. "No Bases? Assessing the Impact of Social Movements Challenging US Foreign Military Bases." *Current Anthropology* 60, no. S19 (2019): S158–S172.

Waltz, Kenneth N. *Theory of International Politics.* Long Grove: Waveland Press, 1979.

Warren, Stephen. *The Worlds the Shawnee Made: Migration and Violence in Early America.* Chapel Hill: University of North Carolina Press, 2014.

Washington, George. "Diary Entry: 4 October 1784." National Archives. *Founders Online,* October 4, 1784. https://founders.archives.gov/documents/Washington /01-04-02-0001-0002-0004

———. "George Washington to Arthur Campbell." National Archives. *Founders Online,* September 15, 1789. https://founders.archives.gov/documents/Washing ton/05-04-02-0022

———. "George Washington to James Duane." National Archives. *Founders Online,* September 7, 1783. https://founders.archives.gov/documents/Washington/99-01 -02-11798

———. "George Washington to Samuel Holden Parsons." In *George Washington Papers,* Series 2, Letterbooks 1754–1799, Letterbook 15. *Library of Congress,* July 15, 1788. http://www.loc.gov/resource/mgw2.015

———. "George Washington to Timothy Pickering." In *George Washington Papers,* Series 2 Letterbooks 1754–1799, Letterbook 30. *Library of Congress,* October 11, 1794. https://www.loc.gov/item/mgw2.030/

———. "Sixth Annual Address to Congress." *The American Presidency Project,* November 19, 1794. http://www.presidency.ucsb.edu/ws/index.php?pid=29436

———. "Third Annual Address to Congress." *The American Presidency Project,* October 25, 1791. http://www.presidency.ucsb.edu/ws/index.php?pid=29433

Waxman, Matthew. "Remembering St. Clair's Defeat." *Lawfare* (blog), November 4, 2018. https://www.lawfaremedia.org/article/remembering-st-clairs-defeat

Wedeen, Lisa. "Acting 'As If': Symbolic Politics and Social Control in Syria." *Comparative Studies in Society and History* 40, no. 3 (1998): 503–523.

Weeks, William Earl. *Building the Continental Empire: American Expansion from the Revolution to the Civil War.* Chicago: Ivan R. Dee, 1996.

———. *Dimensions of the Early American Empire, 1754–1865. Vol. 1. The New Cambridge History of American Foreign Relations.* Cambridge, UK: Cambridge University Press, 2013.

Weigley, Russell F. *The American Way of War: A History of United States Military Strategy and Policy.* Bloomington: Indiana University Press, 1977.

Weinberg, Albert Katz. *Manifest Destiny: A Study of Nationalist Expansionism in American History.* Baltimore: Johns Hopkins University Press, 1935.

Weldes, Jutta. "Going Cultural: Star Trek, State Action, and Popular Culture." *Millennium* 28, no. 1 (1999): 117–134.

———. "High Politics and Low Data." In *Interpretation and Method: Empirical Research Methods and the Interpretive Turn,* edited by Dvora Yanow and Peregrine Schwartz-Shea, 228 238. Abingdon: Routledge, 2014.

Wendt, Alexander. "Anarchy Is What States Make of It: The Social Construction of Power Politics." *International Organization* 46, no. 2 (1992): 391–425.

———. "On Constitution and Causation in International Relations." *Review of International Studies* 24, no. 5 (1998): 101–118.

Williams, Walter L. "A Southerner in the Philippines, 1901–1903." *Research Studies* 39 (1971): 156–165.

———. "United States Indian Policy and the Debate over Philippine Annexation: Implications for the Origins of American Imperialism." *Journal of American History* 66, no. 4 (1980): 810–831.

Williams, William Appleman. "The Legend of Isolationism in the 1920's." *Science and Society* 18, no. 1 (1954): 1–20.

Witgen, Michael John. *Seeing Red: Indigenous Land, American Expansion, and the Political Economy of Plunder in North America.* Chapel Hill: University of North Carolina Press, 2021.

Wolfe, Patrick. *Settler Colonialism and the Transformation of Anthropology: The Politics and Poetics of an Ethnographic Event.* London: Cassell, 1999.

Wooster, Robert. *The American Military Frontiers: The United States Army in the West, 1783–1900.* Albuquerque: University of New Mexico Press, 2009.

Wright, Darrin. "Council Removes Language Prohibiting Firearms from City Parks." *WOWO Radio* (blog), October 18, 2016a. https://wowo.com/council-removes-language-prohibiting-firearms-city-parks/

———. "Fort Wayne Councilman Raises Questions with State Rep over Mayor's

Salary." *WOWO Radio* (blog), October 6, 2016b. https://wowo.com/councilman
   -raises-questions-over-mayor-salary/
Yeo, Andrew I. "The Politics of Overseas Military Bases." *Perspectives on Politics* 15,
   no. 1 (2017): 129–136.
Yeo, Andrew, and Stacie Pettyjohn. "Bases of Empire? The Logic of Overseas U.S.
   Military Base Expansion, 1870–2016." *Comparative Strategy* 40, no. 1 (2021): 18–35.
Zak, Dan. "At Creech Air Force Base, Drones Land, Protesters Chant, and One Man
   Waves a Flag." *Washington Post,* April 21, 2014. https://www.washingtonpost.com
   /lifestyle/style/at-creech-air-force-base-drones-land-protesters-chant-and-one
   -man-waves-a-flag/2014/04/21/ad6603a2-c956-11e3-95f7-7ecdde72d2ea_story
   .html

INDEX

The authorized representative in the EU for product safety and compliance is:
Mare Nostrum Group
B.V Doelen 72
4831 GR Breda
The Netherlands

www.ingramcontent.com/pod-product-compliance
Lightning Source LLC
Chambersburg PA
CBHW030817270326
41928CB00007B/774